MAKING MUSIC WITH
Logic Pro

Stephen Bennett

PC Publishing

PC Publishing
Keeper's House
Merton
Thetford
Norfolk IP25 6QH
UK

Tel 01953 889900
Fax 01953 889901
email info@pc-publishing.com
web site http://www.pc-publishing.com

First published 2005

© PC Publishing

ISBN 1 870775 92 9

British Library Cataloguing in Publication Data
A catalogue record for this book is available from the British Library

Cover design by Hilary Norman Design Ltd

Printed and bound in Great Britain by Biddles, Kings Lynn, Norfolk

Contents

WITHDRAWN
UTSA Libraries

Introduction

Logic Pro was developed by the team of programmers that created the popular Notator and Creator sequencers for the Atari ST. It was the first 'object orientated' sequencer, and was designed to be very flexible and 'customisable'. The Atari version also introduced the concept of the 'Environment'. These features still form the centre of the current version, and make Logic Pro a very different beast from other sequencers. They are also amongst the most often stated reasons why Logic Pro is a complicated program to master. However, by following a few simple steps you can easily get to grips with Logic Pro without your brain imploding. Logic Pro was also amongst the first 'real time' programs, allowing the user to record, play, save and edit MIDI and Audio without stopping the sequencer or, indeed, to sleep.

Logic Pro tightly integrates MIDI, Virtual instrument, audio recording and virtual plug-in processing. For most day-to-day use, audio data is treated in the same manner as MIDI. You can copy, cut, drag, paste and double click audio sequences to edit, just like MIDI sequences. But of course, Logic Pro provides many specific audio-editing tools in addition. You can use Logic Pro like a multi-track audio/MIDI recorder, a non-linear audio editing system, a postproduction facility for work with visuals, or even a replacement for a traditional multi-track tape recorder.

Logic Pro audio also contains some high quality real time 'plug-ins', These can be used on audio tracks as virtual effects units, providing the usual Reverb, echo, compression along with more esoteric effects. Logic pro ships with many high quality Virtual instruments which cover sampling to analog synthesis. Logic Pro also allows you to utilise Audio Unit (AU) plug-ins to use alongside the plethora included with the program. Digidesign's TDM real is also supported. The beauty of Logic Pro is that all these formats are available simultaneously.

Figure 1.1 shows an overview of Logic Pro. As you can see the Environment is the centre of Logic Pro – all data passes through here. However, each window and editor is also intimately connected with each other. These days, Logic Pro shields you from the Environment as much as possible making the program easier than ever to use. But the power is still there if you need it.

Figure 1.1
Overview of Logic

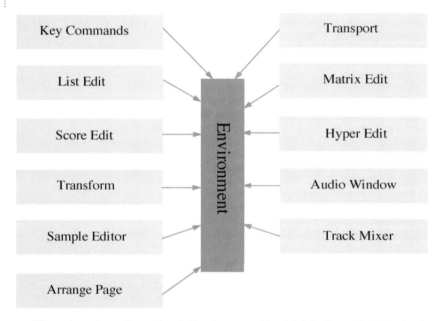

Although each section of Logic Pro is covered in detail in the rest of the book, here's an overview of the major components of the program.

Screensets

Logic Pro can open many windows at the same time. Figure 1.2 has the following windows open:

- An Arrange page, showing sequences
- A Matrix edit page showing the MIDI information in one highlighted sequence
- A List edit page showing the same data
- A Hyper edit page showing controller information
- An Environment page showing a MIDI mixer
- An Environment page showing an Arpeggiator
- Several Transport windows

As you can imagine, it would be very tedious to set up an arrangement like this every time you booted Logic Pro and loaded this song! This is where the Screensets feature of Logic Pro is essential. A Screenset is a 'snapshot' of the screen and its contents. You can store up to 99 Screensets and call them up by simply typing in their number.

Combine this with 'Linked windows' and you begin to see the flexibility of Logic Pro.

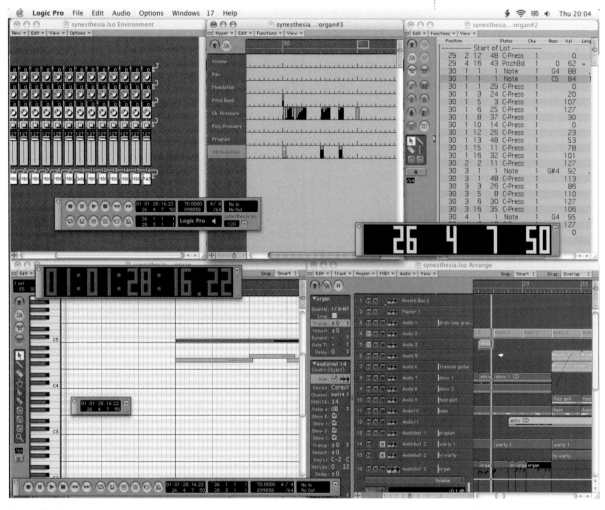

Linked windows

Each open window can be linked so that changes in one window are instantly reflected in another. So you can, for example, have several editors open, of the same or different types, all reflecting the changes made in one of them.

Figure 1.2
Logic Pro can open many windows at the same time.

Window zooming

The information available in some windows depends on the zoom or magnification of that window. For example, zooming the Arrange window out (i.e. making sequences larger) will show the positions of notes, MIDI and audio information in the individual sequences. These zoom settings can be stored in Screensets, so you can have several linked windows of the same type open at the same time, but with different zoom settings.

Figure 1.3
You can have several linked windows of the same type open at the same time, but with different zoom settings.

You can even set individual zoom setting for each track by dragging the track at the left hand corner.

Figure 1.4
Set individual zoom setting for each track

Hyperdraw and Track Automation

If you zoom the arrange window out enough, you can draw controller data directly onto the regions. You can define this data, so it could be volume, pan or any other controller data.

Hyperdraw can also be used to edit Automation data.

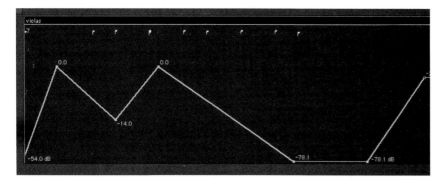

Figure 1.5

Touch tracks

These little beasties let you play whole sequences at the touch of MIDI keyboard. Play your whole song from a C#! At present Touch Tracks do not work with Audio files.

Always in record (MIDI recording only)

Logic Pro is always in record, and anything you play is stored in a buffer to be recalled at the touch of a programmable key. Never miss that great take again! Again, this doesn't apply to audio recordings, only MIDI and Virtual instrument recordings (which are actually MIDI data anyway.).

Key commands

Most of Logic Pro's functions can be assigned to a key on the computer keyboard. Which keys you use are up to you. So you could, for example, emulate the commands for start, stop, record etc. from other sequencer packages you have previously been used to. Logic Pro's functions can also be controlled by a MIDI keyboard or other MIDI controller.

MIDI editors

Logic Pro can now display multiple regions in an editor at the same time. You can also edit several sequences together by opening up more editors. You can link them so they all play together and show related MIDI data.

The MIDI editors available in Logic Pro are:

- Matrix editor: A 'piano roll' style editor
- Event editor: A list-style editor useful for displaying notes, controller and Sysex

data. Logic Pro calls these 'events', hence the name.

- Hyper editor: Used to edit controller data mostly, but can be brought into service as a drum editor.
- Score editor: Traditional notation editor and the place you lay out and print a score.
- Transformer: Changes one type of MIDI data into another.

Audio editor

Logic Pro has a powerful audio editor that allows fine editing of audio sequences and audio files. It is in this editor that you apply non real time effects and processing such as time stretching, tempo manipulation and pitch changing.

The Transport bar

The Transport bar in Logic Pro is particularly flexible as shown in Figure 1.6. All these different types of transport can be saved in a Screenset.

Figure 1.6
The Transport bar.

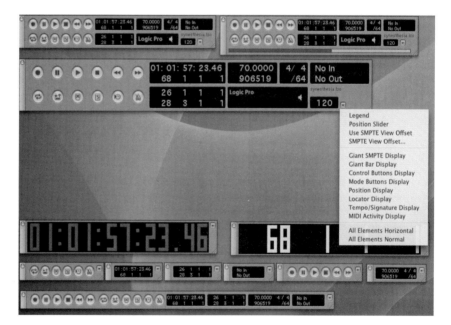

The Environment

The Environment is the place where you can;

- Connect your MIDI inputs to your MIDI outputs
- Set up your MIDI devices. Logic allows you to select patches on them by name rather than number
- Create virtual controller panels for all your MIDI devices
- Patch in MIDI modifiers such as arpeggiators, transformers and delay lines
- See what MIDI information is passing through your system
- Use the 'Touch Tracks' Feature
- Create and manipulate audio, Virtual Instrument, bus and auxes

Like all the windows in Logic Pro, the Environment can be linked so it displays information relating to other open windows. Once you have set up your Environment to suit yourself, you can then use it in all your compositions. It's easy to modify your Environment whenever you buy new MIDI gear or want to incorporate one of Logic Pro's more esoteric features.

The Environment can be as simple as a connection from your instruments to your MIDI interface, or as complex as a complete control and editing system for all of your MIDI and audio devices. You can use it as a virtual interface for programming your synthesisers in real time, and record the results into Logic Pro. You can use it as a 'virtual mixing desk' for your audio recordings, including plug-in effects. Don't be put off by its complexity. Start simple. Take it a step at a time and the Environment will reward you by making your work more flexible, easier and more fun!

> **Info**
>
> You can also create Audio, Instrument and Aux tracks from the Arrange page Track>Create Multiple Tracks menu item.

What's next?

There you have a brief overview of Logic Pro. The next chapter takes you through the installation of Logic Pro. Chapter 3 and Chapter 4 include a step by step, practical introduction to setting up and using Logic Pro, along with some tips and pointers to further experimentation. Chapter 4 deals with using the Score Editor to print out your music. Chapters 5 to 17 are handy references for the individual components that make up Logic Pro. Chapter 18 covers various other useful Logic Pro functions. Finally, the Appendices deal with various, more general parts of the program, a Glossary, and the Internet.

Some good advice

Making Music with Logic Pro assumes you are fully conversant with your Macintosh and the OSX operating system. If you aren't, I'd suggest you get a coffee, sit down in front of the computer and write some letters and draw some pictures. The experience you gain in using the computer will pay itself back many times over when you come to use Apple Logic Pro. The book also assumes you have a reasonable grasp of MIDI and your MIDI devices, and any external Audio hardware you're using.

Happy Logic-al sequencing!

2

Installation

Installation of Logic is detailed in this chapter. Logic is protected by a USB dongle, which some people find annoying. However, until everyone in the music community is as honest as, say, a politician, I'm afraid software protection is here to stay. At least dongle protection isn't dependent on the reliability of the CD or Internet based challenge/response installation used with some other packages. You can freely back up both the Logic program and any associated folders. In fact I recommend you do just that

The Logic dongle is a USB based device called an XSkey, which stores the authorisation for Logic.

Logic itself comes on DVD disks. This is a great medium as Apple are always tempted to stuff onto the DVD examples of Environments, samples and other fun things to fill up the space.

To install Logic on your Mac

To install Logic on your Mac you simply

- Place the XSKey into a spare USB port on your computer.
- Run the Logic installer from the Logic DVD.

If you are installing Logic for the first time, you can use the program right away. If you are upgrading from an earlier version you may need to obtain an authorisation code from Apple. Details will be in your upgrade box.

Now you have Logic installed on your computer, you will need to set it up for use with your MIDI and Audio equipment.

Logic uses the Mac OSX Core Audio and Core Midi protocols for communication with external MIDI and Audio hardware. What this means, in practice, is that the OS handles all communication between programs and these devices. Once installed, Core Audio and Core MIDI drivers are available to all software on your Mac.

Installing audio and MIDI hardware

Your hardware will come with instructions for installing the drivers. Once installed, you can use the Audio MIDI setup utility in the /Applications/Utilities folder to view

and manage your devices.

Figure 2.1a

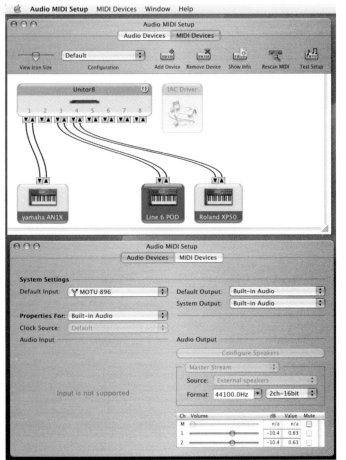

Figure 2.1b

If you now run Logic, these devices will appear in the Audio hardware and the MIDI section of a MIDI track Parameter window.

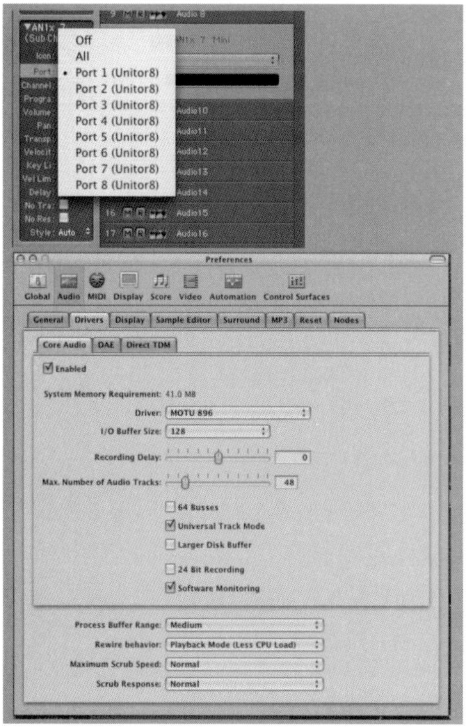

Figure 2.2
These devices will appear in the Audio hardware and the MIDI section of a MIDI track Parameter window.

That's it for the installation of Logic! The next chapter shows you how to start using Logic.

Getting started

In the past, one of the main cries from the new Logic user is 'How the hell do I do this?' Logic is a very flexible program, and it can be tailored to produce a close virtual emulation of your actual studio set-up. Consequently, there is no 'generic' set-up that will work on everyone's system, but there are certain rules one can follow when setting up Logic Pro that greatly simplify the process. This chapter takes you through getting Logic Pro to work with your MIDI and audio equipment and suggests some tips to help you make the most of the program.

Booting Logic Pro for the first time

The first time Logic Pro runs, you will get an Arrange page window labeled 'Untitled'. Logic Pro saves its files as 'songs' or 'templates'. Both are identical in structure, but a 'song' is referred to when it contains a composition and can be stored anywhere on any hard drive, whereas a 'template' is a particular setup that can be used to start a session. Templates are stored in the Library/Application support/Logic/Song Templates folder. You can create many Templates with different numbers of tracks, plug-ins, Environments and Screensets and use them for particular jobs.

Logic Pro has a tool to help you easily set up your MIDI and Audio devices – It's called the Logic Setup Assistant. You can also configure Logic Pro manually this is covered in more detail in Appendix 1. Before running the assistant make sure your MIDI and Audio interfaces are installed and powered up.

Using the Logic Setup Assistant

Run the Logic Setup Assistant from the menu item Logic Pro>Preferences>Start Logic Setup Assistant. A window will appear asking you if you wish to run the program. Click on 'Start Assistant'. Logic Pro will close and the assistant will load.

Figure 3.1
The Logic Setup Assistant

Follow through the questions and click on 'Next' at each window to continue. The assistant will run you through the various stages detailed below.

Detect devices

The assistant will ask if you have your MIDI and Audio interfaces are connected. As this information is derived from the CoreAudio drivers detailed in the previous chapter, it's essential that these have been installed properly.

Audio

This will ask you which Audio devices you wish to use.

Core Audio Mixer setup

This window allows you to choose the basic setup for the Logic Pro session that is loaded on Logic Pro boot up – the 'Untitled' project.

Audio inputs

What you choose here will depend on the way you want to work. Choose the option nearest your ideal situation.

Remember, you can change all the settings in the Logic setup Assistant manually at a later date.

Key commands

If you have used Logic before, select 'Do not change existing Key commands'. Otherwise, select a suitable option. You can also import Key commands from another preferences file here.

Screensets

You will want to adjust these to your personal preference later, so just click 'Next' here.

MIDI devices

If you have powered up and connected your MIDI devices (synthesizers, effects etc) they will show up here. You can also add devices manually.

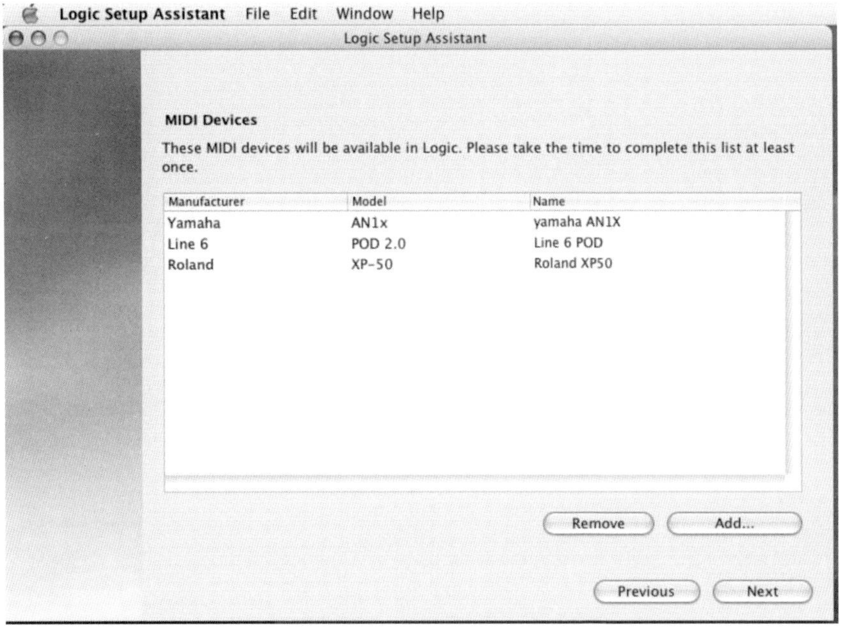

Figure 3.2
Your MIDI devices appear in the window.

When the summary window appears, click on Finish.

Logic Pro will reload. To load the setup just created choose the File>new menu item. Make sure 'Use song template is checked'.

Next go to the 'File' menu, choose 'Save as Template', and save this song as a template named 'Autoload' in the Library/Application support/Logic/Song Templates folder. Logic Pro stores its files as 'songs'. The Autoload song is the 'default' Logic Pro song that the program will load when it boots. You may also want to save in the Autoload song some default screensets, an Arrange page with default instruments and so on. These songs can also be saved as Templates for easy retrieval. Use the File>Save as Template menu item.

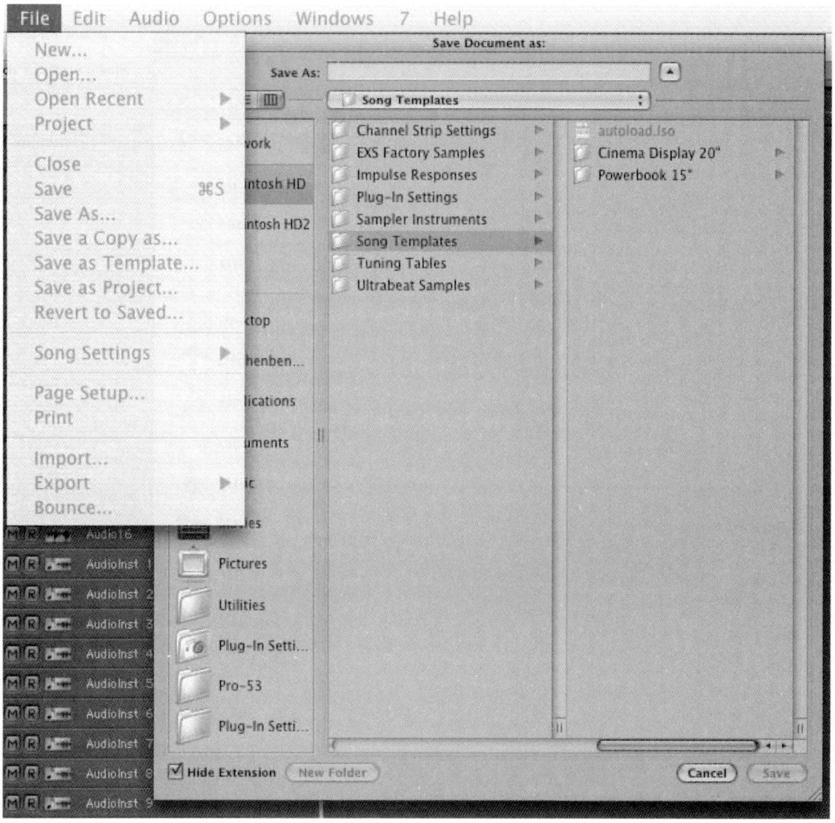

Figure 3.3
Save as 'Autoload'.

You can then open these templates from the File>New menu.

Figure 3.4

The structure of Logic Pro songs

While saving songs as templates should be done as described above, the saving of songs as compositions should be approached in a slightly different fashion. Logic pro songs could be using the following files;

- The Logic Pro song file
- The audio files
- EXS24 sampler instruments and samples
- Space Designer impulse files
- Movie files
- Freeze files

It's convenient to store all (or most) of these files in a single folder. This makes the song easier to backup. You should get into the habit of saving a Logic Pro song as a Project.

Logic Pro projects

A project is a folder that contains the Logic Pro song file and associated files as described above. When you want to save a new session you should always use the File>Save as Project menu item.

What you decide to save into your Project folder depends on various criteria.

If you are going to be using the project on the same computer all the time

In this case, you probably just want to save the song file and audio files into the project folder.

If you will want to take the project to another computer or studio

In this case, you'll probably want to save Sampler information, impulse response files and movies as well. You can always re-freeze tracks later if you want to save disk space. More on freezing in Appendix 8.

Logic Pro' Setup assistant will fill the Arrange page with lots of instruments and tracks. You can delete those you wont need using the ' 'Track>Delete unused' menu item. These aren't removed from the song, only from the Arrange page.

That concludes the basic Logic Pro setup. If you have a simple set-up, you can probably move on to the next chapter. If you wish to modify the basic setup song further, you'll need to use the Environment. More details of this in Chapter 14 and Appendix 1.

Info

Save Logic songs pre-version 7 as Projects to make backing up easier. You can choose to leave unused audio files behind to save disk space.

Once you have saved a song as a project, you can just use the usual File>Save to save further changes.

Audio in Logic

Overview

Audio recorded into Logic Pro can be treated, to a great extent, in the same way as MIDI data. Audio is stored as files on a hard drive, and these files contain areas that can be used as regions within Logic Pro. Appendix 5 has more details on audio files and regions. Figure 3.5 shows MIDI and Audio regions together on an Arrange page.

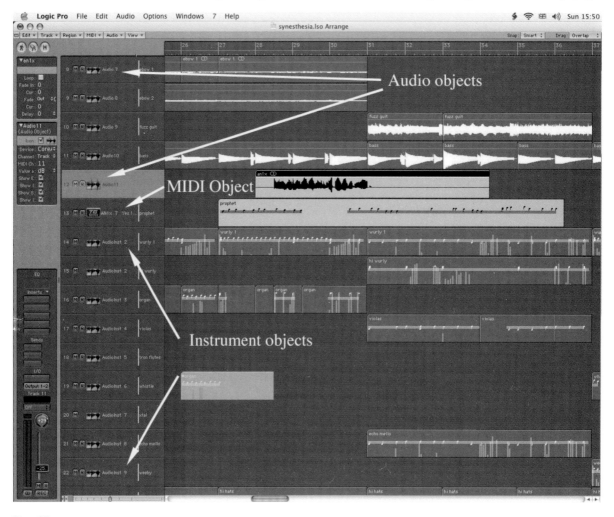

Figure 3.5
MIDI and Audio regions together on an Arrange page.

As you can see, at high window zoom settings you can display waveforms alongside notes on the Arrange page.

Audio regions within Logic Pro are recorded and played back via Audio objects, which are created in the Environment window. This is covered in more detail in Chapter 6 and their use within Logic Pro is covered in Chapter 4.

Logic uses tracks to record. These tracks are linked to Objects, which are actually on an Environment page, which are selected from the Arrange page. Here's a guide to the various objects in Logic.

Instrument objects

These are used for controlling Logic Pro's Virtual instruments. These are software versions of traditional instruments such as synthesisers and samplers.

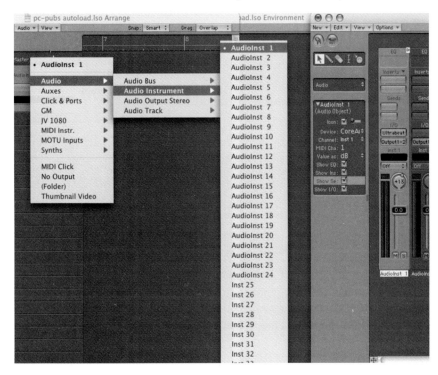

Figure 3.6
Instrument objects are used for controlling Logic Pro's Virtual instruments.

Audio objects

These are used for playing back and recording audio files and Apple Loops.

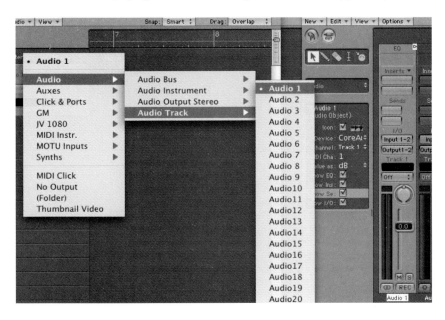

Figure 3.7
Audio objects are used for playing back and recording audio files and Apple Loops.

Buss objects

The output of Audio objects can be sent either to an output of the audio card you are using, or to Buss objects. You could, for example send the output of several Audio faders to a single Buss object, and thus control their overall gain with a single fader. Or add a plug-in effect to the Buss object that is then applied to the group of Audio objects to reduce the demand on the computer processor.

Figure 3.8
The output of Audio objects can be sent either to an output of the audio card you are using, or to Buss objects.

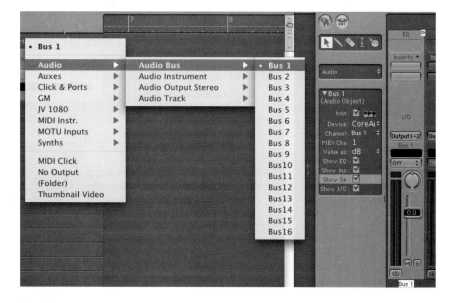

Aux objects

These are specialized Bus objects that are used with the outputs of Multi-channel Virtual instruments.

Figure 3.9
Aux objects are specialized Bus objects that are used with the outputs of Multi-channel Virtual instruments.

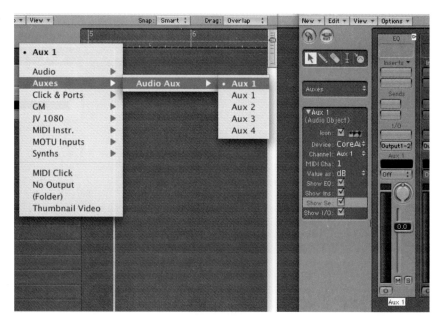

MIDI objects

These allow you to record and playback external MIDI devices such as synthesisers or samplers.

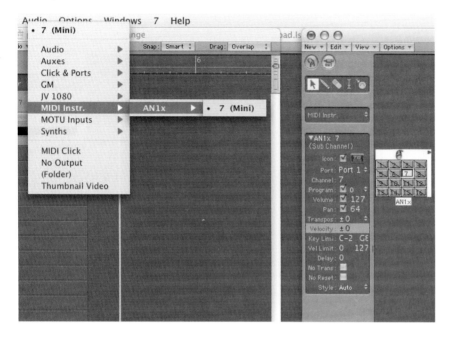

Figure 3.10
MIDI objects allow you to record and playback external MIDI devices such as synthesisers or samplers.

External instruments

These are specialized versions of Live inputs. You can route the outputs from your external hardware (Synthesisers etc) to the inputs of your Audio interface and then onto the Arrange page in Logic.

Figure 3.11
External instruments are specialized versions of Live inputs. You can route the outputs from your external hardware

Master fader objects

These control the overall output of the Audio side of Logic Pro.

Figure 3.12
Master fader objects.

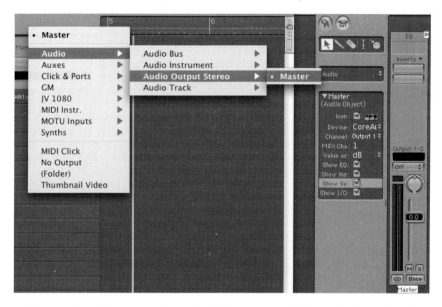

The beauty of the above objects is that you can add EQ and Plug-ins to all of them, just like a 'normal' Audio object. You could, for example, add EQ and Compression to the Master fader object to process a mixdown.

Effects plug-ins

Logic Pro is supplied with several plug-ins. These are software equivalents of traditional external processors, such as reverb, delay and modulation. Some plug-ins have no hardware equivalent – they are purely available as plug-ins. Logic Pro can also use the following additional plug-in types.

Plug-ins are covered in more detail in Chapter 15.

MIDI, Virtual instruments and audio together

All audio recorded into Logic Pro passes through the Audio objects and the Master fader Audio object. Virtual instruments sounds are generated from plug-ins and are controlled via MIDI data on Virtual instrument tracks. The sounds produced from MIDI devices playing back MIDI data from Logic Pro are output from the jacks on the back of those devices. So how do we hear the audio and MIDI together? This depends on what kind of audio interface you have. The following diagrams illustrate various options available. Remember, the connections in these diagrams are Audio not MIDI.

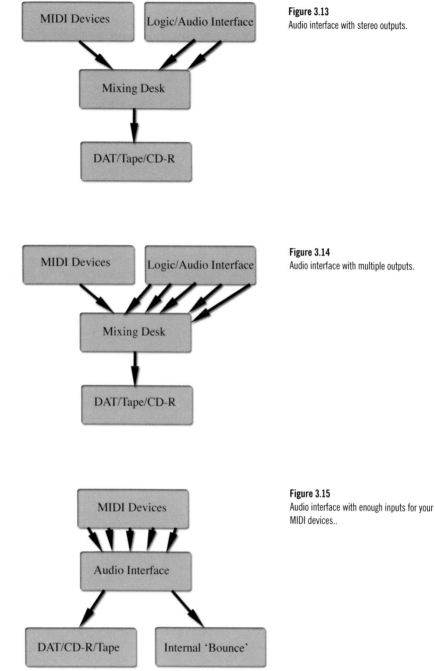

Figure 3.13
Audio interface with stereo outputs.

Figure 3.14
Audio interface with multiple outputs.

Figure 3.15
Audio interface with enough inputs for your MIDI devices..

Using Logic Pro

Making music is what Logic Pro is all about, and this chapter will take you through your first recording and then from there and on to the editing and mixing of the MIDI, Audio and Virtual instrument recordings. Before you start however, there are a few things you should know, and a couple of preparations you can make, which will make working with Logic Pro smoother and easier – not to mention more fun.

Some Logic Pro terminology

Logic Pro has its own particular, and sometimes peculiar, names for many of its features. These are detailed below and displayed in Figure 4.1.

- Logic Pro splits its time line into bars : beats : divisions : ticks.
- Logic Pro has 3840 ticks per division, which is one of the highest resolutions of any sequencer.
- the parts that Logic Pro records are called 'Regions'.
- MIDI data (notes, control data, SysEx data etc.) are called 'Events'.
- Regions are recorded into a 'Song'. This is saved as a 'Logic Pro song file' and/or a 'Logic Pro Project'.
- Regions, notes and faders etc. are called 'Objects'.
- Logic Pro can have many songs open at the same time and objects can be freely copied between them.
- the actual MIDI devices and Virtual Instruments you record with are called 'Instruments' and are chosen in the Instrument list – a pull down menu in the instrument column.
- On the Arrange page, regions are recorded onto 'Tracks', which can be given a 'Track name'.
- the line that moves as Logic Pro plays or records is called the 'Song position line' (SPL).
- 'Float' windows are windows in Logic Pro that cannot be hidden by other windows. The Transport bar is an example. Many other windows can be opened as Float windows.
- Highlighting objects is known as 'Selecting objects'.
- Most Logic Pro windows have 'Parameter boxes' where you can change the values of parameters relating to selected objects.

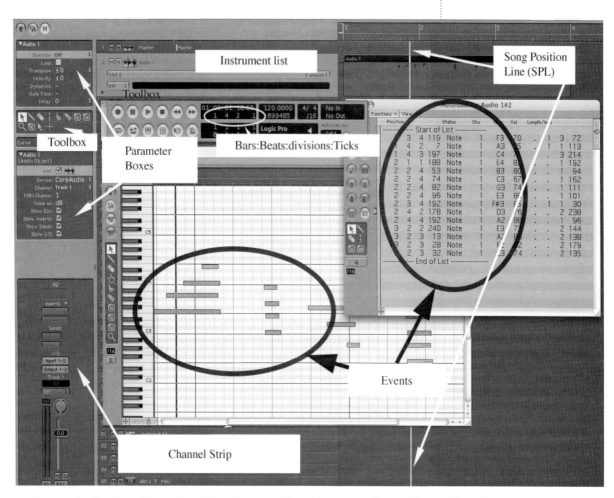

Figure 4.1

- You may be familiar with the term 'Cut, Copy and Paste' in other software. You may use this technique in Logic Pro. For example, you may wish to cut out a section of a song, close the gap and paste it into another position. Logic Pro uses the terms 'Snip, Splice and insert' instead, just to confuse you!

Info

'Normalize' and 'Normalizing' in Logic mean making the changes to certain playback parameters of a region or track, such as quantization and transpose, permanent. Normally within Logic, when you change these parameters they are 'non destructive'' changes or 'playback only'. *Normalizing* or *Fixing* parameters means that you cannot retrieve their original values. This is used when exporting MIDI files and the means to do it is found in the MIDI > Region Parameters > Normalize Region Parameter menu in the Arrange page. Don't confuse this type of Normalising with maximizing the level of audio recordings in the sample editor.

Useful Logic Pro stuff

Everything is connected to everything else. When you change a value in a Logic Pro window, the change will be reflected in all other open windows in the same song, as far as possible.

Changing values

You can use a two-button mouse and a scroll wheel in Logic Pro to change values and scroll. Values within fields in Parameter boxes or dialog boxes can be changed in several ways in Logic Pro. Most can be changed by:

- Double clicking on the field and entering the values, holding down the mouse key and dragging the value up or down to increment or decrement values,

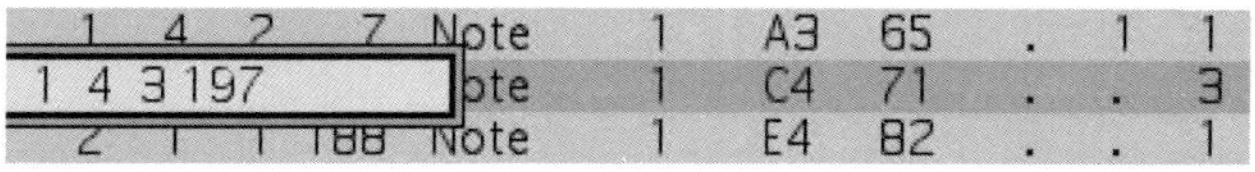

Figure 4.2

1	4	2	7	Note	1	A3	65	.	1	1
1	4	3	197	Note	1	C4	71	.	.	3
2	1	1	188	Note	1	E4	82	.	.	1

- Holding down the mouse key and selecting from the pop up menu that appears (Figure 4.3).

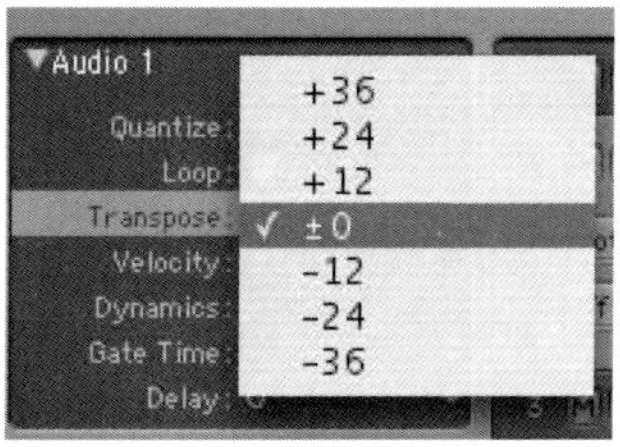

Figure 4.3

Selecting objects

This is done within Logic Pro by using the usual computer methods:

- Clicking on an object highlights it,
- Shift clicking on multiple objects selects them all,
- Rubber banding, or dragging the mouse with the mouse key down over all objects selects them all.
- Select all the regions on a track by making sure no region is selected then click on the track name column itself. If you have a cycle region defined, regions are selected in this area only.
- Use the Select all (and its many variants) from the Edit menu

Figure 4.4

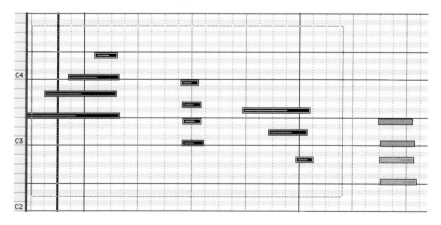

All the windows have several useful items in their Edit menus. These are particularly useful in editor windows for selecting various notes or other MIDI data. You could for example:

- Select all the regions in a track by making sure no region is selected then click on the track itself. If you have a cycle area defined, regions are selected in this area.
- Use the Select all (and its many variants) from the Edit menu. All the windows have several useful functions existing in the Edit menu. These are particularly useful in editor windows for selecting various notes or other MIDI data. You could for example
- Select all the empty regions in the arrange window (Edit >Select empty regions)
- Select all objects within the left and right locators (Edit >Select inside Locators)
- Select all muted objects (Edit >Select muted regions/events). When selected, they can be deleted.
- Select all the notes played by a given note in the matrix or List editors. (Edit >Select Equal regions/events or Edit >Select Similar regions/events). Then cut these notes and paste them into a new region.

Deselecting objects is done by clicking on the background of the window.

Tip

This could be useful for extracting a bass drum from a region and pasting into a new region on a new track, played by a different instrument.

Parameter boxes

Logic Pro windows often have Parameter boxes which show parameters relating to selected objects (Figure 4.5).

The parameters can be changed directly on the screen. These changes are non-destructive and operate in real time.

Scroll bars

Logic Pro's scroll bars work in exactly the same way as in most applications. However, if you drag the bottom left box up and down, both X and Y scroll bars are moved together (Figure 4.6).

Figure 4.5
You can resize Parameter boxes by dragging the two vertical lines to the right of the box.

Figure 4.6
Both X and Y scroll bars are moved together

Zoom sliders

Most Logic Pro windows have one or two Zoom sliders at the top right and bottom left of the window. These change the magnification within the box so you can either see more or less data, or more or less of the contents of objects.

Figure 4,7

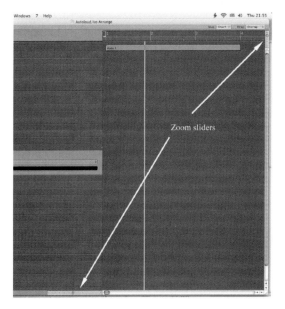

Zoom sliders

There are also several zoom Key commands available to help you navigate around the program.

Figure 4.8.

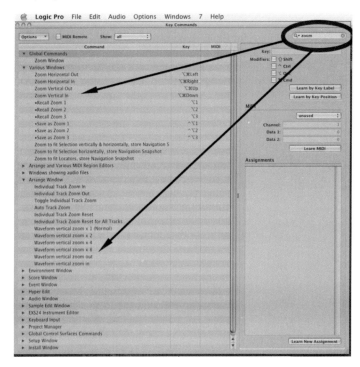

View menu

Most windows have a View menu. This menu allows you to hide or show various window items like Parameter boxes, Toolboxes, mute buttons and the like. Use these where screen real estate is at a premium.

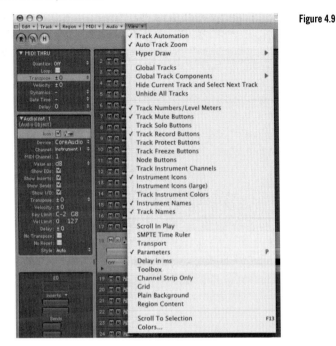

Figure 4.9

Toolboxes

Most Logic Pro windows have toolboxes. The tools perform the same or similar functions in every window. You can select tools by either:

Figure 4.10
Logic toolboxes

- Making sure the toolbox is visible. You can select it in the VIEW menu of many windows. Click on the tool you require. The Mouse pointer changes to the tool.

  Or

- Press the ESC key. A toolbox will be displayed at the mouse cursor position. Select the tool.

  Or

- Right-click on the background of a window if you have a 2-button mouse. The Global Editing>Right Mouse Opens Toolbox preference must be set.

The tools have the following functions:

Pointer

This is the 'default tool'. When using this tool to perform actions, such as dragging and resizing. The cursor will automatically change its icon to the correct shape.

Pencil

Use this to add new objects, such as drawing notes in the Matrix and Score editors, to create blank empty regions in the Arrange page, or draw MIDI controller data in the Hyper editor.

Eraser

Deletes selected objects. All currently selected objects are deleted. Same function as the DEL key.

Text

Add text or rename objects

Scissors

Cuts selected objects

Glue

This is the opposite of scissors. All selected objects are merged or mixed into a single object.

Solo

Solos all selected objects. If you move the Solo tool vertically over a region, the notes and other MIDI data are output even when the region is stopped. Use the Solo tool to listen to regions when Logic Pro isn't running.

Mute

Mutes selected objects. A dot appears on the object. Clicking on the objects again de-mutes them.

Magnifying glass

Drag around objects to magnify them. Double click on the background to return the magnification to normal.

Audio crossfade tool

Use this tool to draw crossfades.

Automation tool

Use this tool to draw various Automation curves.

Marquee tool

Use this tool to select any part of a region or regions for editing.

Finger

Use the hand to resize objects. Useful when objects are too small to be reliably resized using the pointer tool.

Crosshair

Draws a linear series of values in the Hyper Editor.

MIDI Thru tool

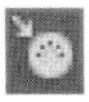

Click on any object in the Environment with this tool. Logic Pro will make this the default instrument in the Arrange page, so you can play it.

Layout pointer

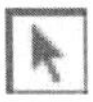

Use this to move objects in the Score editor without editing MIDI events.

Size tool

Use to adjust the size of graphic elements in the score editor.

Voice Splitter

Separates polyphonic voices in the Score Editor.

Camera

Use to outline and export sections of the Score Editor display as graphics files.

Quantize tool

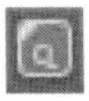

Use to quantize notes to the most recently set value in the Matrix and Score Editors.

Velocity tool

Use to change the velocity of notes in the Matrix and Score Editors.

Using the tools

When operating many of the tools, for example using the finger to drag a region, details of the object can be seen in a box next to the object being adjusted (assuming the Logic Pro>preferences>Display>Show help tags preference in set.

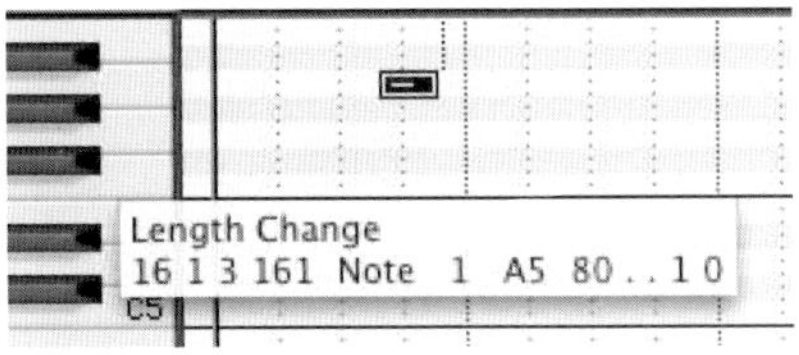
Length Change
16 1 3 161 Note 1 A5 80 . . 1 0
C5

Figure 4.11

Info

If you click on a tool with the Apple key held down, you can then change the cursor to this alternative tool by pressing the Apple key.

Editing more than one region simultaneously in the Matrix editor

- Select the first region you want to include. Color it from the Arrange page View>Colors menu
- Select the second region you want to include. Color it from the Arrange page View>Colors menu. Make it a different color from the first region.
- Select the two regions in the Arrange page and open the Matrix editor from the Windows menu.
- Select the Matrix editor menu item View>Region Colors so each region has its own color
- Double click on the Matrix editor background. You can now see the regions selected – the noters from eache region being colored the same as the region itself.
- Double click on a note to revert to single region editing

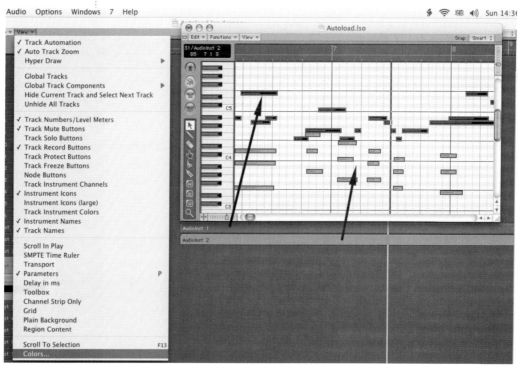

Figure 4.12

You can also open up edit windows for each region and arrange them on the page. Store this layout as a Screenset for easy access.

Figure 4.13

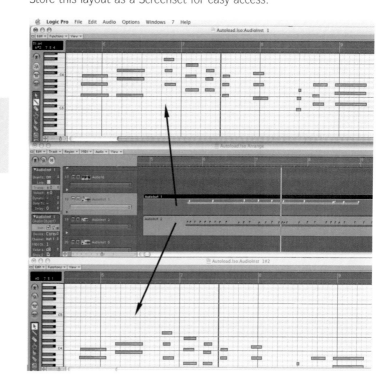

Info

The Score editor can be used to edit multiple regions displayed as multiple staves.

Some basic functions

There are usually many ways to do things in Logic Pro. The methods described here usually aren't the only way to achieve a given end.

- Logic can have an unlimited number of windows open at any one time.
- Logic can perform most of its functions while playing and recording.
- Most things in Logic can be undone using the EDIT>UNDO menu item. There's also a REDO and an UNDO history window too.
- In any of Logic's windows, you can move objects around by grabbing and dragging the object with the mouse. Hold down the mouse key over the object to do this.

Multiple Undo and Redo is available in most editors and the Arrange page. Opening the Edit>Undo history window allows you to get back to previous edits quickly.

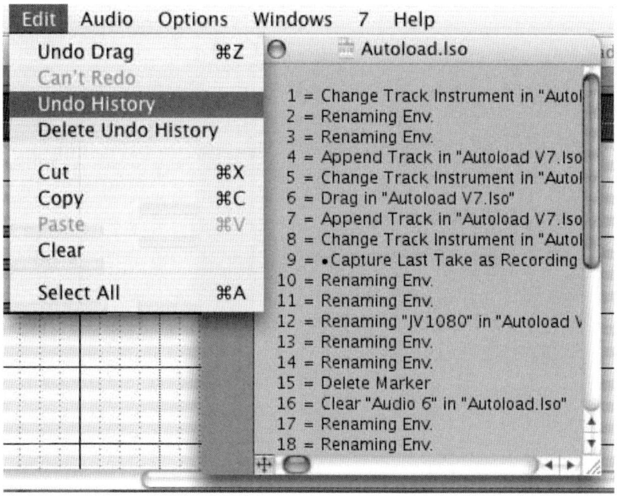

Figure 4.14

- The Toolbox can be usually displayed at the mouse cursor position by holding down the Esc key or clicking the right mouse key if you have one.
- Recording can be done in all of the editor windows
- Double clicking on a region opens the editor selected in Logic Pro>Preferences>Global>Editing menu
- Double clicking on a note opens the Event List editor
- Most of Logic's functions can be assigned to a key on the computer keyboard

Many objects can be resized by either grabbing the bottom right of the object (the mouse pointer changes to thet in the figure below or by choosing the Finger tool-box icon in the Matrix editor.

Future music

Logic Pro is always in record. Even if you haven't pressed the record button, Logic Pro is trundling away in the background recording the MIDI data you are inputting.

What this means in essence, is that if you are just doodling along in play mode and you come up a corking synth solo, all you need to do is press a key and Logic Pro will create a region, just as if you had recorded it. This feature is for MIDI data only.

Which key? Well the command for Logic Pro to 'Capture last take as recording' exists only as a Key command. If you don't know what Key commands are, you skipped here before reading all of Chapter 3. Creating Key commands are covered in that chapter and also, more fully, in Chapter 11.

So create a Key command for 'Capture last take as recording'. You know it makes sense. While you are in the Key command window, you could also usefully set up Key commands for the following:

Record Toggle   Make this the Space bar
Play   Make this the numeric keypad 0 key
Stop   Make this the numeric keypad Enter key
Record   Make this the numeric keypad * key

Setting up your first screenset

You may have noticed the number next to the Windows menu. This is the Screenset number. Screensets are Logic Pro's way of storing the positions and contents of windows on your screen. Logic Pro can store up to 99 Screensets, which are accessed by the numbers on the main keypad.

Figure 4.15

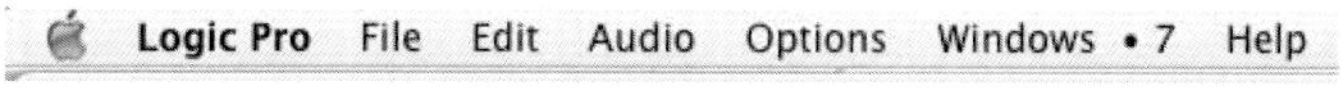

So how do you set up and save a Screenset? Lets make a 'Basic Recording' Screenset. Here's what you do. First, close all the windows and the Transport bar if there is one, so that only the main menus are visible.

Now open an Arrange window using the Windows>Arrange menu item. Drag the window and lay it out as shown in Figure 4.16. Open a Transport bar from the Windows>Transport menu item. The essential areas of the Arrange Page are:

a   Song position line (SPL)
b   Bar ruler
c   Zoom
d   Transport in Arrange window
e   Track list area
f   Instrument icons, track level meters, mute buttons
g   Instrument column
h   Track name column
i   Sequence parameter box
j   Toolbox
k   Instrument parameter box
l   Sequence area
m   Transport Bar

Make sure the Toolbox, Transport, Instrument Name; Track name, Mute switch and Parameters are visible. Select these from the Arrange page View menu.

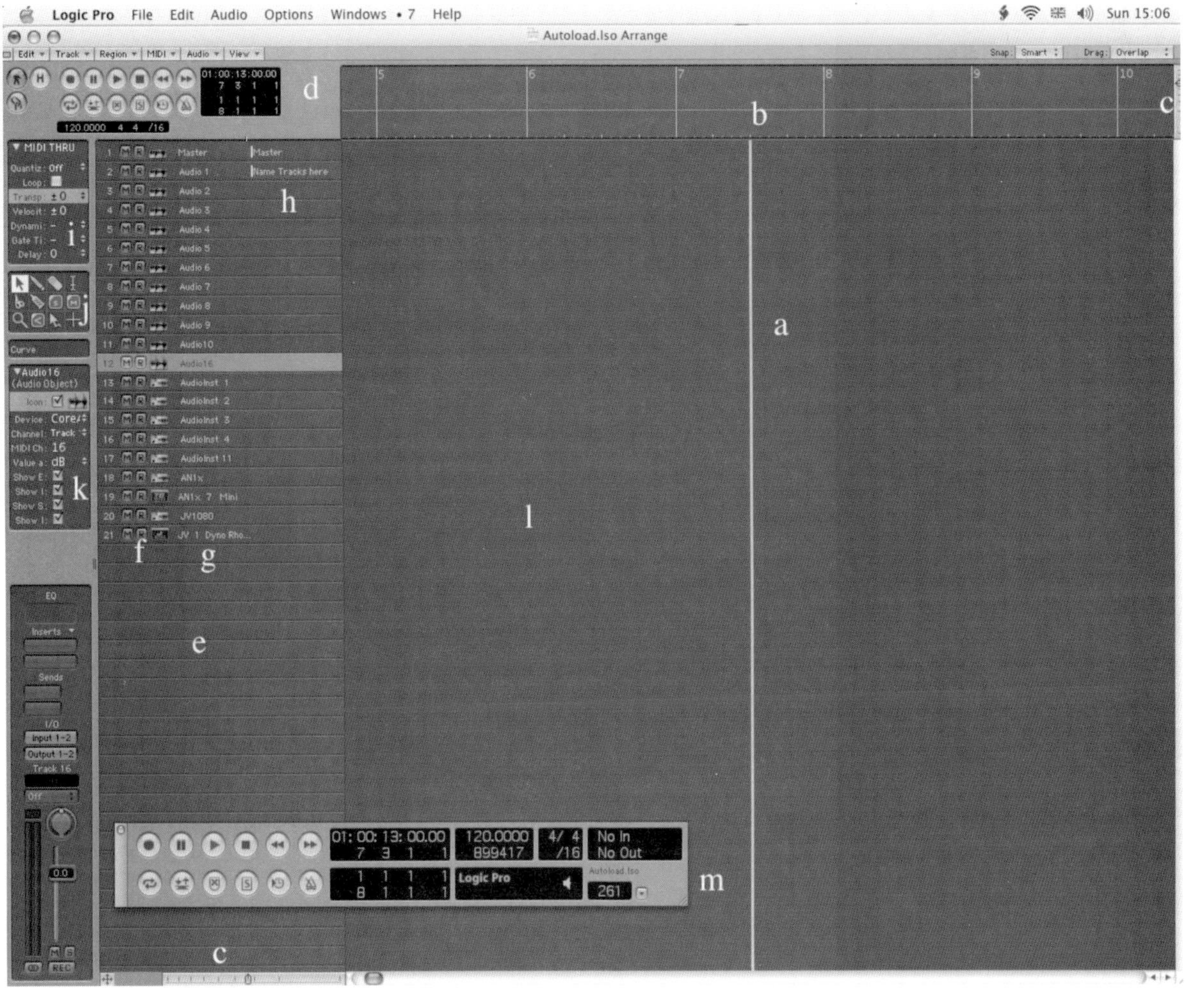

Logic Pro   File   Edit   Audio   Options   Windows • 7   Help   Sun 15:06

Autoload.lso Arrange

Drag the bar ruler down and the Track list area across so it looks something like Figure 4.17. You do this by moving the mouse over the position shown and dragging the cross to the required position.

Figure 4.16
The essential areas of the Arrange Page

Figure 4.17

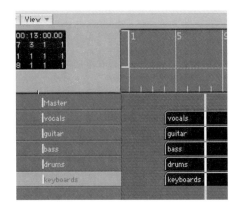

You may want to drag the Instrument name column to the right to make more of the Instrument name visible, by dragging as shown in Figure 4.18.

Figure 4,18

Now Zoom the window so it looks like Figure 4.16. The zoom controls in the top and bottom left of the window (Figure 4.19) allow you to zoom the Arrange page in and out. The tool shown in Figure 4.20 zooms in the X or time direction.

Figure 4.19 (below) and 4.20 (right)

You can zoom out to make more of the song available, or zoom in to make the regions larger and easier to grab, move and resize. The tool shown in Figure 4.21 zooms in the Y direction, allowing you to either make regions larger so you can see their contents or smaller, so you can fit more tracks on one arrange page.

So how do you save the Screenset? Well, it's already saved! Every time you open a window or move an Editor, Logic Pro saves a 'snapshot' of the screen as the number next to the Windows menu. You can return to that current screen 'snapshot' by selecting the Screenset number. You may want to Lock the Screenset by pressing the 'Lock/unlock current Screenset' key that you set up earlier or do it from the Windows>Screensets>Copy Screenset meu item. A dot appears next to the Screenset to show it's locked.

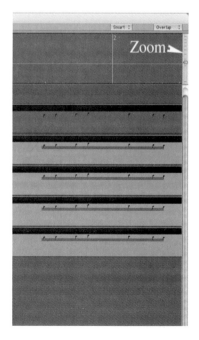

Figure 4.21

Pressing the 'lock/unlock current Screenset' key, or toggling the Windows>Screensets>Lock Screenset menu item unlocks the Screenset and removes the locked symbol. Lock it again. If you now change the position of any windows, or add another transport bar or whatever, pressing the '1' key above the QWERTY keyboard the screen will revert to the layout in Figure 4.21 again. Type '2', to change to Screenset 2 and then '1' to get back to Screenset 1. Fun isn't it? But think, you can set up complex screen layouts with many editors open and revert back to that exact set up at the touch of a key.

You can copy the current screen to a Screenset of your choosing from the Windows>Screensets>Copy Screenset menu item. Then use the Paste Screenset menu item.

You may want to save your new song at this point.

Saving songs

The first rule when using any computer program is 'Save Often'. In fact it should be 'Save often, copy the file to another hard disk, then onto a CD-R and store that in a bank vault. Every minute'. Computer crashes are a way of life, and saving often is the sensible thing to do. Logic Pro can save up to 100 backup versions of each song. So if you do decide that you have really made a mistake in turning the song from a ballad into a jungle/trance/rave/techno/Frank Sinatra cover track, you can recover your previous versions.

The first time you save your song, you should save it as a Project. The advantages of this are that all the files associated with the song are collected together in the same folder. This makes backing up easier.

Saving your song as a Project.

Use the File>Save as Project menu item and save your song. After you've saved your song as a Project, you only need to use the File>Save menu item to save the song.

Set the number of backups you want to save from the menu item Logic Pro>Preferences>Global Preferences>Song Handling. The backup files are saved within a folder created in the same folder as the song.

If you make a complete mess of an edit on a loaded song, you can use: File>Revert to Saved, to get back to the last saved version.

Opening a song

You can either open a song from within Logic Pro using the File>Open menu item. Alternatively you can double click on a song file, or an alias of one, from the Finder. If Logic Pro isn't loaded, it will be – automatically.

Your first recording

Now you have your 'Recording' Screenset, and you can record MIDI data into Logic Pro. In this chapter we will be using the Transport bar features extensively. Here's a handy diagram describing the Transport bar functions.

Figure 4.22
Transport bar features

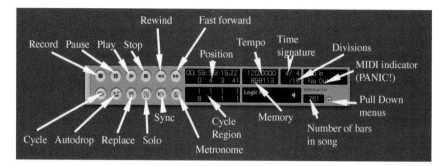

Select an instrument

Often, you'll want to start the recording with a rhythm track. So select a drum instrument from the menu in the Instrument column. A MIDI track or a Virtual instrument will do. (hold and click on the Instrument column in the Arrange page).

Figure 4.23
Select a drum instrument

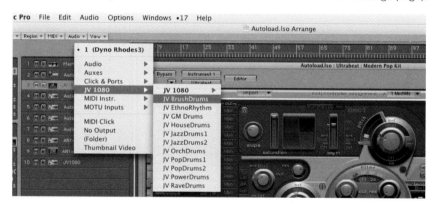

Switch on the metronome, by clicking on the metronome button on the Transport bar. The metronome is 'played' by the KlopfGeis, which you can insert on an Instrument track.

Figure 4.24

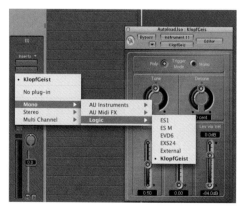

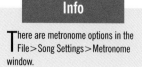

Info

There are metronome options in the File > Song Settings > Metronome window.

Set your tempo and time signature to the desired values in the Transport bar (Figure 4.25). If you want the whole song to have the same values, move the song position line to bar 1 and change the values there. Make sure Cycle and Autodrop are off (Figure 4.26).

Figure 4.25

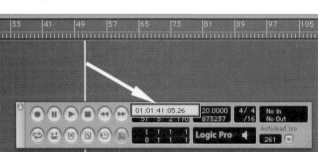

Figure 4.26

Next move the song position line by either dragging it to the place you want to start recording from, or entering the position in the song position line field on the Transport bar. (Figure 4.27).

Figure 4.27

Now from the File>Song Settings>Recording menu, select the count-in – 'No Count-In'.

There are several ways to record MIDI note data into Logic Pro.

The 'Oh damn, I forgot to press record' method

Move the song position line to the required bar. Click on the Play button on the Transport bar and play along to the click. When you have finished playing, click on the Stop button (Figure 4.28).

Press the 'Capture last take as recording' key that you set up as a Key Command earlier in the Chapter. A region will be created (Figure 4.29).

Figure 4.28

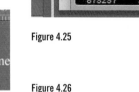

Info

Remember: MIDI data is used to record and play back both external and Virtual instruments.

Figure 4.29

The 'Just press record' method.

If Logic Pro is playing, clicking on the Record button drops Logic Pro into record. As recording progresses, Logic Pro draws little notes on the screen. Pressing Record again drops Logic Pro out of record.

The 'Press record and go' method

Move the song Position line to the required bar. Press the Pause button on the Transport bar. Now press the Record button to put Logic Pro into Record/Ready mode (Figure 4.30).

To start recording, click on the Play or Pause buttons. When you click on Stop, a region is created.

Figure 4.30

The 'Count me in' method

From the File>Song Settings>Recording menu, select the number of bars you want the count-in to be, the time signature you want it to be and whether you want the click to carry on playing when you are recording. Move the song position line to where you want the recording to start. Logic Pro will give you the selected count in before the song position line. However, Logic Pro will record anything you play during the count-in too.

The 'loop' method

Logic Pro can loop around a pre-defined area and record on each pass. First set up the left and right locators. There are several ways to do this.

You can drag the mouse over the bar ruler. This automatically switches the Transport bar's cycle button on.

Figure 4..31

You can drag the whole cycle area to the left or right

Figure 4..32

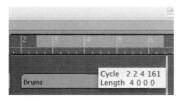

Change the beginning or end of the area with the mouse.

Figure 4..33

You can switch the cycle button 'on' and 'off' on the Transport bar and enter the values directly into the locator positions.

Figure 4.34

You can highlight an existing region, or group of regions and select the Region>Set Locators by Regions Arrange page menu item. Switch on the Cycle button on the Transport bar to switch Logic Pro into cycle mode.

So now you have set up a cycle region. Next, from the File>Song Settings>Recording Options menu, select the number of bars you want the count-in to be, what time signature it should be and whether you want the click to carry on playing when you are recording.

Press the Record button on the Transport bar. Logic Pro will count in and drop into record at the left locator. When the song position line reaches the right locator, it loops back to the left locator and the recording continues. You can 'overdub' while looping by selecting the File>Song Settings>Recording>Merge New Recording with Selected Region menu item when you record.

Tip

Set up Key commands for easy access to transport bar functions.

Recording modes

What happens depends on certain options you set within Logic Pro. These options also work in non-cycle mode. They are all chosen from the File>Song Settings>Recording menu.

If you want Logic Pro to merge each new pass of the recording into one region, click on 'Merge only new regions in Cycle Record'. If you want to create a new track each time the cycle completes, select 'Auto create tracks in cycle record'.

If you want Logic Pro to mute each previous cycle of the recording, click on 'Auto mute in cycle record'. A new region is created on each pass, each one on top of the other. However, as the song position line reaches the right locator, the last recorded region is muted and a new region recorded

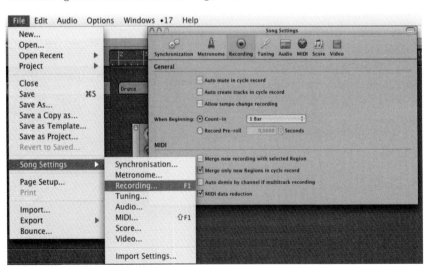

Figure 4..35

Tip

You can also destructively replace each sequence by clicking on the ERASE button on the Transport bar. This erases any MIDI or audio data, and replaces it with the latest recording.

Replace

Figure 4.37

Combining the last two options is very useful if you want to do several takes. Loop round the part of the song you desire and play away. As you start a new cycle, the previous region is muted and placed on a new track. Then, after you have pressed Stop you can choose the best parts of each region, to create the 'perfect' take!

The 'Drop in while looping' method

Logic Pro can drop in and out of a predefined part of a song. This is also known as 'punch in'. You set the autodrop region by dragging the mouse along the bar ruler while holding down the Alt key.

Figure 4.38

It can be moved and resized just like the cycle region. The autodrop region can be set within the cycle region, and switched on and off with the Transport bar button.

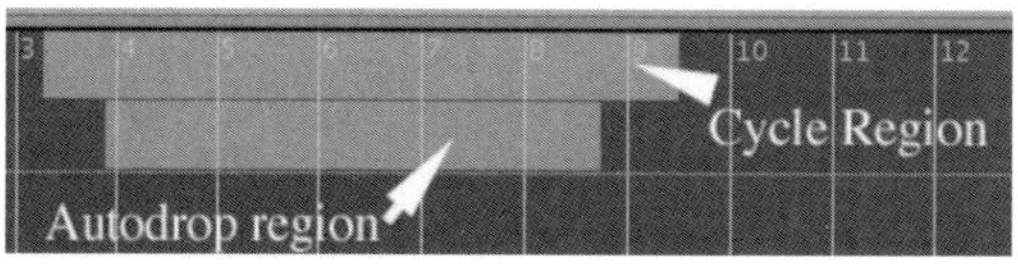

Figure 4.39

Figure 4.40

When both regions are set, the Transport bar shows both the cycle regions and the autodrop regions. These can be directly changed on the Transport bar.

Now Logic Pro will cycle between the left and right locators in record mode but record only in the autodrop region. You can use the Erase button and the File>Song Settings>Recording menu as for other recording methods.

The 'Drop in' method

You can drop in as above, without being in cycle mode. Make sure the cycle button is off on the transport bar, otherwise Logic Pro will loop.If you click the Erase button on the Transport bar, any new recording will overwrite any previous recording on the same track.

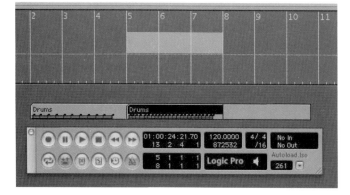

Figure 4.41

Keyboard as step entry

Using step entry you can add notes when Logic is stopped, rather than playing in 'real time'. You can add single notes or chords of different lengths and volumes. Using step input it's easy to produce bass lines and pads even if you have no keyboard skills. It's particularly useful for entering drum parts or any type of music where you're looking for a steady tempo feel, such as dance or electro pop.

The centre of the step input feature is the on-screen Keyboard. This is accessed from the Windows>Step input Keyboard Window main menu item.

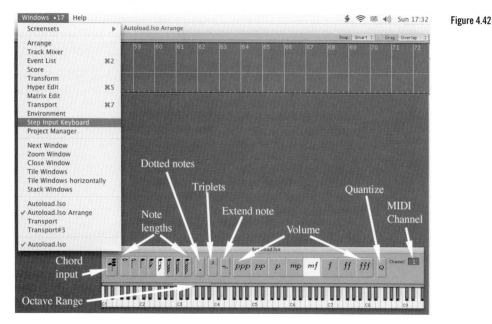

Figure 4.42

There are also a whole group of new Key commands that correspond to the controls on the keyboard window. You can also use the computer keyboard itself to enter step note data using these Key commands.

Here's how you use the step input features.

- Create an empty MIDI sequence using the Pencil tool.
- Open the Matrix or Event list editor.
- Open the Step input Keyboard window.

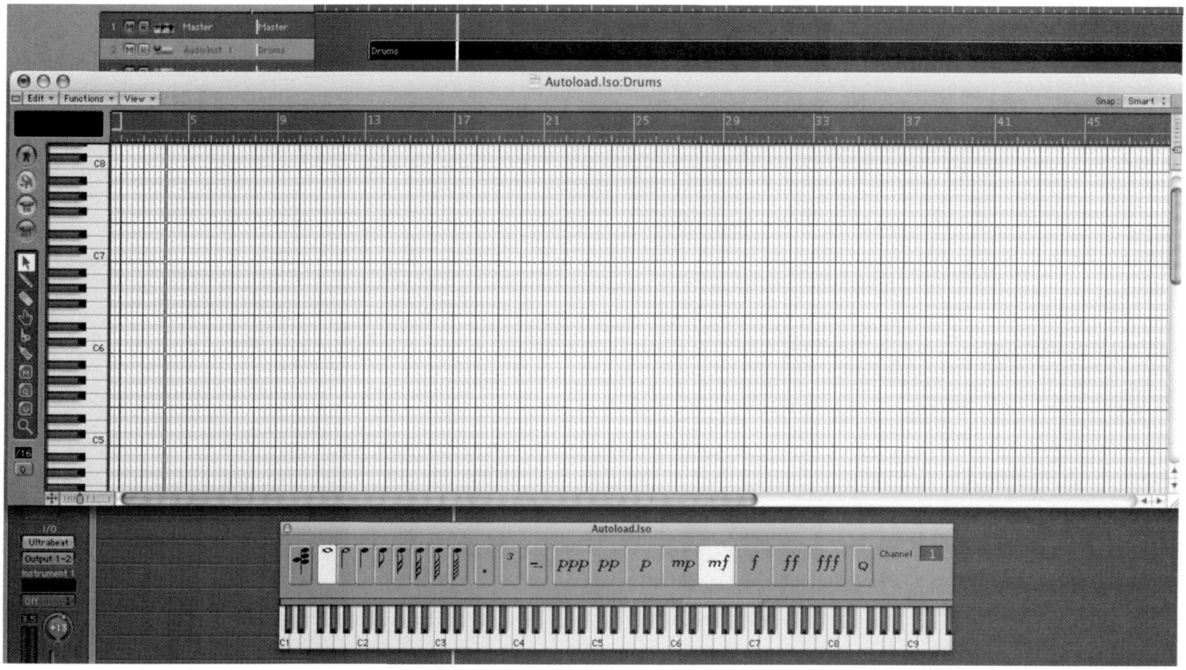

Figure 4.43
The Step input Keyboard window.

Select the note length you want and the volume of the note. The volume is set in MIDI data levels, the maximum being 128.

ppp=16
pp=32
p=48
mp=64
mf=80
f=96
ff=112
fff=128

Figure 4.44
Select the MIDI channel

Now select the MIDI channel you want the data to play back on (Figure 4.44).

Place the SPL at the start of the sequence. Click on the note on the on-screen Keyboard. As each note is created on the Matrix editor the SPL moves along the required note length. The length and pitch are defined by the settings on the Keyboard. You can change these at any note entry. You can continue to add notes as required, changing the volume and note length as you go along.

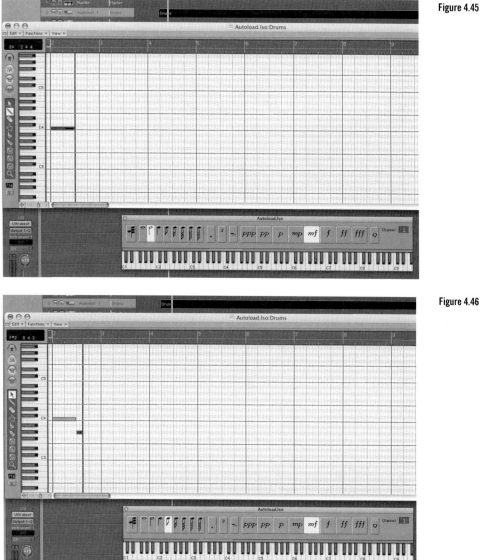

Figure 4.45

Figure 4.46

Figure 4.47

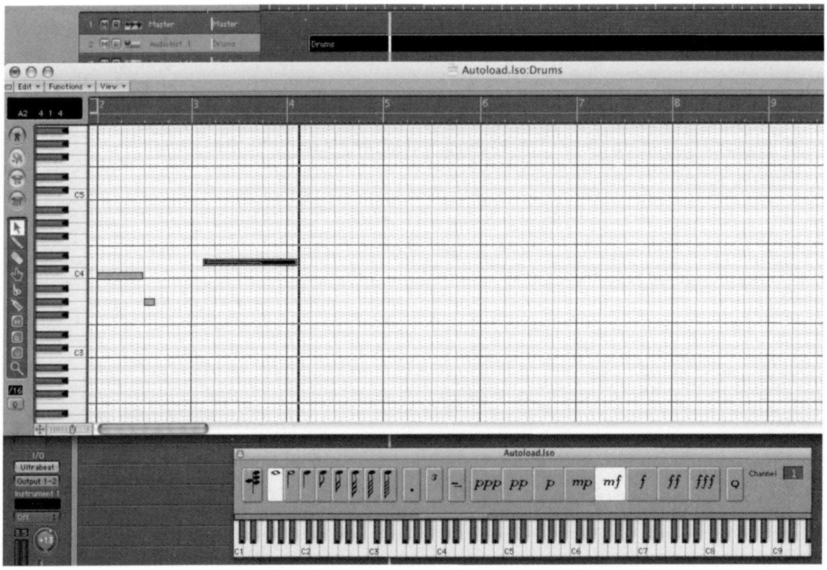

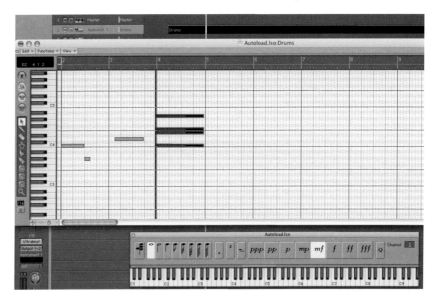

If you want to add chords, click the chord icon on the keyboard.

Now add as many notes the chord needs. Before you enter the last note, deselect the chord icon. The SPL will move on for note entry after last note is entered.

Figure 4.48

Info

You can also use the on-screen keyboard obtained by pressing the Caps lock key to perform step input.

If you want to add rests or dotted notes, you'll need to use the step input Key Commands. These are located in the Keyboard Input section of the Logic Pro>Preferences>Key Commands window.

You can also add triplets and dotted notes, in the same fashion.

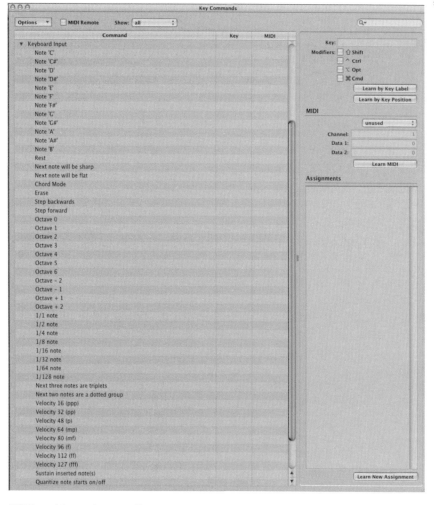

Figure 4.49
Step input Key Commands window.

Figure 4.49
Step input Key Commands window.

MIDI multi-track recording

You can record several MIDI or Virtual Instrument tracks together, just like Audio multi track recording. MIDI and Instrument tracks have a record button. When you do this, you'll hear all the selected Instruments playing, making it easy to layer parts (Figure 4.50).

There are two types of Multi-track MIDI recording, selected from the File>Song Settings>Recording menu

Figure 4.50

File > Song Settings > Recording > Audo Demix by Channel if Multitrack recording is ON

This is MultiPlayer recording. If you have different MIDI controllers, say MIDI Keyboard, Guitar and Drum pads, they will all be recorded onto separate regions on the record enabled tracks. This is really useful if you are recording a MIDI equipped band! (Figure 4.51).

Figure 4.51

File > Song Settings > Recording > Audo Demix by Channel if Multitrack recording is OFF

This is Layer recording. In this mode, only one region is recorded (on the selected

Instrument track). The other recorded instruments just have aliases of the one recording.

Figure 4.52

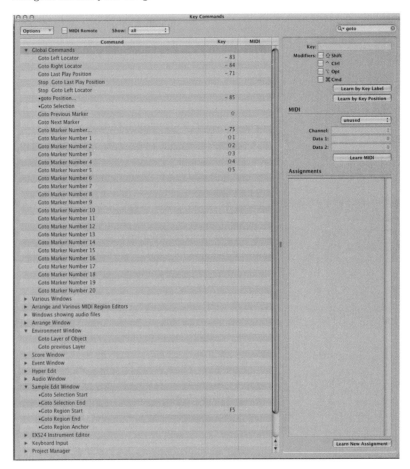

Playing back the recording

Using the transport bar

Drag the song position line to a point before the recording and press Play on the Transport bar. Of course, you don't have to play back the region with the instrument you used to record it! Select another instrument from the instrument list in the Arrange page if you wish.

If you have a cycle region defined, pressing the Stop button once will take the song position line to the left locator. Press the Stop button twice to take the song position line to bar 1. See 'Markers' later in the chapter.

There are many options that can be set as Key commands that can help you to navigate around your song.

Tip

Logic can sometimes slip into cycle mode if you mis-click on the bar ruler. Just check the Transport bar button status before you start playback or recording and save much frustration!

Figure 4. 53
Using the 'Find' feature in the Key commands window to view all Key commands with a 'Goto' function.

Skip cycle

If you drag or set the right locator before the left in the song, the region shown by the thin bar (Figure 4.54) will be skipped when the song position pointer reaches the right locator.

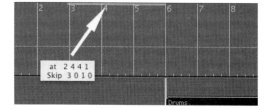

Figure 4.54

Scrubbing

You can 'scrub through' the song and hear the note data output at a speed proportional to the movement of the mouse. This is just like a tape recorder in wind mode:

Tip

You can start playback of a song by double clicking on the bar ruler.

- Press the PAUSE button on the Transport bar
- Press the PLAY button on the Transport bar
- Dragging the song position line up and down in the song will 'scrub' any sequences the line passes over. This is useful for finding specific positions within a song.

Working with tracks

Moving tracks

Grab the track to the left of the Track number. A hand appears. Drag the track to the desired position.

Deleting empty tracks

Select the Arrange page Track>Delete Unused menu item

Deleting tracks with regions on them

Highlight the track to be deleted. Select Arrange page Track>Delete Unused menu item Logic Pro will ask you if you want to clear the regions on the track.

Naming tracks

Make sure Track names has a tick by it in the View menu. Double click on the Track name column to the right of the instrument name. Enter a track name. The track name can be anything useful. (Figure 4.55).

Figure 4.55

Muting tracks

Click on the mute button to the left of the instrument icon (make sure they are visible. If not, switch it on in the View menu). Clicking on it again de-mutes the track and any regions on it.

Info

You can click and drag the mouse across many mute buttons to mute several tracks at the same time.

Working with regions

You will probably have made some errors while recording (what do you mean, 'No

I haven't'!). Perhaps you haven't kept time as well as you may have liked, hit a few bum notes, or played a bit too much. So you'll want to edit your recording.

All of these editing functions are non destructive and can be changed at any time. Many of these features are available in the other editor windows. Regions can be dragged and cut 'n pasted between songs.

Renaming regions

If you copy a region to another track or another position, you may want to rename it to reflect its new status in life. Select a region. Double click on the name field to the right of the down arrow in the region playback Parameter box and rename the region. Multiple selected regions can be renamed in the same way.

Renaming all regions on a track

Figure 4.56

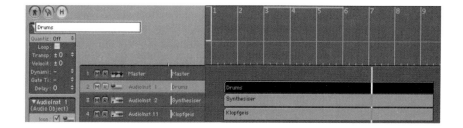

Use the Arrange page Region>Track Names to Objects menu item to rename all regions on a track to the same as the track name. Just deselect all the regions, make sure the cycle button is off and select the track. All the regions on the track are highlighted and can be renamed using the above. Another useful command to make into a Key command. If the cycle button is on, regions between the left and right locators are renamed.

Moving, copying, cutting, deleting and resizing regions

Moving, copying and resizing are all done on an invisible grid set by the bar and beat settings in the Transport bar (left). You can change how fine this grid is holding down the following modifier keys while performing the required function.

Figure 4.57

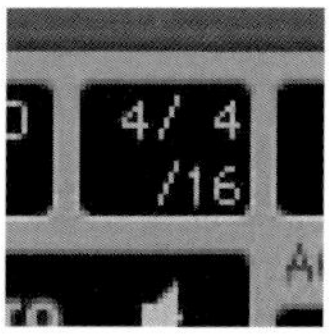

CTRL	Moves in ticks
CTRL + SHIFT	No Grid. Movement is unrestrained

Snap menu

Using this menu you can determine the behaviour of the drag.

Figure 4.58

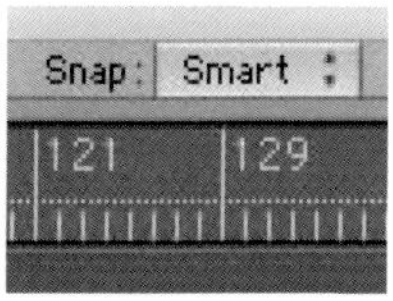

- Smart – this will usually allow you to drag a region where you need to. You can always make the movement finer using the modifier keys described above.
- Bar – this limits the dragging to individual bars.
- Beat – this limits the dragging to individual beats.
- Format – if you have the View>SMPTE Time ruler switched on, you can drag and snap to using the SMPTE values.

You can also snap to ticks, frames and quarter frames (QF)

Drag menu

This defines how regions butt up to regions they are dragged against.

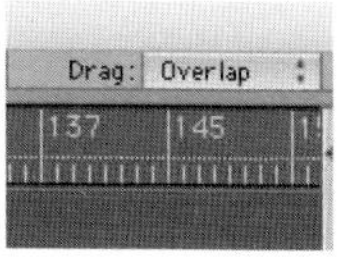

Figure 4.59

Overlap

This mode preserves the region size when dragged – even if overlapping another region.

Figure 4.60

Figure 4.61

No Overlap

If you drag a region over another region using this mode, the second region is truncated in size.

Figure 4.62

X-fade

This mode automatically cross-fades two adjacent regions. It's useful if you want to remove clicks from the transition. You can also use the crossfade tool for more complex fades.

Shuffle L and Shuffle R

These two modes will automatically butt up a dragged region to the left and right of another region automatically.

Moving and copying regions

Regions can be dragged with the mouse to a new point on the same track, or to a new track where they will then playback the new instrument. Holding down the Alt key while moving, creates a copy. Multiple selected regions can be created in this way

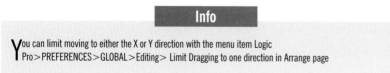

Info

You can limit moving to either the X or Y direction with the menu item Logic Pro>PREFERENCES>GLOBAL>Editing> Limit Dragging to one direction in Arrange page

Regions can be highlighted and copied to the clipboard using the Edit>Copy menu item. From here they can be pasted at the song position line, or back at their original position. All these editing features are in the Edit menu. Multiple selected regions can be copied in this way.

Aliases

Tip

Use aliases when you have many copies of the same sequence in a song, so that they are easy to keep the same when you edit the original

You can make aliases of regions in Logic Pro using the MIDI>Alias menu items. These are very similar to the alias in the Finder. Aliases are created by selecting the desired region and dragging while holding down the Shift and Alt keys. Aliases are recognized by the text within them being written in italics.

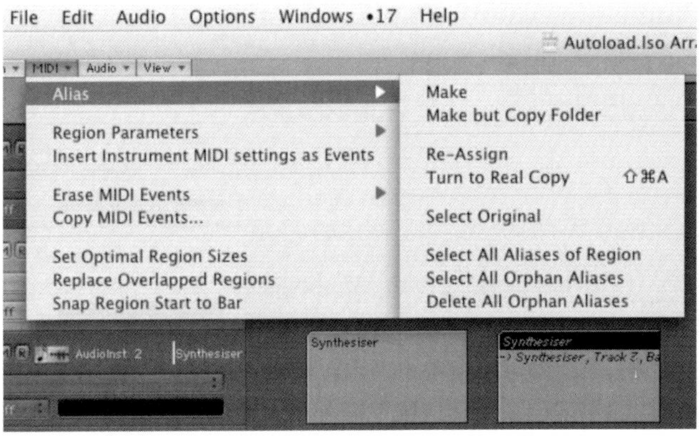

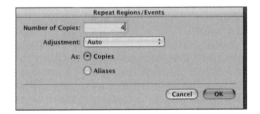

Figure 4.63

Aliases can be moved independently and have independent sequencer playback parameters, except quantization. However if you move any notes, or delete any, in the original region, the alias is also changed. You can change aliases into independent, editable regions by selecting and using the MIDI>Alias>Turn to Real Copy menu item.

Repeating regions

Highlight the desired region and select the Region>Repeat regions menu item. A dialogue box opens

Figure 4.
Basic interface

The repeat parameters are:

- Number of copies – enter the number of copies you want to make
- Adjustment – auto is the default and quantizes the repeat so that the start time is 'on the beat'. None makes the repeat start exactly at the end of the previous copy
- As – repeats can be real copies or Aliases

Cutting regions

Regions can be cut by highlighting the desired region(s) and selecting the Scissors tool. The regions are cut at that position.

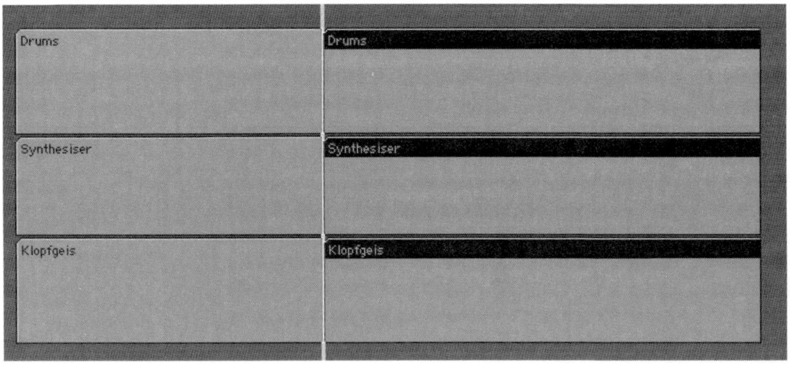

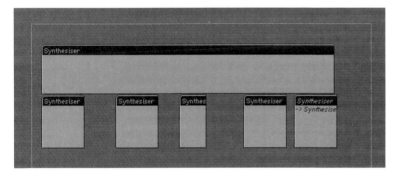

Figure 4.65

Gluing regions

Regions can be glued together by selecting them and clicking on them using the Glue tool. If you select regions on different tracks, they are 'mixed' together.

Figure 4.66

Info

You can cut sequences at the song position line using the REGIONN>SPLIT/DEMIX>SPLIT OBJECTS BY SONG POSITION menu item.

Deleting regions

Select the regions you want to delete and press the delete key. Or Select the Edit>Cut menu item.

Info

You can always Undo a deleted region using the EDIT>UNDO menu item.

Resizing regions

Grab the bottom right or left of a region and drag it to resize it. The mouse cursor turns into a resizing tool.

Muting regions

Select the region(s) you want to mute and choose the mute tool from the toolbox. Click on them again with the tool to un-mute them.

Other ways to modify regions – the region playback Parameter box

The region playback Parameter box contains many parameters you can use to modify highlighted regions. These changes are all non-destructive and are performed in real time. You can modify single regions, or groups of selected regions simultaneously.

Figure 4.67
The region playback Parameter box

Figure 4.68
Quantization menu

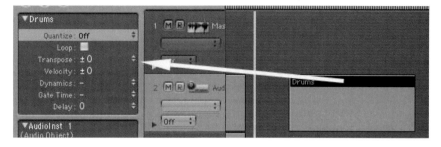

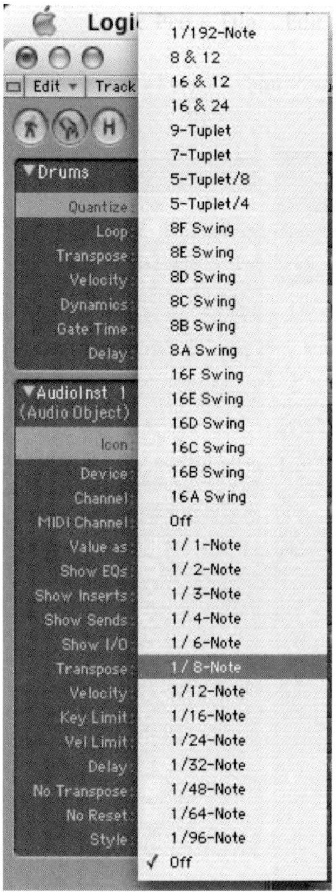

Quantization

You can quantize, or 'bring notes into time' in Logic Pro. In the Arrange window, whole regions can be quantized using the Region Playback Parameter box. This shows the details of any highlighted region.

Clicking and holding with the mouse key over the field to the right of 'Quantize' brings up a quantization menu where you can choose the desired quantization value. All selected regions will be quantized. This quantization is 'non-destructive' and can be changed, or switched off at any time.

Looping

Logic Pro's regions can be looped, i.e. repeated indefinitely or until another region is found on the same track. Multiple regions can be looped.

Select the region(s) to be looped. Turn on the loop value in the region playback parameter box 'Loop' field. Looped regions appear as grey boxes.

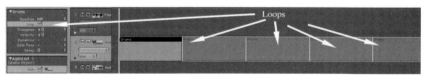

Figure 4.69
Turn on the loop value in the region playback parameter box

Transposing

Regions can be transposed. Either change the value directly in the Transpose field of the Region Parameter box or click and hold on the field, which brings up a transpose menu (right).

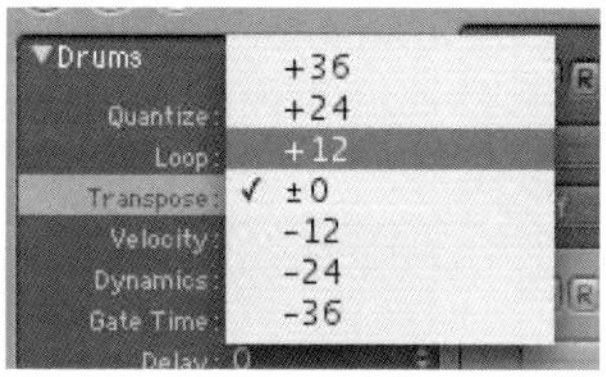

Figure 4.70
Transpose menu

Info

ou can also loop by dragging the top right of a region.

Recording more tracks

Double click on the next track area or select the Track>Create menu item. If you need to create more Audio, Instrument or Aux tracks, you can do so from the Track>Create Multiple menu item. This opens a window where you can create as many new tracks as you need. These will also be placed in the Audio page of the Environment window.

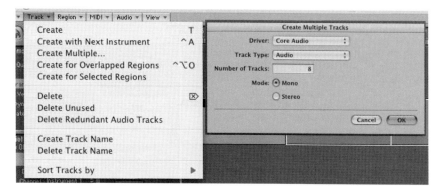

Figure 4.71
Creating tracks.

Choose the next instrument you want to use to record. Let's try a bass line next. Select an instrument or Virtual Instrument from the instrument list in the Arrange page.

Figure 4.72
Select an instrument or Virtual Instrument from the instrument list in the Arrange page.

If you're using an external MIDI device, such as a synthesizer, choose a patch by clicking On the name of the instrument on the Track parameter box. Click on the Parameter box, to the right of the down arrow to bring up the Patch change box. Choose the patch you require and close the window.

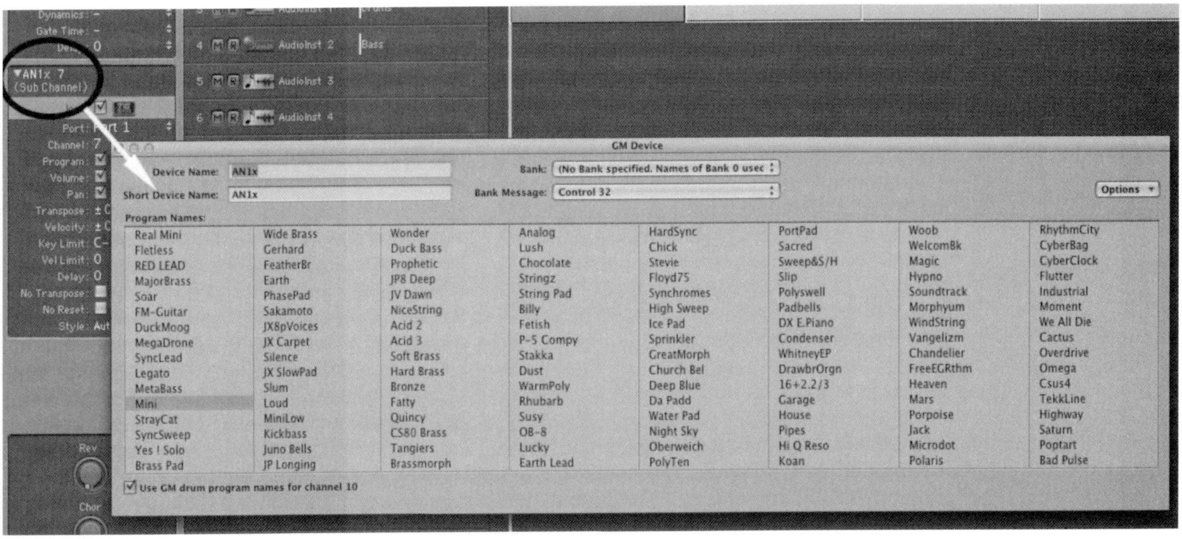

Figure 4.73
Click on the Parameter box, to the right of the down arrow to bring up the Patch change box.

Now record using the selected instrument. Continue adding tracks and instruments until you have recorded several parts. The Arrange page should look something like Figure 4.74.

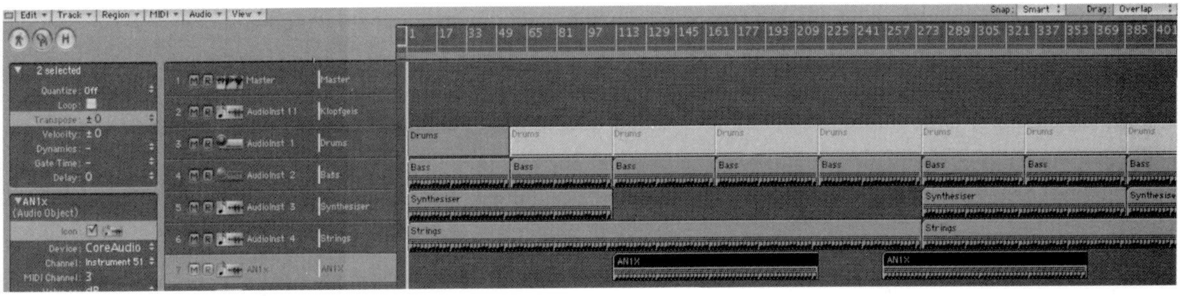

Figure 4.74

More detailed editing

Of course, you may want to edit individual notes within a region. To do this you will usually use the Matrix or Event editors.

Matrix editor

This is a 'piano roll' type editor mainly used to graphically edit note data. See Chapter 9.

Event list editor

All types of MIDI data recorded into Logic Pro can be edited here. See Chapter 8. Before we get down to any serious editing we have to discuss the 'Running man' and 'Link' icons. You may have noticed these in most of the windows in Logic Pro.

They are the thread that runs between Logic Pro's windows and pages, allowing you to choose how they work together. Open an Arrange page. Matrix editor and event list (as shown in Figure 4.76).

Running man

When this is on (man is blue), the windows' display follows the song position line. In our example, when we press start, the running man switches on and both Arrange and Matrix edit song position lines move together. If you switch the Matrix editor running man off, the Matrix editor's song position line will stop but the Arrange pages' will continue. This only happens if the Logic Pro>Preferences> Catch>Allow content Catch if Catch and Link are enabled menu item is on.

Figure 4.75

Link mode

If you click once on the Link Icon, the window always displays the same contents as the top window, if that is possible. Here's an example of what this means.

    If you have a Matrix editor, an Event editor and an Arrange page open, and the Link icon is, clicking on a region on the Arrange page will show the following Event editor window. Note that the Event editor shows the same 'level' of data as the Arrange page.

Figure 4.76

Now click on a note in the Matrix editor. You will see the Event list editor will change to show the same notes as the Matrix editor, i.e. it is at the same 'level' of data.

Figure 4.78

Link – Show Contents mode

If you double click on the Link icon the behaviour of the windows changes. If you have the same Matrix editor, Event editor and Arrange page open and the Link icon is yellow, clicking on the Arrange page will show the following Event editor window (Figure 4.79).

Note that the Event editor shows data one 'level' below that of the Arrange page, i.e. the note data of the selected region in the Arrange page. Now click on a note in the Matrix editor. You will see the Event list editor will keep the same data as the Matrix editor. You cannot have one 'level' below that of MIDI events!

Info

If you want the Editors to show the notes within a sequence as the song position passes over that sequence, make sure the Running man is ON and The Link icon is double clicked.

If you switch on both the Running man and the Link icon in 'Link-Show Contents mode' you can force the editors to display the notes of each region currently being played on a selected track as the song position line passes over it.

Figure 4.79

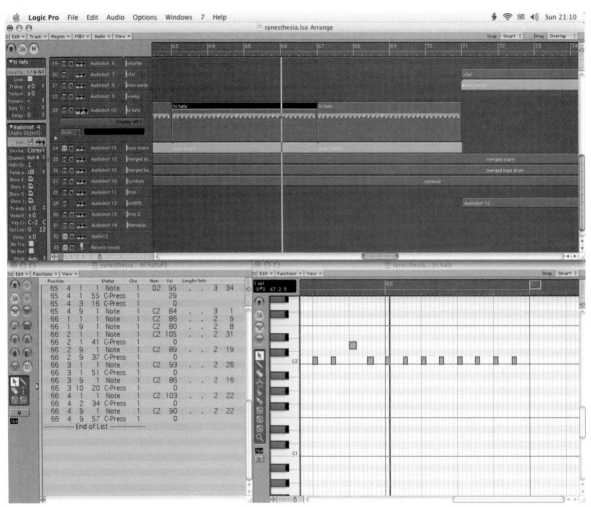

Linking and the Environment

If you click once on the Link icon in the Environment, selecting an instrument in the Arrange window will select that instrument object in the Environment even if it has to change layers to do it. This is useful if you select a modifier, such as an arpeggiator in the Arrange page, and you want to modify its parameters from the Environments Parameter box. You can have many windows open with different Link Settings saved as a Screenset

Info

You can set the Matrix editor as the default editor by selecting it from the Logic Pro>Preferences>Editing menu item. Double clicking on a sequence will open the Matrix editor.

Figure 4.80

Editing with the Matrix editor

Open the editor by highlighting a region and selecting the Windows>Open Matrix Edit menu item. Or double click on the region if the Preference is set.

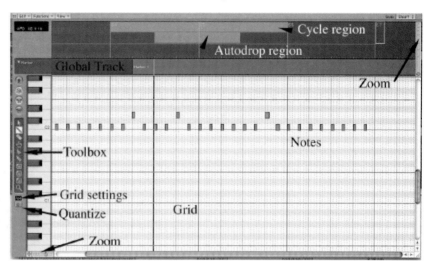

Info

There are several Goto Key commands available for moving around in windows. Open the Key Commands window and use the Find: command to see all the Goto commands.

Drag and resize the Matrix editor window to a convenient size and place. Use the slider to the right of the window to bring the notes within the editor into View. You can also zoom the window using the zoom tools. You may notice that this page is very like the Arrange page. In fact, the Matrix editor behaves like the Arrange page in many ways. The notes in the Matrix editor are analogous to regions in the Arrange page.

Notes in the Matrix window can be moved, cut, copied, pasted, resized and deleted in exactly the same way as regions in the Arrange page. When you drag a note it will 'snap' into a position which is defined by the grid setting, which can be changed with the mouse. This change is instantly displayed on the grid in the editor window. You can move objects in finer steps, as in the Arrange page.

Figures 4.81 and 4.82

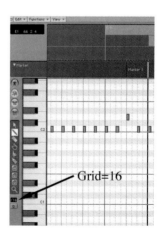

If you hold the mouse key down on a note, the details of that note are displayed in an info box.

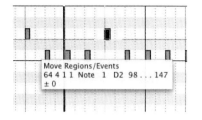

Figure 4.83

If you wish to edit a single note numerically, open the Event Float from the View menu. This window shows the properties of a single note when highlighted, and the values in it can be edited directly with the mouse.

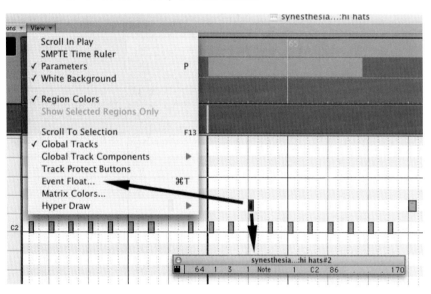

Figure 4.84

Figure 4.86

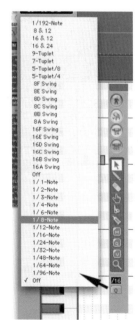

Selecting notes

You can, of course, select notes in the usual way in the Matrix editor, i.e. rubber banding, clicking shift clicking. If the Out button (right) is on then you will hear the notes as they are selected.

Quantizing notes

Select the notes you wish to quantize. Choose the quantize value from the pull down menu (right).

Quantizing is non destructive and can be changed at anytime, or reset to off. Alternatively you can deselect all the notes, choose the quantize value in the pull down menu and select the quantize tool. Then clicking on a note, or selected notes will quantize those notes.

Changing the velocity of notes

You can see that each note is a different colour (or shade of grey), with a line through it. This is a representation of their velocity value. You can change this value by selecting the velocity tool (left) and dragging it vertically over the note

Figure 4.87

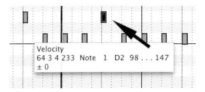

Changing the velocity of several notes

Select the notes you wish to change and select the velocity tool. If the velocity value of any of the notes reaches 127 or 0, you cannot further increase or decrease of any of the notes. If you hold down the Alt and Shift keys while you do this, all notes are given the same velocity value. If you hold down the Alt key while you do this, all notes will eventually reach the extreme velocity value.

Editing with the Event list editor

Use the Event list editor when you want to finely edit all types of MIDI data. You can edit notes, controller data, SysEx, patch changes, aftertouch and pitchbend. You can either type in the data directly or use the mouse to alter values. Open the editor by highlighting a region and selecting the Windows>Open Event List menu item. (Double clicking on a note in the Matrix editor will open up the Event list editor and select that note.)

Figure 4.88

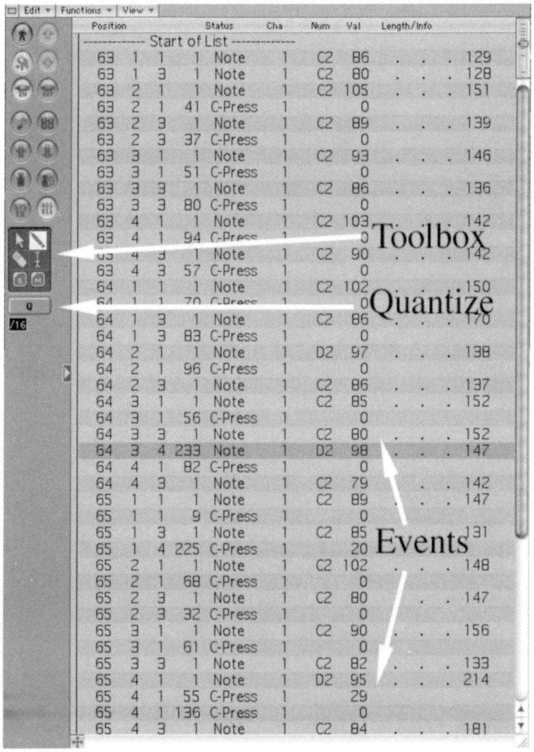

Move and resize the editor to a convenient size and position. Note that the Event list editor only has a Y direction zoom icon at the top of the window. There is a Link icon and a Running man icon here as in the Matrix editor and Arrange pages.

The Event list editor shows MIDI data in a vertical list with the earliest events at the top, the later events at the bottom. The data displayed depends on the status of the following buttons:

 Displays note data

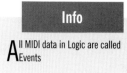
Info

All MIDI data in Logic are called Events

Displays program change data

Displays Pitch bend data

Displays controller data (Pan, volume etc.)

Displays Channel pressure (Aftertouch) data

 Displays polyphonic aftertouch data

 Displays SysEx data

Meta events

Meta events are generated internally by Logic Pro. You can use them to do things like change Screensets, start and stop playback etc. For examples on how to use Meta events, try out the Logic Pro tutorial song that is supplied on the Installation disks.

Let's edit some data. Look at notes first. Make sure just the note icon (right) is on. This is a drum region.

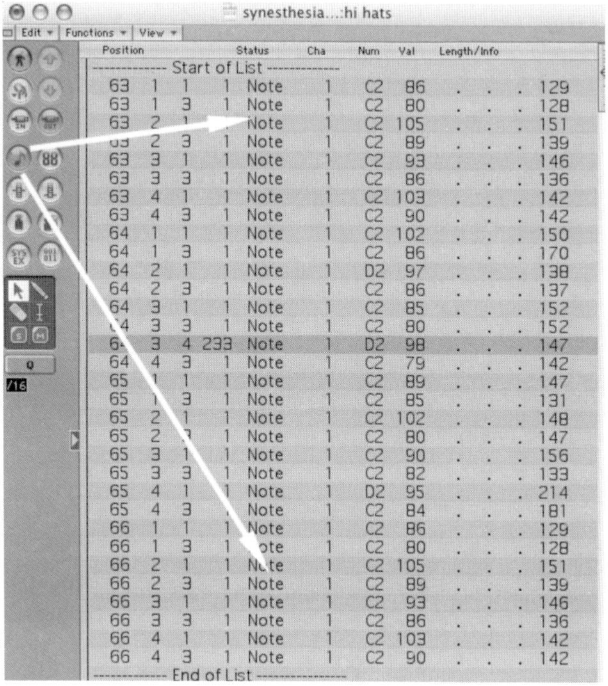

Figure 4.98
Drum region

Changing the position of a note (Position column)

You can change the position of a note either directly with the mouse or by double clicking on the Position value and entering the values.

Figure 4.99

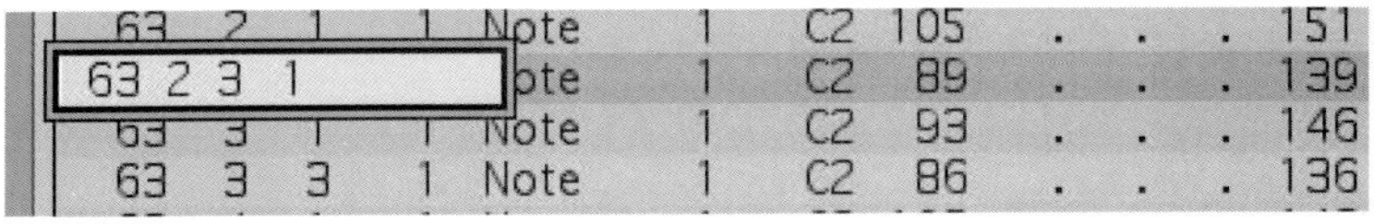

63	2	1	1	Note	1	C2	105	.	.	.	151
63	2	3	1			C2	89	.	.	.	139
63	3	1	1	Note	1	C2	93	.	.	.	146
63	3	3	1	Note	1	C2	86	.	.	.	136

The note will be moved in the list to maintain the Lists' time structure. If you change positions with the mouse, the value changes with reference to an 'invisible' grid, set by the 'divison' value as in the Matrix editor.

Changing the MIDI channel (Cha column)

You can change the MIDI channel of the note either directly with the mouse or by double clicking on the Cha value and entering number directly.

Changing the note (Num column)

You can change actual note either directly with the mouse or by double clicking on the NUM value and entering the note directly.

Changing the velocity of a note (Val column)

You can change the velocity of the note either directly with the mouse or by double clicking on the Val value and entering the value directly.

Changing the length of the note (Length)

You can change the length of the note either directly with the mouse or by double clicking on the Length/Info value and entering the length directly.

The parameters these fields address vary depending on what type of MIDI data you are editing or viewing.

Selecting events

You can select one event by just clicking on it. There are several ways to select multiple events. Obviously, you cannot 'Rubber band' in the Event list. You can however Shift and click on multiple events or use the Edit menus selection parameters, as in the Matrix editor and Arrange page.

Changing multiple events

Select the notes you wish to change. Change one of them as described above. If the value of any of the MIDI events reaches 127 or 0, there will be no further increase or decrease of the events. If you hold down the Option/Alt and Shift keys while you do this, all events are given the same value. If you hold down the Option/Alt key while you do this, all events will eventually reach the extreme values.

Quantizing

Select the notes you wish to quantize and select the quantize value from the 'Q' pull down menu.

Editing other data

To view other data, click on the relevant icon. For example, if you want to edit pitch-bend, click on the pitchbend icon (right). If you leave the note icon on too, you will see both types of data.

See Chapter 8 for more on the Event List editor.

Other features you may find useful while recording and editing

Recording and editing program changes

In Logic Pro it is very easy to record program changes. Here's how to do it: Select the instrument you want the program change to affect. If necessary, create a new track.

Figure 4.101

Move the song position line to where you want the program change to occur. As with most sequencers, it's a good idea to have the program change a tad before the music begins.

Put Logic Pro in Record/Ready mode, either by pressing the space bar, or clicking on the pause button, then the record button. Logic Pro should now be in record mode but not moving.

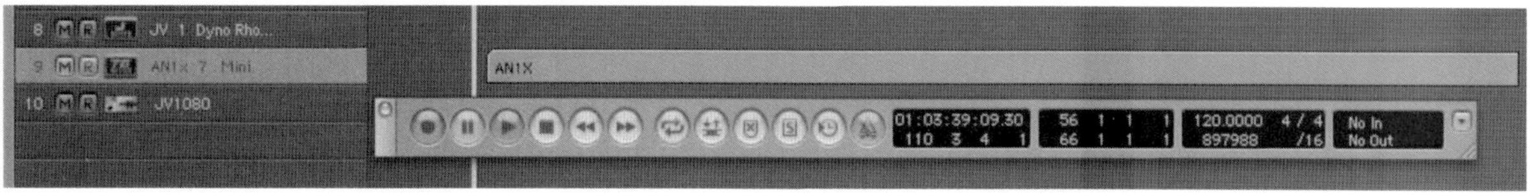

Figure 4.102

Click and hold on the MIDI device name on the Track parameter box. The patch window opens.

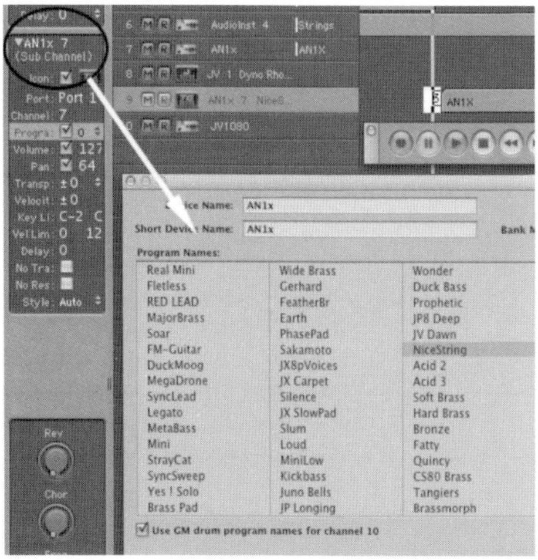

Figure 4.103

Select the patch you want. Click on the stop button. A region will be created containing the program change. Rename it 'Program Change'. You can edit the program change by selecting the region, and opening the Event list from the Windows>Open Event List menu. Click on the program change icon to view the program change value. You may want to switch off all the other icons to only see program change events.

Figure 4.104

Program Change Icon

You can edit the position and MIDI channel of the event in the usual way. Hold and click on the Length/Info column to change the patch. Select it from the pull down menu.

Figure 4.105

Info

If you want to make sure the actual patches on your synth match those in the instruments in a song when it is loaded, make sure that File>Song settings>MIDI Send used Instrument. MIDI settings after loading is on.

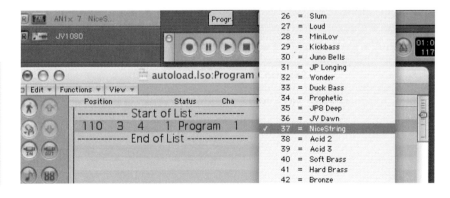

Solo mode

There are times you will want to listen to a part or parts in isolation to the others. There are several ways to use solo in Logic Pro. Select regions you want to solo and either click on the Solo button on the Transport bar, or select the Solo tool from the toolbox (right) and click on the regions with it. For more on soloing see Chapter 6.

Figure 4.106

Markers

When working on a complex song, it's easy to get lost. Wouldn't it be useful if you could put markers at certain positions of a song, name them something like 'Chorus 1', perhaps even make some text notes and have a way to easily jump to these markers? Logic Pro has such a feature, and they are called Markers and you create them on the Arrange page. See also Chapter 13 on 'Global Tracks' for more on Markers.

To create a marker

Move the song position line to where you want the Marker to be created. Create a marker at this point by selecting the Options>Marker>Create menu item.

Figure 4.107

A marker is created at this position.

Figure 4. 108

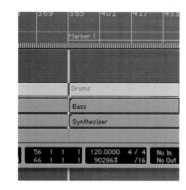

Open the marker list from the Options>Marker>Open List menu item. You can also create a Key command to open the list. As you can see, the marker list box is very like the Event list editor. You can edit the position and length of the marker directly here.

Figure 4.109

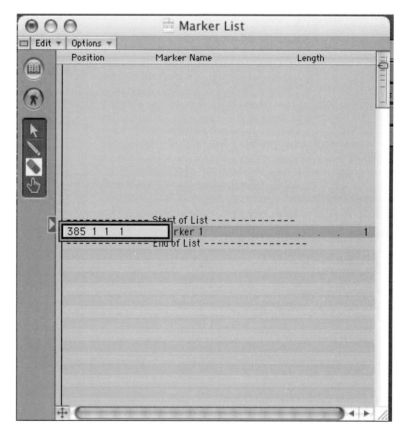

You can move the position of the marker directly on the bar line on the Arrange page. Grab the marker while holding down the Apple key and drag the marker to the left or right.

To edit the name of the marker, click on the book icon or double click on the marker name in the list. This opens a text editor window.

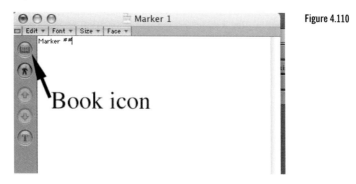

Figure 4.110

You can rename a marker directly in the Arrange page. Double click on the marker while holding the Apple and Ctrl keys down.

Figure 4.111

The Top line is the marker name. You can edit this directly. The change is reflected straight away in the Arrange page.

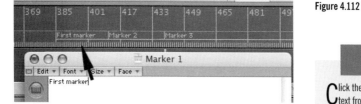

Figure 4.112

As you can see, this marker window is a little text editor, and you can add text notes here. You may want to make some comments about the song, which will help you when you come back to it in the future, or add lyrics or whatever. Close the window when you have finished. Create some more markers!

You can use the menu item Options>Marker>Open Text to bypass the event list style box and go directly to the Text editor.

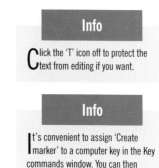

Info

Click the 'T' icon off to protect the text from editing if you want.

Info

It's convenient to assign 'Create marker' to a computer key in the Key commands window. You can then create them 'on the fly' as Logic plays

Using the marker list box

Open the marker list box. The box has a 'running man' icon, which means as Logic Pro plays it will scroll along with the Arrange page (Figure 4.113).

Figure 4.113

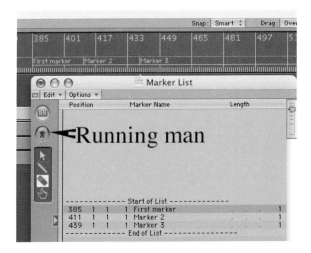

Moving the song position line to a specific marker

As is usual in Logic Pro, there are several ways to do this. Use the menu commands Goto Next, Goto Previous and Goto Number (see Tip) in the Options>Marker menu. Goto Marker Number opens a dialog window where you can enter the number. The song position line will be moved to the correct marker, or click on the marker name in the marker list. The song position line is moved to the beginning of the new marker on the Arrange page.

If you click on a marker on the bar ruler while holding down the Apple key, the song position line is moved to the start of the marker.

Tip

Make these three commands into Key commands for convenience.

To delete a marker

Drag the marker downwards (a thumb appears). Release the mouse key and the marker is deleted. Markers can also be cleared or cut using the Edit menu in the marker box.

Other useful marker functions

If you select regions, you can create a marker that encompasses them all from the menu item Options>Marker>Create by regions. If you have a cycle region set up you can create a marker the between the left and right locators. Drag the cycle bar down (an upwards thumb appears). Release the mouse key over the marker region of the bar ruler and a marker is created. If you drag the cycle region onto an existing marker, the marker is adjusted to fit the cycle region.

Folders

A folder in Logic Pro is an Arrange page object that can contain other objects, i.e. regions. It's directly analogous to a folder on your computer and can be used in the same fashion; to group together items in a useful way. Folders are a kind of song within a song. A folder can contain as many tracks and regions as you like.

To create a folder
Highlight the regions you want to put into a folder.

Figure 4.114

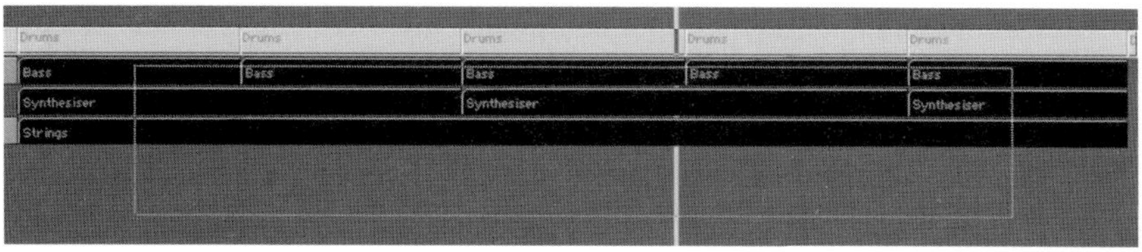

Select the Region>Folder>Pack Folder menu item. A folder is created containing the regions previously selected.

Figure 4.115

Folders can be renamed, moved, cut, copied, pasted, resized, and deleted in exactly the same way as regions in the Arrange page.

To open a folder
Double click on the Folder to open it. You can see the regions in it. Note that the instrument Settings are the same as they were in the main Arrange page.

To close a folder
Double click on the background to close a folder.

To copy regions to and from a folder
Open two Arrange windows like this. Make sure the Link icon is off.

Figure 4.116

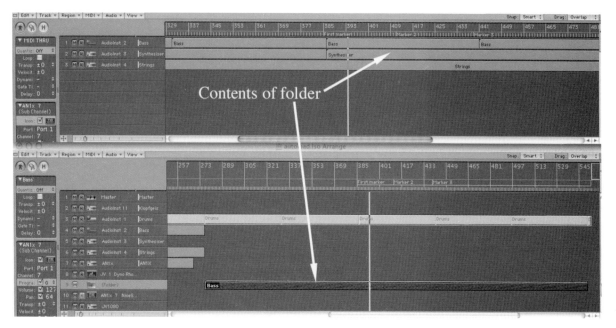

Contents of folder

Open the folder in the top window by double clicking on the folder. You can drag regions to and from the two windows. Note: Markers and instruments are visible in the folder in exactly the same way as the Arrange page.

Unpacking a folder

Select the folder to unpack. Select the Region>Folder>Unpack Folder menu item. If the appropriate tracks and instruments are not there they will be created by Logic Pro.

Working with songs

Once you have recorded several regions your song may look something like the figure below. The window has been zoomed out so all the regions and tracks in a song can be seen at the same time. Note that all the drum parts have been grouped into a folder and markers set up to define parts of the song.

Figure 4.117

You can copy the current screen to a Screenset of your choosing as follows: Hold down the Shift key. While keeping the Shift key down, change to a new Screenset using the number keys above the qwerty keyboard. To access Screensets with numbers over 9, hold down Ctrl and type in the number desired. This new Screenset is a copy of the original screenset.

Use the 'protect Screenset' Key command to prevent the Screenset being changed. You can now get to this 'overview' by simply selecting the Screenset number.. You can also use the Windows>Screenset menus to perform these tasks.

Moving whole parts of songs around

We have seen earlier how it is possible to copy individual and groups of regions around the Arrange page. However, sometimes you may want to copy whole areas of the song around. You may want to:

- Copy and paste a chorus from the middle to the end of a song
- Cut out a whole portion a song and join up the gap
- Insert a whole section of a song into the middle of the song
- Cut a whole section from a song and paste it into another song

The first thing you need to do is select the portion of the song you wish to cut. You could select the regions in the usual way, but Logic Pro provides several helpful commands in the Edit menu to make selection easier.

Here's how to select 'Chorus 1' in our example. Set the left and right locators to the start and end of the region you want to cut. You can do this by either, entering the left locator and right locator directly into the Transport bar (above right), or dragging the marker named 'Chorus 1' up to the top of the ruler bar (below right).

The left and right locators are set to the same as the start and end of the Marker. Here's how you move this section around.

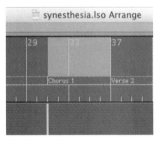

Adding 'Chorus 1' to the end of the song

Select the whole song from the Edit>Select All menu item. Snip out the 'Chorus 1' section of the song using the Region>Cut/Insert Time>Snip: Cut Time and Move by Locators menu item.

Figure 4.120

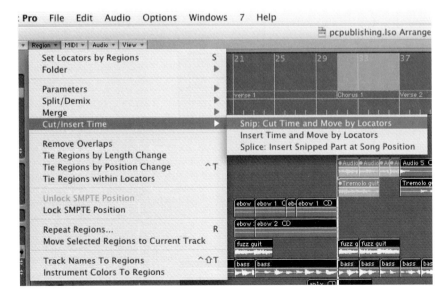

If you want to keep the original 'Chorus 1' select Edit>Undo or the Region>Cut/Insert Time>Splice: Insert Snipped Part at Song Position item immediately, to paste it back in place. Move the song position line to the end of the song. Paste the region into the song at this point using the Region>Cut/Insert Time>Splice: Insert Snipped Part at Song Position menu item.

Figure 4.121

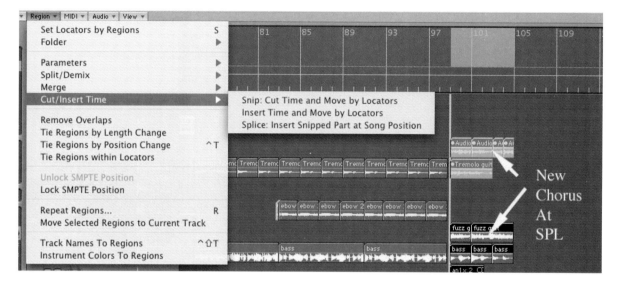

You can use the above technique to insert the same region into a song. The song will be cut and the regions moved up to make way for the new region. Just place the song position line at the point you want to insert the section.

Removing 'Chorus 1' and closing the gap created.
Select the whole song from the Edit>Select All menu item. Select Region>Cut/Insert Time>Snip: Cut Time and Move by Locators.

This completely removes the section between the left and right locators, and moves the whole song to the left to fill the gap.

Figures 4.122 and 4.123

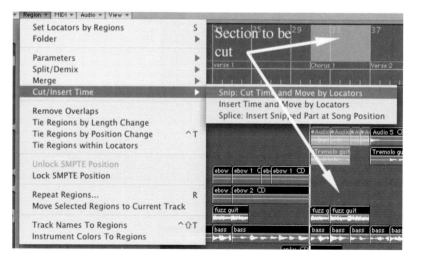

Creating a gap in the song

Select the whole song from Edit>Select All. Select Region>Cut/Insert Time>Insert Time and Move by Locators. A gap the length of the cycle region will be inserted. All the regions in the song are moved to the right.

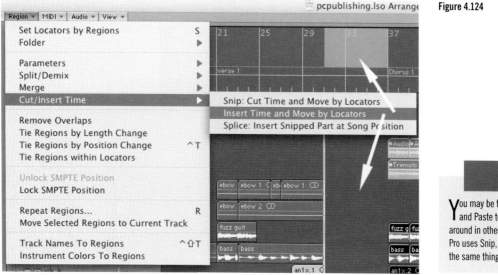

Figure 4.124

> **Info**
>
> You may be familiar with Cut, Copy and Paste to move parts of a song around in other music software. Logic Pro uses Snip, Insert and Splice to do the same thing.

Moving parts of one song to another

Logic Pro can load many songs at the same time. You can use all the methods for copying data within a song to move data between songs. You can also drag regions between arrange windows of different songs, if you align them on the screen like this.

Figure 4.125

Info

The Automation data used in Logic Pro can be edited in the same way as Hyperdraw. See Chapter 16 for more on Automation.

Graphically mixing your MIDI data – Hyperdraw

Hyperdraw is a way of drawing controller information directly on the regions themselves. You can draw any controller information but the most useful are obviously volume, pan, modulation, aftertouch and pitchbend.

Hyperdraw curves can only be seen if the regions are large enough. This obviously makes it easier to draw on them with the mouse too! You can make the regions larger in two ways. Zoom the window out using the zoom tools at the top right and bottom left of the Arrange page, or select the magnifying tool (left) from the Toolbox and drag the tool around the regions you want to enlarge.

Figure 4.127

Figure 4.128

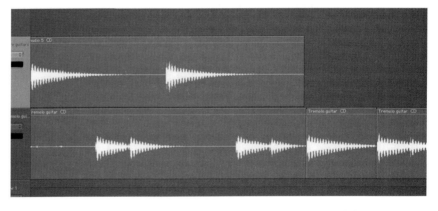

Release the mouse key and the regions will be enlarged. Double click on the background to revert the Arrange page to normal.

Create a Screenset with a magnified Arrange page

Here's how you do it.

- Type 2 on the numeric keys above the qwerty keyboard (for example)
- Open two Arrange pages, and drag and resize them as shown (Figure 4.130)
- Zoom out the lower Arrange page
- Lock the Screenset with the Key command you set up earlier in the chapter.
- Now pressing the 2 key will bring up this Hyperdraw Screenset
- Make sure the Running man icon (right) is ON, so the two windows play back in sync.

Figure 4.130

Select the region you want to draw the controller data onto.

Adjusting the volume of the region

Select the View>Hyperdraw>Volume Arrange page menu item. The region will turn blue and the controller number appears at the top left of the region (In this case, 7).

Figure 4.131

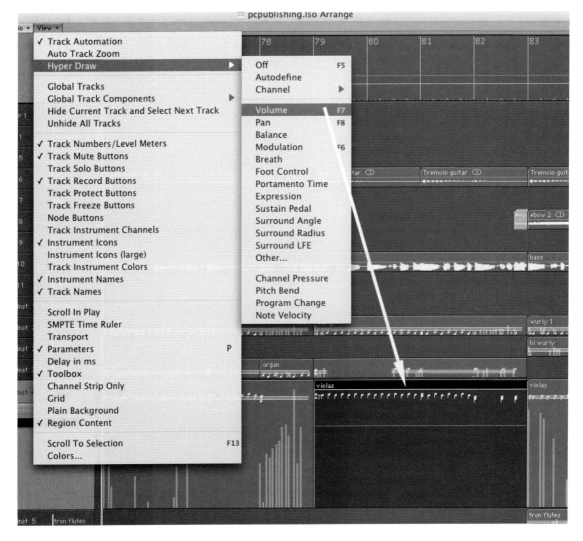

Now click on the region to draw a Hyperdraw curve. At each click, a MIDI Volume (controller number 7) event is created and a line drawn between them. Events can be dragged and moved at will (Figure 4.132).

Holding down the Ctrl key while dragging makes the movement finer. You will only be able to move vertically though.

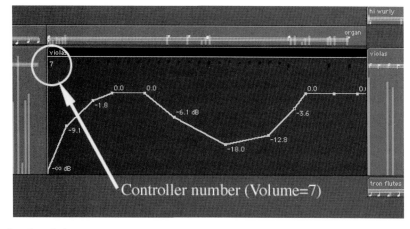

Figure 4.132

Controller number (Volume=7)

Moving the whole curve

Holding down the Alt while you drag a Hyperdraw event, moves all the Hyperdraw events to the right of the node you click on.

Deleting individual Hyperdraw events

Click on each event to delete it. The line is re-drawn between the nearest 2 events.

Deleting all the Hyperdraw events

Hold down the ALT and double click on a node to delete all the events.

Finer editing of Hyperdraw events

Highlight the region. Open the Event List editor. Make sure just the controller data icon is on and the Note icon is OFF. This will ensure only controller events are displayed. You can see all and edit all the events you have just created by drawing on the region.

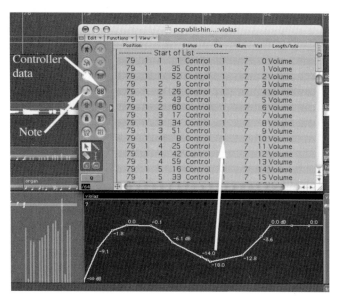

Figure 4.133

If you want to draw the curve for a different controller number, let's say pan (controller number 10), select it from the View>Hyperdraw> menu item. The volume data curve on the region is greyed out. Draw on the region in the same fashion as for the volume curve.

Figure 4.134

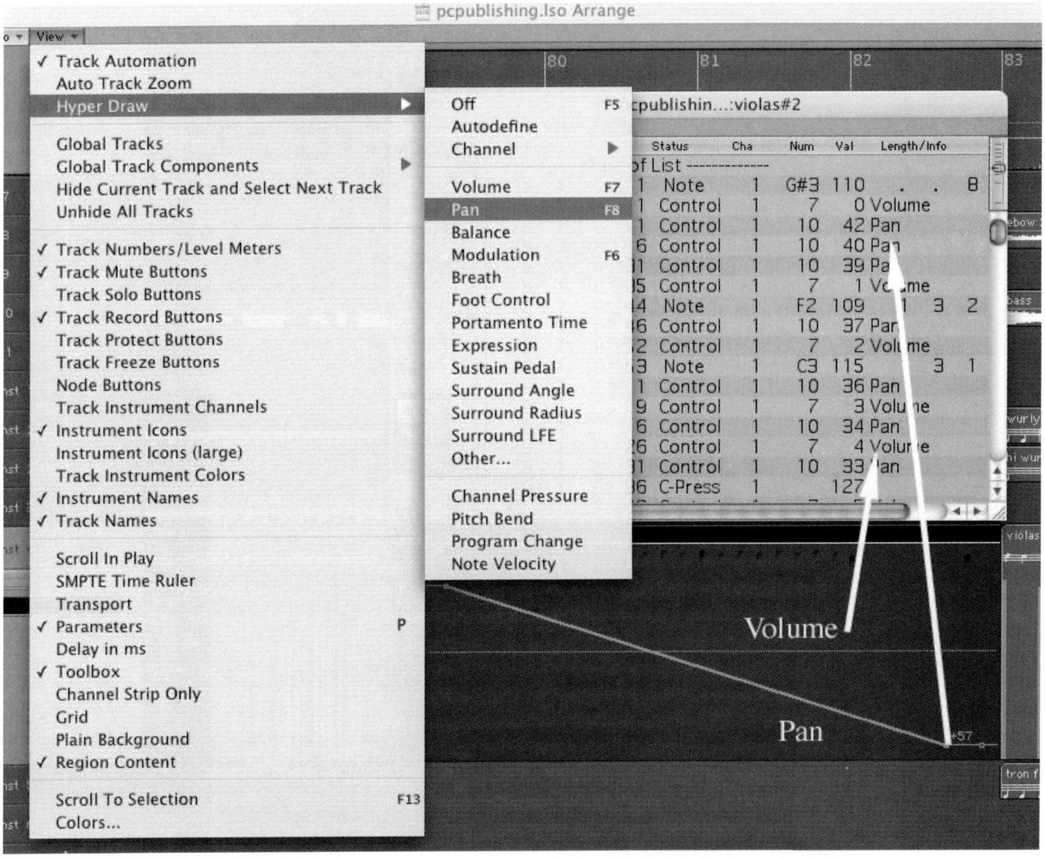

You can re-edit the previous Volume curve by choosing the View>Hyperdraw> Volume menu item.

Tip

If you want to use Hyperdraw to control the volume, pan etc. throughout a song:

- Create a new track and assign it the same instrument as the instrument you wish to control
- Zoom the Arrange page out so you can see the whole song
- Create an empty sequence by selecting the pencil tool and clicking on the Arrange page at the start of the song
- Select the arrow tool and drag to resize the sequence to the length of the song. Rename it 'Mixer Sequence'
- Now draw the hyperdraw curve on this sequence. This, along with markers, can make it easier to keep track of
- Create a new sequence for each of the instruments you wish to control
- You could pack all these in a folder and call it 'Mixdown'

Info

It's easier to use Logic's Track-based automation system. See Chapter 16 for more on this.

Using folders and markers makes it easy to automate your song and find your way around it.

Logic Pro time signatures and tempo

Setting time signatures

Move the song position line to where you want the time signature change to be. Change the time signature value in the Transport bar. You will see the new signature appear in the bar ruler.

Info

You may want to use Global tracks to deal with Tempo and Time signature events using Global Tracks (see Chapter 13) – but you can edit Global Track data using the information here, and vice versa.

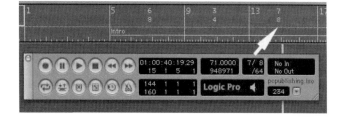

Figure 4.135

Setting the tempo and time signature of a whole Logic Pro song

Move the song position line to bar 1. Set the tempo and time signature in the Transport bar.

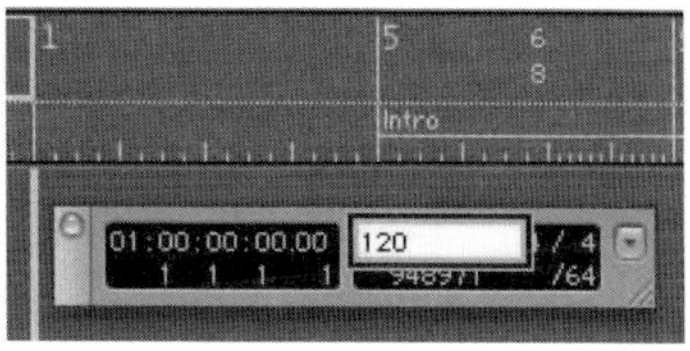

Figure 4.136

Time Signature and Key Editor

This editor is accessed from the Options>Signature/Key Change List Editor main menu item.

Figure 4.137

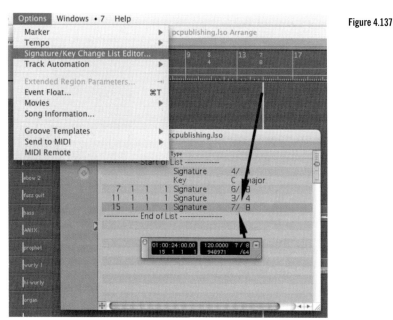

Key changes can be added at the SPL in the Arrange page by changing the values in the Transport window. These are immediately added to the Signature/Key Change List Editor window. You can edit the position and the keys directly in the editor using the mouse just like the Event List editor.

Figure 4.138

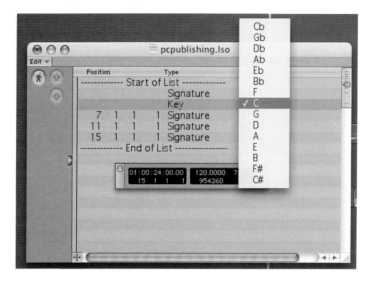

You can cut, copy and paste key changes using the Edit menu item and it also has the usual running man icon so you can keep the window synchronised when the SPL is playing.

You can change the overall key of the song by clicking and holding on the key parameters. You can chose major or minor keys in the same way. This key defines the key in the score editor.

Creating tempo changes in a Logic Pro song

Open the tempo list by holding down the mouse key over the sync button on the Transport bar (4.139).

Select Open Tempo List from the menu. A Tempo list box will open

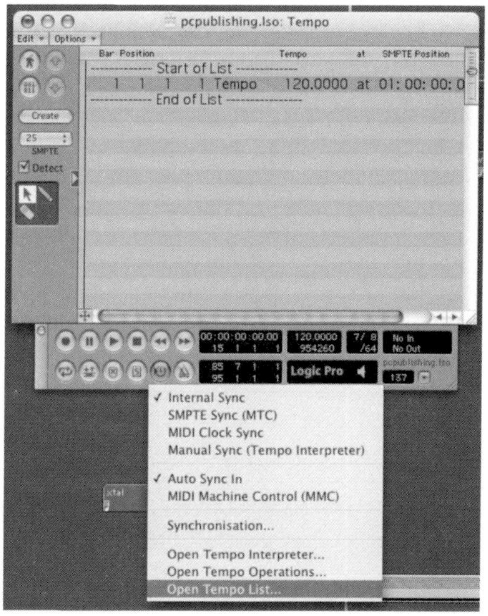

Figure 4.140

Creating tempo changes

Move the song position line to where you want the tempo change to occur. Click on Create in the tempo list box. A new tempo event will be created at that position. Or, click anywhere in the window with the pencil tool. A new tempo event is created along with a box for you to type in the position of the event.

Figure 4.141

Creating continuous tempo changes

This is dealt with in more detail in Chapter 13 – Global tracks. However, any tempo changes created there are also editable in the Tempo List box.

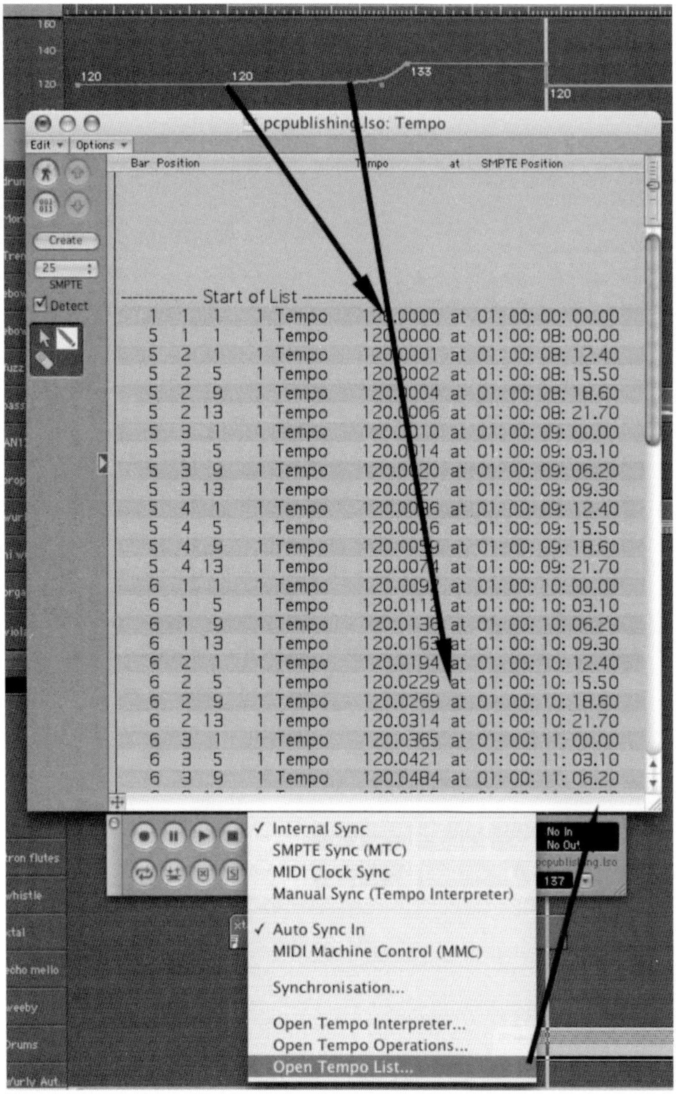

Figure 4.142

Editing Tempo Changes

There is a further editor available to modify tempo changes. You open this window by selecting Option>Tempo>Open Tempo Operations or select it from the Transport bar pull down menu. A window opens. This acts on any selected Tempo events. It has the following pull down menu parameters, which allows you to vary the tempo in different ways.

Figure 4.143

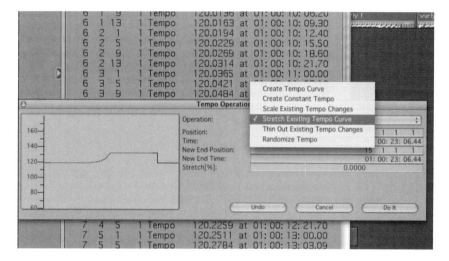

Using the computer keyboard or external MIDI events to set the tempo

Say, for example you have pre-recorded music on tape and you want to set the tempo of Logic Pro to the same tempo. You can use a computer keyboard key to enter this tempo by tapping or an incoming MIDI event.

Using the tempo interpreter

Assign the Key command Tap tempo in the Key Commands window. Put Logic Pro in manual sync mode from the menu on the Transport bar and open the Tempo interpreter from the list.

Info

Using a device that translates a percussive sound (say a hi-hat) into a MIDI note, you can easily set the tempo within Logic.

Figure 4. 144

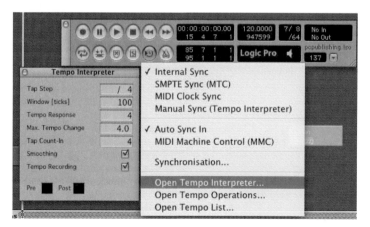

You can set the following parameter values:

- Tap step – sets the note value that the taps will be describing. Best results will be obtained by using larger values. Try 1/4 note to start.
- Window (ticks) – sets a window within which incoming taps are used. Taps outside this window are ignored. The narrower the window you can use, the better.
- Tempo response – this adjusts the sensitivity to tempo changes. The larger the values the greater the sensitivity. Start with 4.
- Max Tempo change – sets the maximum tempo change possible. Select as small a value as possible to reduce the tempo fluctuations to a minimum.
- Tap Count-in – Logic starts responding to incoming taps after this count-in period has passed.
- Smoothing – when on, smoothes out large changes in the incoming tempo.
- Tempo recording – when on, a tempo list is created as you tap.
- Pre – displays all the incoming taps
- Post – displays only taps that fall in the above set parameters

Close the tap tempo windows. Now start tapping on the key you set up in the Key command window, or set the percussive input. After the count-in, Logic Pro will start at the tempo of the tapping. The tempo determined is displayed in the Transport bar.

Setting the tempo after recording – re-clocking the Song

If you record a region without using the metronome, you can match Logic Pro's tempo afterwards. Why might you want to do this? Well, if you want to quantize the results or play some groovy drums along with the recording, you'll need to know its tempo. The recording is not changed by re-clocking (unless you quantize that is!), instead an invisible tempo grid is overlaid onto the recording.

It's always best to have some idea of the general tempo of your playing before you start! If your playing is pretty strict, you may find that using the tap tempo facilities described above is a quicker way to insert the tempo.

Here's how to do it. You need to know the number of bars in the freely record-ed region. You also need to know the exact bar position of one note right at the beginning and end of the region. You can find this out from the Event list editor.

Info

While you can re-clock using this method, it's easier to use the Beat Mapping feature of the Global Tracks. See Chapter 13 for more information. However, some of the information here is relevant to Beat Mapping too.

- Open the Reclock Song window from the Options>Tempo>Reclock Song menu item.
- Enter the positions of the start and end notes. You can find these out by opening an event list.
- Enter the desired destination of the start and end notes.
- Use only selected events in a sequence at source means only selected events in a sequence are used in reclocking.
- Reclock only within left and right source means that any tempo changes ONLY affect the selected sequence. The rest of the songs tempo remains unchanged.

Figure 4. 145
Open the Reclock Song window

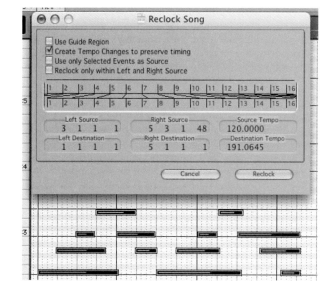

Using a guide region

If you can, record a region containing 1/4 or 1/8 notes with the same timing as the freely played region. You can then use this to reclock the song. The guide region should be the same length as the original region. Select this new region and open the Reclock Song window as before. Tick the 'Use Guide region' field. Enter the left destination and the step increment and Reclock the song.

Figure 4.146
Reclock the song

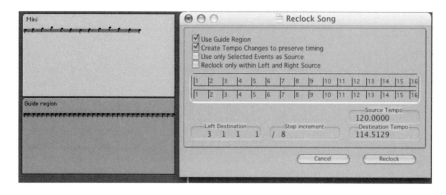

Logic Pro and synchronisation

Figure 4.147
The synchronisation menus

Logic Pro can be synchronized to run in time with other devices (acting as a slave) or other devices can run in time with it (acting as a master). Mostly you'll want Logic Pro to run as a slave to a drum machine or timecode entering Logic Pro from an external tape or video machine. There are several synchronisation possibilities.

Internal sync

Logic Pro's tempo is set from within the sequencer itself i.e., it's following a tempo event list or the tempo value in the Transport bar

MIDI clock (SPP)

MIDI clock is sent by older drum machines and MIDI hardware sequencers. This code consists of clock events sent by the master device at 24 times per quarter note. The slave receives the clock via its MIDI input and follows at the same tempo.

An addition to MIDI clock is SPP or Song Position Pointer which allows a slave responding to MIDI clock to know where in the song the master is, allowing the slave to start from the same point. Before this, you had to start the song from the beginning each time. Most MIDI synchronisers using this technique combine the two. It's sometimes called PPS or 'Poor Person's Synchroniser' by PWLA or 'People Who Like Acronyms'.

SMPTE/EBU (MIDI time code)

SMPTE was laid down as a standard for synchronization by the American Society of Motion Picture and Television Engineers and adopted by the European Broadcast Union. Basically, SMPTE time code contains exact time code information for a 24 hour period. SMPTE code has the format:

hours:minutes:seconds:frames

The number of frames per second depends on the frame rate of the incoming code. Several frame rates are in use in various locations around the world.

24 Frames per Second (FPS)
25
29.97 (drop)
29.97
30 Drop
30

In Europe 25 FPS is used for Audio and Video and TV synchronisation. In the United States 30 FPS is used for audio. Film uses 24 FPS.

MIDI time code is a translation of SMPTE into a code MIDI devices can read.

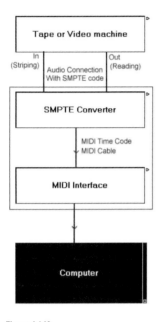

Figure 4.148

Luckily, Logic Pro can automatically detect the incoming frame rate of any SMPTE time code it receives. Figure 4.148 shows a typical synchronisation set up.

The SMPTE code from the video or tape machine is sent out to the input of a SMPTE to MIDI converter. This audio signal (it sounds like a modem twittering) is converted into MIDI time code data which is then passed to the MIDI IN on the MIDI interface. You can buy MIDI interfaces combined with SMPTE synchronisers. The MIDI data is then passed into Logic Pro.

Logic Pro can either automatically detect the type and form of time code it receives, or you can select it manually from the Transport bar drop down menu.

The upshot of this is that when the external tape or video machine is started, Logic Pro will start from the same position. You can record, edit, save and perform all of Logic Pro's other functions whilst Logic Pro is synchronised to time code. SMPTE time can be viewed in most windows by selecting the option in the View menu. For example, in the Arrange page, selecting View>SMPTE Time ruler displays the SMPTE position in the bar ruler.

Figure 4.149

Making sure regions or notes always stay at the same SMPTE time position

If you are writing music for visuals you may want certain notes or regions to be locked at a certain time, even if you change the tempo of the song. Select the region in the Arrange page or the notes in the Matrix editor. Select the SMPTE position>Lock in the Functions menu. You can unlock the SMPTE position from this menu too.

Groove

Logic Pro's resolution is amongst the highest of any sequencer on the market. Its 3840 pulses per quarter note is practically non quantized, and what you play in should come out of Logic Pro pretty much the same – unless you quantize that is!

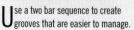
Groove templates

These are special quantization templates that allow you to impose a groove or timing feel of a certain region to another region. Here's how you do it:

- Create a region which has the groove you want.
- Select the region. Select the Options>Template>Make Groove Template from the Main window
- The template, named after the region, appears in the Quantize field in the Region Parameters box.

Figures 4.150 and 4.151

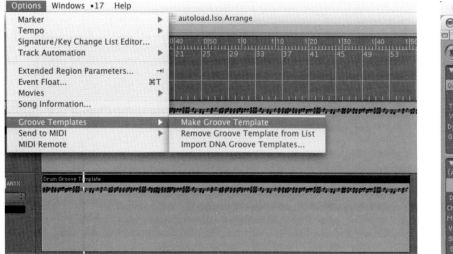

You can now use this like any other quantization value.

Deleting groove templates

Select the template from the Quantize menu. Select the Options>Groove Template>Remove Groove Template from List menu item. If you look in the Quantize menu, you will see that the template has gone

Using third party templates

You can use third party groove templates, such as those created by DNA in Logic Pro.

Drag the DNA or other templates into the /Library/Application support/Logic/Grooves folder. Import the templates from the Options>Groove Template>Import DNA Groove Template menu item. A window opens containing the templates.

To use a template on the selected region, click on a groove template to apply it to the selected region.

Adding an imported template to the Quantize menu

Double click on the template you want to add. The template is added to the Qua menu in the Region Parameter box.

Quantization in Logic Pro

Quantize is basically pulling your played notes into time onto an invisible grid. Like everything in Logic Pro, quantization can appear complicated at first, with an over-whelming number of choices available. However, remember that the results of quantize, like many functions in a sequencer, are best judged by ear. So select a region, solo it, create a cycle region – switch on the cycle mode on the Transport bar and select Functions>Objects>Set Locators by Objects in the Arrange page menu to do this – then press play and adjust the quantize value in the Region Parameters box as Logic Pro loops. If it sounds good, it's right!

Figure 4.153

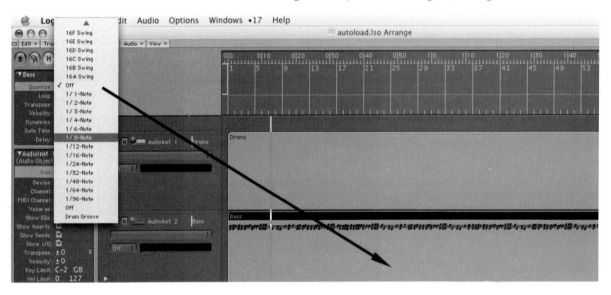

You can change the quantize value at any time. If you want to undo the quan-tize completely, select 'off'. It's totally non destructive. Logic Pro has the following groups of quantize values.

Off – Quantize is off (the highest Logic Pro resolution).

Normal quantization

1/1 note to 1/64 note. These values quantize the region to the equivalent note value. For example take a region like Figure 4.154. The grid resolution is set to 1/4. Quantize is Off.

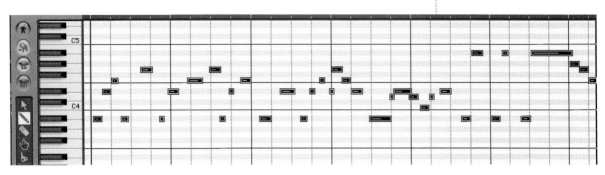

Quantizing to 1/1 would make the region look like the Figure 4.155, i.e. all notes
moved onto the bar.

Figure 4.154

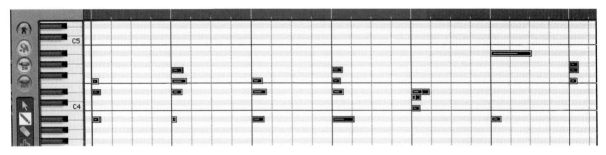

Quantizing by a 1/4 would look like the next figure, i.e. all notes moved to a 1/4
of a bar.

Figure 4.155

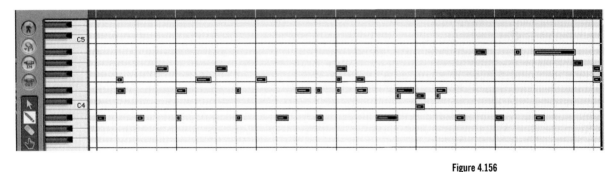

Figure 4.156

And 1/16 would look like this, i.e. all notes moved to 1/16 of a bar, and so on.

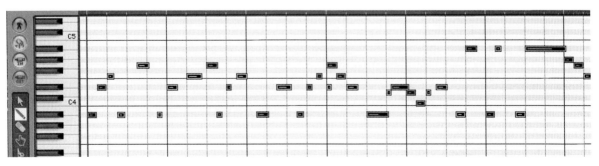

Figure 4.157

There are some further quantization values in the Qua menu.

Triplet quantization
The settings 1/3 to 1/96 quantize the region to triplet values.

Mixed quantization
These settings combine the above two quantizations.

ODD quantization
If you are going to use these quantizations it's likely that you are possessed by Frank Zappa's ghost and I'd suggest the services of a medium!

Fix quantize
Normally quantize is a playback-only non-destructive method of editing notes. You may wish however want to make the quantize permanent if you want to export the song to a MIDI file. This is another 'Normalization' parameter and is selected via the Functions>Region Parameter Fix Quantize menu item.

Extended Region Parameters

This box is opened from the menu item Options>Extended Region Parameters. Its values affect all selected regions. You can view the effect that these quantize parameters have on individual notes if you also open a Matrix editor window.

The Extended Region Parameter box has several extra parameters affecting quantize over the standard Region Parameter box. Again remember, your ears are the best judge of what sounds right! The parameters are:

Q-Swing
This % value alters the position of every second point in the quantization grid. Use settings between 50% and 75% to give your quantization a 'swing' feel.

Q-Strength
This determines how far a note is shifted towards the nearest quantize grid position. 100% is full quantization, 0% is no quantization.

Q-Range
All notes, whose distance from the nearest quantize grid position is the number of ticks set here, are not quantized. A value of 0 means every note is quantized. If you enter negative values (Far Quantize) only notes outside the selected region are quantized. Use this to bring the worst played notes in a region into time. If you enter positive values (Linear quantize) notes that are more 'laid back' that the rest of the region are brought into line. This value is connected to the Q-strength setting

Q-Flam
Chords get spread out by this parameter. Positive values produce an upwards arpeggio, negative values a downward one. The first note is unaltered.

Q-Velocity
This parameter affects how much the velocity values of the region are affected by velocity values in a Groove Template. At 0% the velocity is unaltered. At 100% it

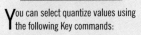

Tip

You can select quantize values using the following Key commands:

Quantize: Again – use to rapidly quantize a recorded part to the set value.
Quantize: Next value
Quantize: Previous value

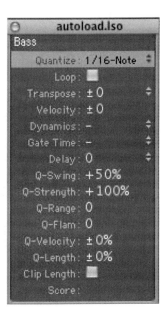

Figure 4.158
Extended Region Parameters box

takes on the velocity values of the Groove template. Negative values make the deviation more extreme.

Q-Length

This is similar to Q-Velocity but affects the note lengths in the region. 0% has no effect, ie the note lengths are unchanged. 100% means the note lengths become the same as the those in the template. negative values make the deviation more extreme.

Clip Length

When this is on, any note stretching past the end of a region will be cut off. This is a playback parameter only. The original note length remains unchanged.

Transforming MIDI events

In Logic Pro you can transform MIDI events in two ways:

1 Select a region and open the Transform window (Windows>Transform):

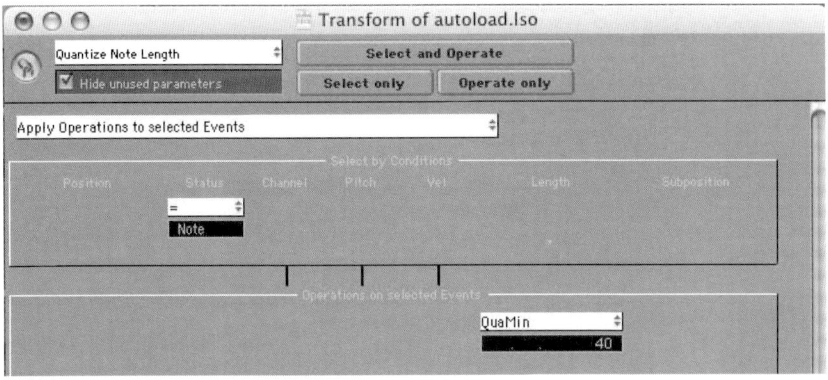

Figure 4.159

2 Use the Transform object cabled within the Environment to transform MIDI in real time.

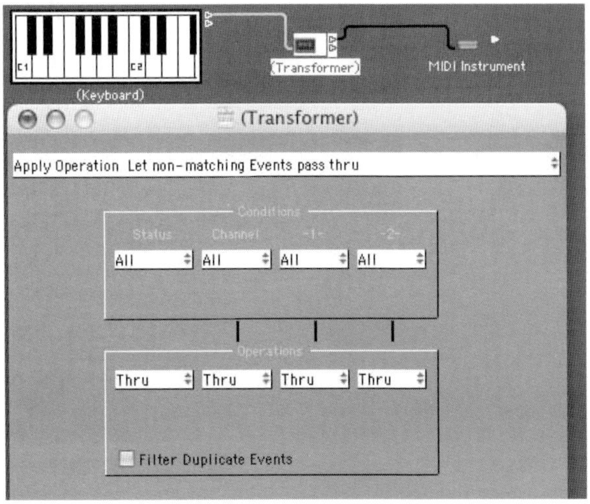

Figure 4.160

The real time transformer has many of the properties of the Transform Window. The Transform windows acts on conditions set up by the user and defines the range over which the transform will apply. The user then defines which type of transform operations will be applied to the events selected by the conditions. Then action is applied to the events to actually transform them.

The pull down menu has a list of Transform sets. These are preset transforms, such as reversing the pitch or changing the apparent speed of MIDI notes. Just under this is a button for hiding unused parameters. If you switch this off and look at the pre-set transform parameter sets, you'll get a feel for how they work.

Info

You can patch a transformer into the Environment *before* MIDI data enters Logic, if it's placed between the Physical input and the sequencer input.

Using the pre-set transform parameter sets

Select a region, or group of notes within a region, to be transformed. Open the transform window. Select the 'Reverse Pitch' pre-set as an example.

Toggle the 'Hide unused parameters' box to see which parameters are set within this pre-set. You can see in this example that the conditions are that all notes (= all) are to be transformed. The action part is actually performing the transform.

Figure 4.162

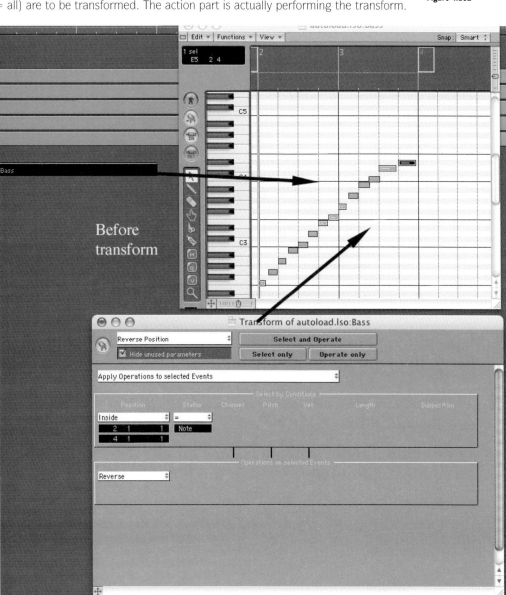

Logic Pro's Transformer actions

Logic Pro's Transformer has three actions:

Select only – Logic Pro will show all events that fulfill the Conditions. Operations has no effect.

Operate only – Performs the operation on all events selected, not just those which fulfill the Conditions.

Select and Operate – This combines both actions. First events are selected according to the Conditions and these events are then transformed by the parameters set up in Operations. After each action, events selected and/or transformed are shown below the title bar.

Figure 4.163

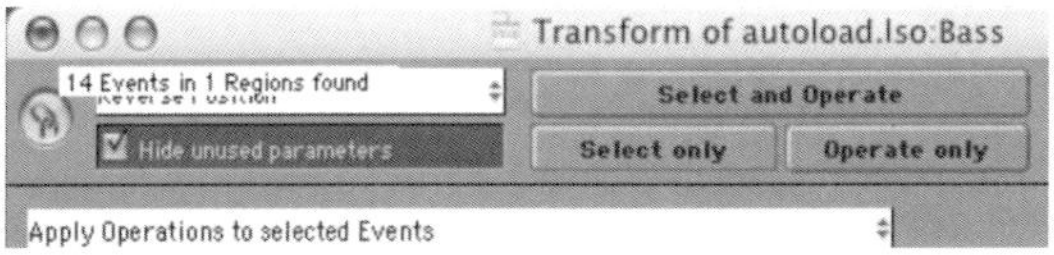

The results of the 'Reverse' transform are shown below.

Figure 4.163a

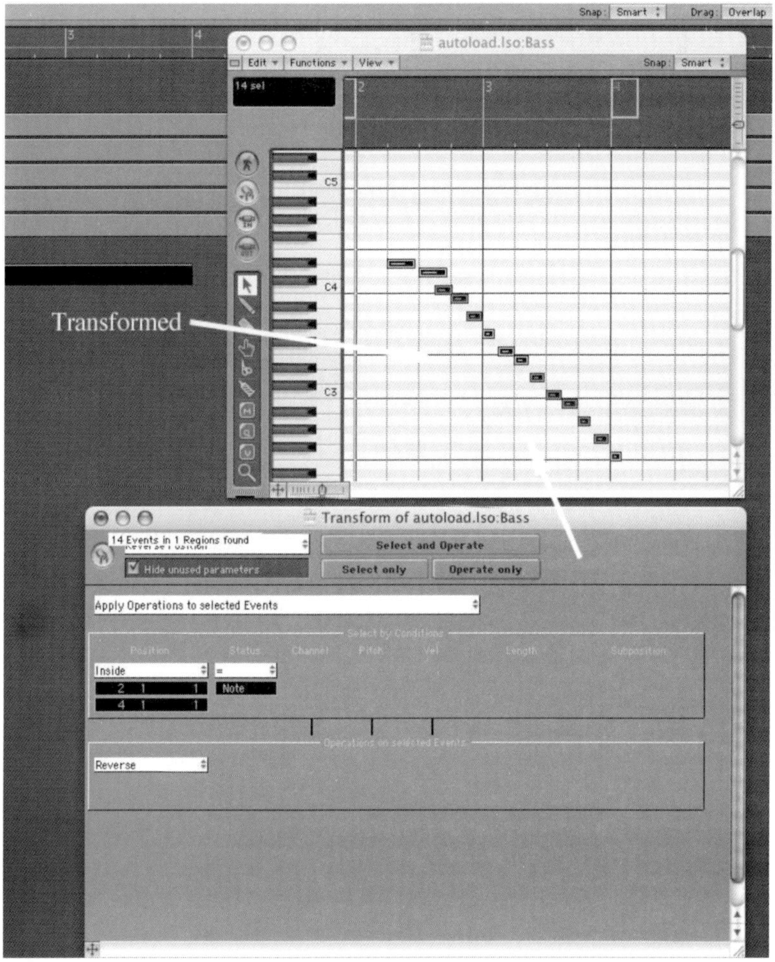

You can also define your own Transform parameter sets. Select ** Create User set **, from the pull down menu. Make sure 'Hide unused parameters' is off.

Figure 4.164

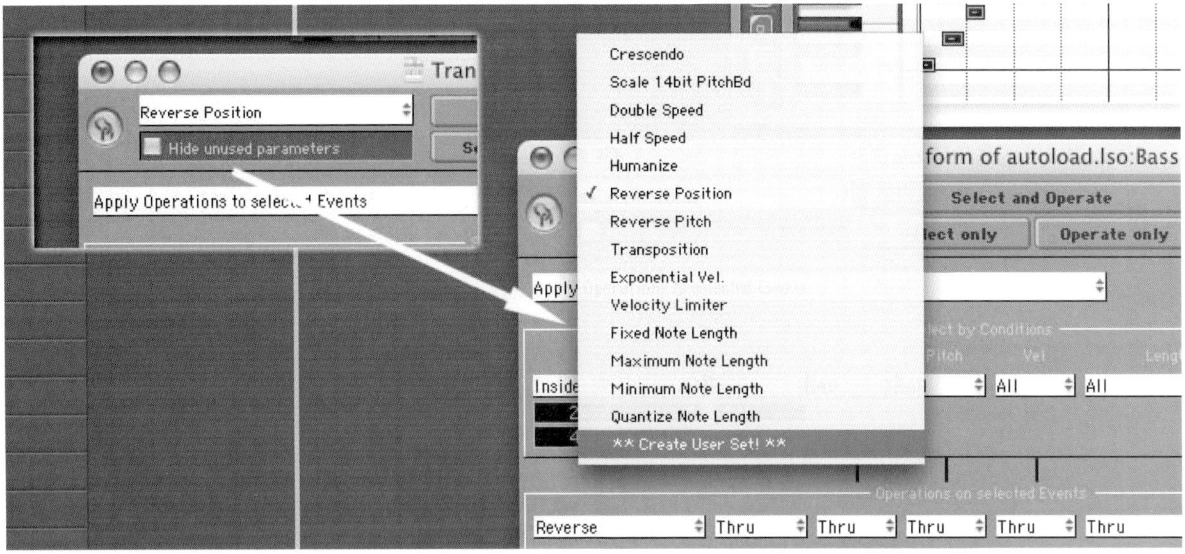

Double click on the line 'Transform parameter set' to rename it.

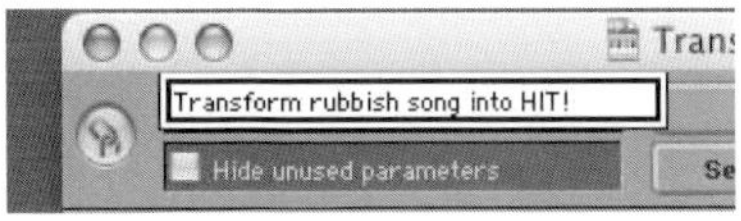

There is a pull down menu to for you to define which events are operated on. Let's make a transform set that will transpose all notes on MIDI channel 7 by 5 semitones and increase their velocities by 13.

Click on the 'Hide unused parameters' box to clear unused parameters. You can now use your transform set along with all the others.

Figure 4.165

Figure 4.165a

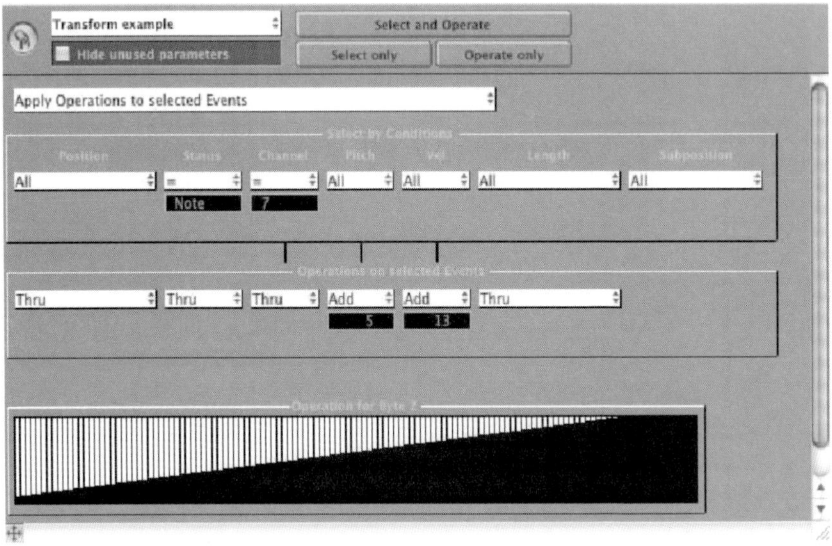

Recording audio

When recording audio into Logic Pro, it's useful to see an Arrange page, The Audio window and perhaps, the Track Mixer. You can save this arrangement in a screenset.

Figure 4.166

Before you start recording

There are a few things you need to do before recording audio into Logic Pro.

Set the input required. This setting will depend upon your audio interface, how many inputs it has, which of them you want to record through and whether the inputs are from an analogue source, such as a guitar or microphone, or a digital source such as DAT or MiniDisc. You can choose the inputs on an Audio object or the control panel provided with your audio hardware, if there is one.

You may want also use the Set Record path (Audio>Set Audio Recording Path) feature. However, if you will be saving your song as a Project, the Recording path is automatically set to the Project folder path.

Figure 4.167

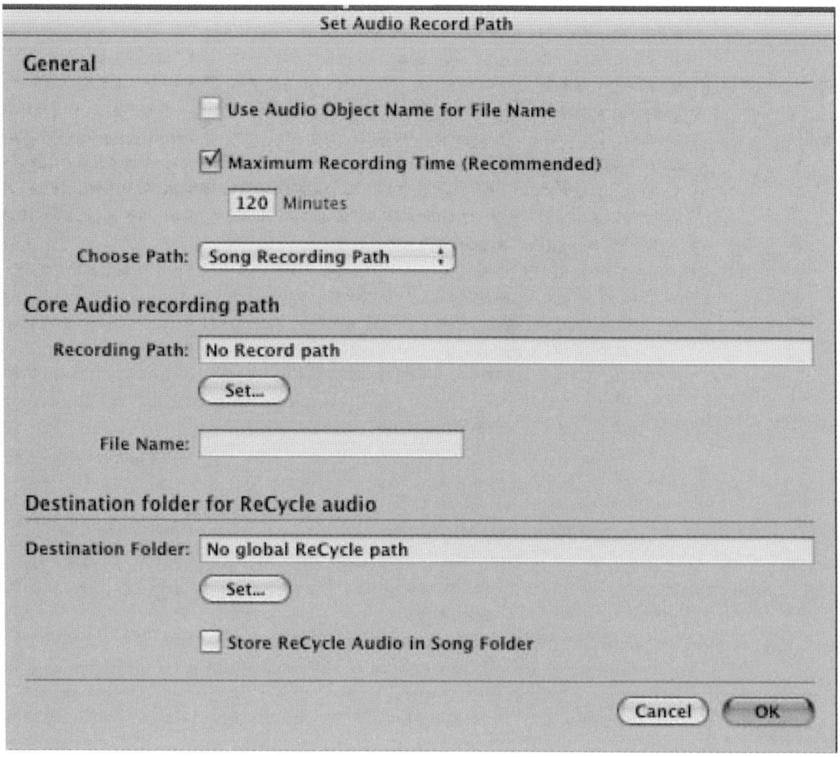

This window allows you to define where Logic Pro will store the recorded audio files. Normally, you'll want to store the files in the same directory as the song file, or a sub directory within the song directory. If you have already Saved your song as a Project, this will be automatically set.

The following parameters are available.

Use Audio object name for filename
If the Audio objects are called Audio 1, Audio 2 etc, the files recorded will have the same filenames. Audio files can be renamed within the Audio window by double clicking on the filename.

Maximum recording time
This sets the longest time you can record for in one go within Logic Pro. The default is the time Logic Pro thinks you have space for on your hard disk – you can freely change this, up to the limits of your hard disk space of course!

Choose path
This has a pull down menu where you can choose the Song recording path or the Global recording path

This pull down menu allows you to set either a recording path that all the audio is stored in, regardless of the song, or to set the path to the same as the song being recorded. The paths are set by the parameters below.

Figure 4.168

Figure 4.169

File name

You can set a 'root' file name for your audio recordings here. If you set it as 'vocals', recording would become 'vocal01', 'vocal02' etc.

Selecting an input

The number of inputs available depends on your audio hardware. If, for example, your audio interface has two inputs, you will only be able to choose up to two. In this example up to six can be chosen. Select an input from the pull down menu under I/O. Stereo objects can chose two inputs at a time.

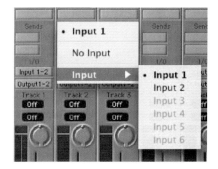

Stereo or mono?

Audio objects can either be in mono or stereo. This can be changed by clicking on the Channel strip Audio object. Note that consecutive audio objects are used as stereo objects.

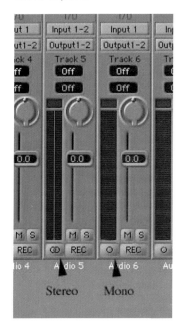

Select an Audio object to record on. Click on the R button to the left of the Audio object name in the Arrange window, or the REC button on the Audio object itself on Channel strip or Track Mixer. This is called record 'Arming'. You can Arm as many Audio objects as your hardware allows. For example if you only have a stereo input card, the maximum number of Audio objects you can arm is two.

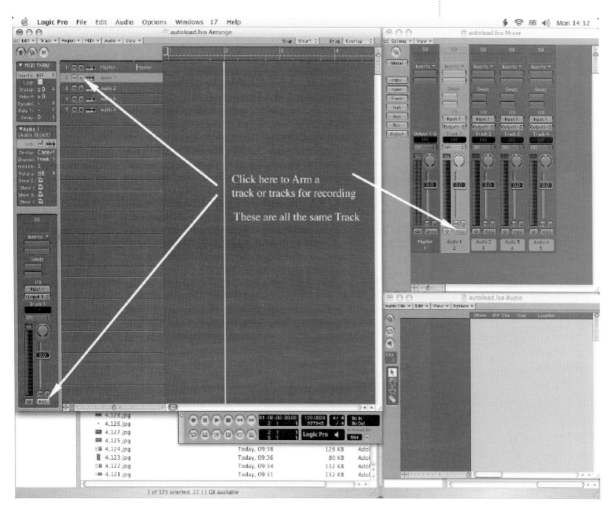

Figure 4.170

Monitoring

Most times when you are recording audio, you will want to hear it alongside a previously recorded track. The way monitoring is set up depends upon the latency of your audio interface. See Chapter 15 and Appendix 2 for more on latency and its implications for monitoring. Usually, you'll want to have Software monitoring ON (Audio>Audio Hardware & Drivers) as you'll want to monitor through effects (such as a reverb for a vocalist).

Auto Input monitoring

This is toggled on and off using the main menu item Audio>Auto Input monitoring. With this switched ON you will be able to hear the old recordings if you are punching in to record new audio.

Setting the recording level

There are some important things to remember when setting the level for recording into Logic Pro.

With digital recording systems, recording levels over 0dB or 'clipping' results in harsh and unpleasant distortion, unlike the softer style overload typically encountered with analogue tape machines. However, it's important to get as 'hot' or high a level as possible to increase signal to noise ratio. The more bits used in a recording the more accurate the sample and the lower the noise level.

The fader in the Audio object is only there for playback or monitoring the audio level. The actual level must be set by an external mixer or physical or software controls on the audio interface used. You'll need to check your interface manual for details.

Making a recording

Recording audio using Logic Pro is almost exactly the same as recording MIDI. Recording audio requires more computer processing power than recording MIDI data and there may be an audible delay before recording starts after the record button is pressed. There are several ways around this, detailed as follows.

- Set the Audio>Punch on the fly main menu item to on. This records audio on a 'hidden' track so it requires one extra recording track. If you have audio playing back on the maximum number of tracks your system can handle, you will need to mute a track to use this feature.
- Use a pre programmed autodrop locator as described for MIDI recording earlier in this chapter.

Audio Cycle recording

If Logic Pro is in cycle mode, recording audio will create a new track for every cycle. This is really useful for recording multiple takes of a solo for compiling into a 'greatest bits' region. Each cycle is muted as a new one is recorded.

After recording

Logic creates a pictorial overview of the recording to be created after recording has stopped. A window pops up to show the progress of these overviews. You don't need to stop Logic Pro while these overviews are being created. Now everything is set up record some audio.

Logic supports up to 24bit, 192kHz recording using hardware that can support those rates.

Handy recording set-up overview

- Select a mono or stereo Audio object
- Select the required input for the object
- Adjust the recording level using an external mixer or your soundcard software for maximum level without clipping
- Set the recording path for the recorded files if needed – not needed if you save as a Project.
- Adjust the Audio objects slider for a comfortable monitoring level
- Record using the record button, punch-in or other methods detailed in the MIDI section

Info

You may want to monitor vocals with some reverb or compression. It's much easier to get a good performance if the singer feels comfortable with his or her own voice.

Info

It will make your like a lot easier if you define the tempo of the song before you start recording audio. While Logic Audio has facilities for changing the tempo of recorded audio files, it rarely works without introducing artifacts into the audio.

If you want to record MIDI and Audio simultaneously you can arm audio recording objects and then highlight a MIDI track for recording as normal.

The figure below shows some recorded audio. Note in the lower Arrange page the Arrange page View>Instrument name menu item is switched on and the Audio tracks have been named without renaming the actual Audio objects themselves. Note the Stereo regions 'Drums'. The top left Arrange window is zoomed so that the actual waveforms are visible.

Figure 4.171

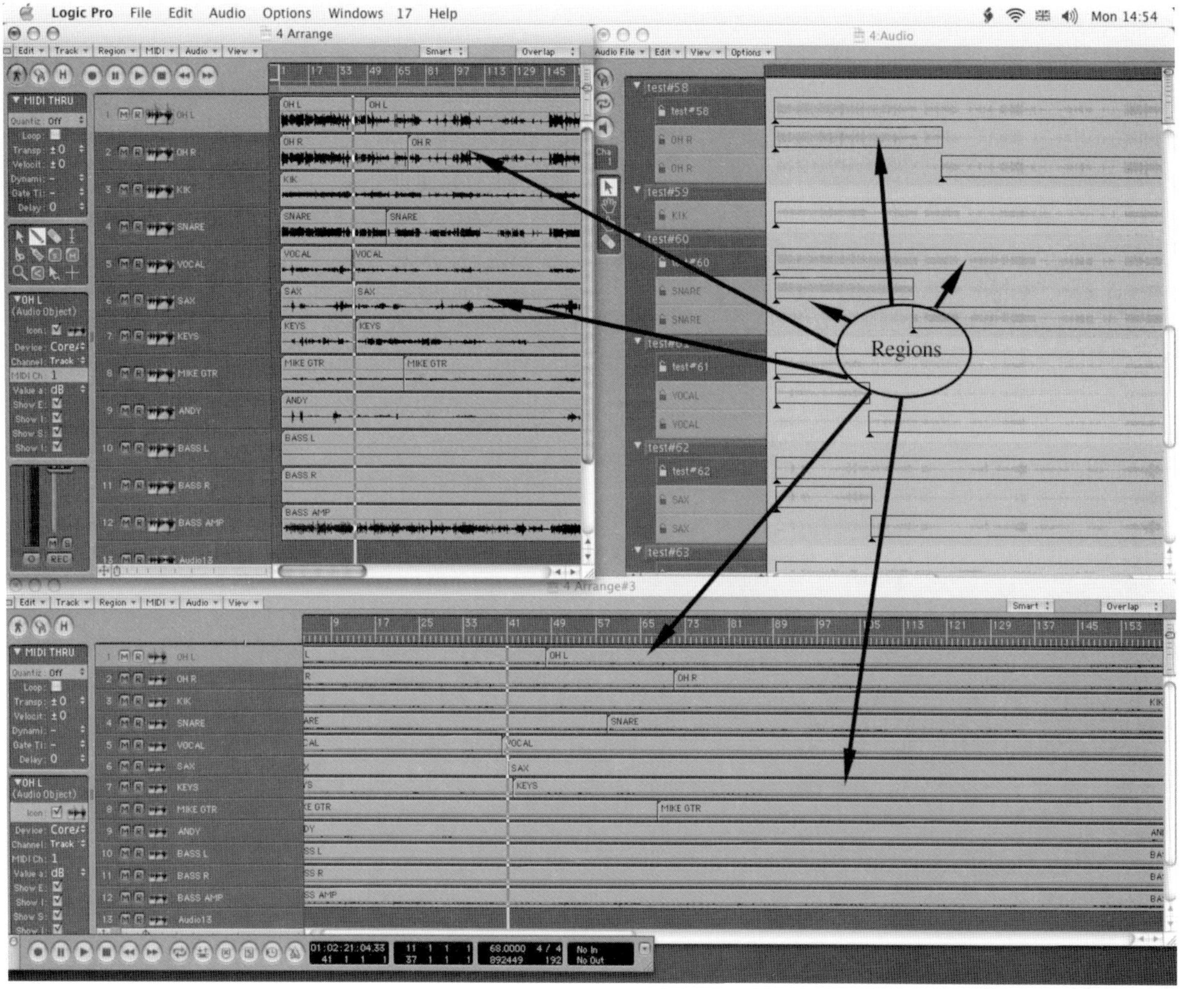

Now set a rough mix of the levels of the recorded tracks using the Audio objects in the Track mixer.

Figure 4.172

Now let's clean up the audio just recorded. Double click on the Guitar.1 region in the Arrange page or the Audio window. This opens up the Sample editor.

As you can see from the Figure 4.173, there was some recorded noise during the main guitar line. Perhaps the cat jumped on your lap just before recording? Let's get rid of it.

Highlight the noise using the mouse. You can zoom in or out using the windows' zoom tools. Silence the audio using the Sample editor Functions>Silence menu item (Figure 4.174). This silences the region selected (Figure 4.175).

Important

If you edit a region on the Arrange page, any region copied from it will also be edited. To make sure you only edit the selected region, highlight it in the Arrange page and make it a separate audio file using the menu item Audio>Convert regions to New Audio files. Save the new file in the same directory as the song. The region in the Arrange page will now be part of the new audio file.

Figure 4.173 (above)

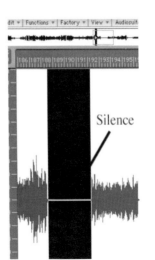

Silence

Figure 4.174 (left)

Figure 4.175 (right)

Info

*A*ll processing in the sample editor window is destructive and there is only one level of undo in the Edit>Undo menu. This means that only the last or ALL the edits can be undone. So first of all you may like to make a copy of the file in case you make a mistake during editing using Audio file >Create Backup or Audio file>Save A Copy As.

Silence the other noise in the same way. Now let's fade the guitar part out. Select the end of the part and use the Functions>Fade out menu item

Figure 4.176

The next figure shows the resultant fade out.

Figure 4.177

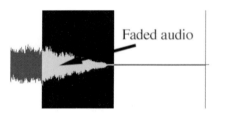

Figure 4.178

The fade out (and in) curve can be modified using the Functions>Settings menu item. Here you can set the duration of the Fades and the shape of the curve.

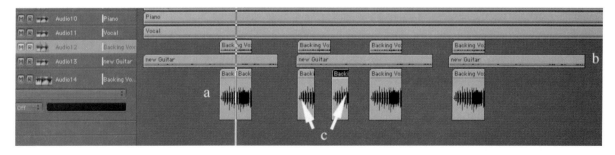

So what next? Chapter 12 details the other functions of the Sample editor and the use of Time machine in particular to manipulate audio pitch and duration. However, here's a brief overview of what you could do in the Sample editor with reference to the guitar part we are editing.

The Time Machine

- Normalize the part so that it's at the maximum possible volume.
- Select the region of the guitar part you want to normalize. In this case it's probably the whole region, so select it using the Edit>Select All menu item. Then use the Functions>Settings menu item to open the window shown above. Set the desired Normalize peak level – this is usually left at 100% or 0dB. Then Normalize the part using the Functions>Normalize menu item.
- Change the pitch of the guitar part with or without changing the tempo using the Time Machine.

You could use this feature to

- Bring the pitch of the guitar into tune if you change the overall pitch or key of a song.
- Bring the tempo of the guitar into a tune if you change the overall tempo or key of a song.
- Work on a copy of the guitar part and detune the copy a small amount for a chorusing effect, or a large amount for a harmony part when played with the original.

Use of the Time Machine is covered in more detail in Chapter 12

When you have performed all the editing you require in the Sample Editor, close it in the usual way. Logic Pro will ask you if you want to make the last change permanent. You can either accept the edits or undo them all.

Now record some new Audio parts

Note that the backing vocals regions have been copied (a) another guitar part (b) has been added. The backing vocal regions have been cut and pasted just like MIDI Regions (c).

Figure 4.169

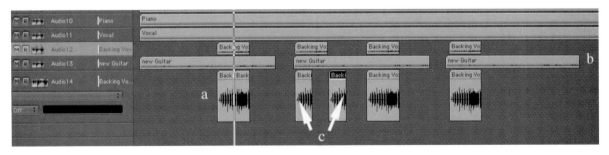

If you open a 'New Guitar' region in the Sample editor you can see that the region is part of a larger audio file.

Figure 4.180

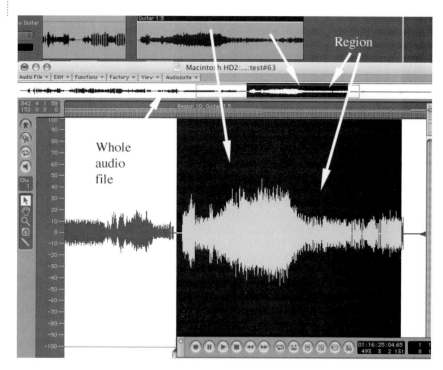

You can copy and paste parts like this very quickly. You can cut and paste regions in the Arrange page as if they were MIDI Regions, using the same tools outlined earlier in this chapter.

More useful audio tricks

Loading in an audio file from a CD
It's a common practice to use a sample from an audio CD in a composition. It's very easy to do this in Logic Pro. Of course, you could just record the audio from CD, tape or vinyl through the audio inputs of your audio interface too. Here's how you do it.

- Place the desired CD in the CDROM drive of your computer. Drag the audio CD file directly to the Arrange page in Logic Pro, Figure 4.181, or
- Drag the audio CD track onto the hard disk and Import into Logic,

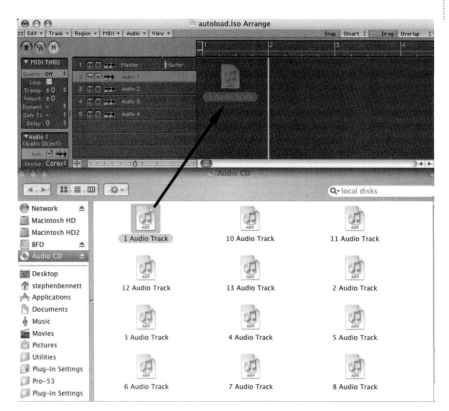

Figure 4.181
Drag the audio CD file directly to the Arrange page in Logic Pro

Importing an audio file

- Use the Audio>Import Audio File from the main menu item, or
- Open the Audio window using the main menu item Audio>Audio window then
- Select the file to be added to Logic Pro using the menu item Audio>Add Audio File. You can audition the files in the file selector box that opens.

Creating a drum loop from the file

- Open the Sample editor
- Select the part of the track you want to loop. Just roughly for now
- Click on the Loop icon (a).
- Click on the Play icon (b) to loop around the highlighted part.
- Adjust the part highlighted until the loop is correct. It's a good idea to choose a whole number of bars in the loop. Drag the ends of the selected area while holding the shift key.

> **Info**
>
> If you want to make the drum loop into an Apple Loop, so it can be matched to Logic's tempo, see Chapter 17.

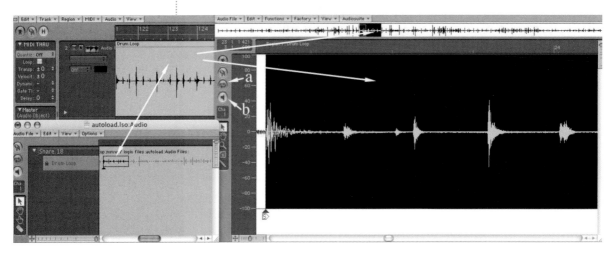

Figure 4.182

• Convert the highlighted part into a region using the menu item Edit>Create new region. The new region is placed in the Audio window.

Figure 4.183

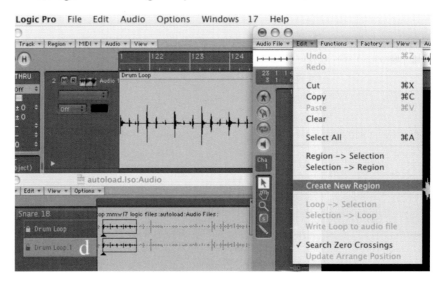

• If you double click on (d) in Figure 4.183 you can rename the region to 'drum loop'
• Now drag the region into the Arrange page by selecting the hand tool and draggong the region across. As it's a mono file use a mono audio object in the Arrange page for playback.

Figure 4.184
The Hand tool

It's a good idea to convert the region to an individual Audio file using the Arrange page menu item Audio>Convert Regions To Individual Audio Files, otherwise you'll affect the original recording if you edit the loop.

Set the song tempo to the tempo of the loop

• Highlight the loop on the Arrange page
• The loop is four bars long, so drag a cycle area of four bars.

Figure 4.186
Basic interface

- Now set the song tempo using the main menu item Options>Tempo>Adjust tempo using region length and locators (Figure 4.187).

You will be asked if you want to change the tempo globally (for the whole song) or create a tempo change at the start of the region (Figure 4.188).

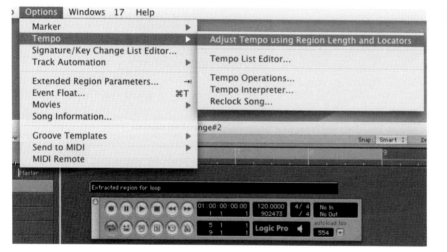

Figure 4.187

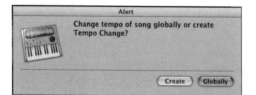

Figure 4.188

The cycle area is set to the same size as the region and the tempo is matched to that of the audio file.

Figure 4.189

Time stretching in the Arrange page

You can change the length, and thus tempo, of audio regions directly in the Arrange page. This doesn't affect the pitch and is useful for getting loops and audio recorded elsewhere into time with a song. When a region is stretched, a new audio file is created – leaving the old one in the Audio window.

There are two ways to do this time stretching:

Audio > Adjust Region length to locators

Figures 4.190 and 4.191

Audio > Adjust Region length to nearest bar

Figures 4.192 and 4.193

There are several time stretching algorithms available in the Audio>Time machine menu. Different algorithms produce different results, so it's worth trying one and listening to the results. If they aren't want you wanted, Undo and try another.

Audio file housekeeping

When recording audio into Logic Pro it's easy to end up with lots of unused regions in the Audio window. You can select regions that are not used in a song with the Audio window menu item Edit>Select Unused. The regions can then be deleted.

Of course, the parts of the audio files that the regions referred to still exist and are wasting hard disk space. You can clean up this unused space using the Audio window menu item Audio File>Optimize File(s).

You can also save a song as a new Project and select the 'Leave Audio files not used in Arrange' item. Only used files will be copied into the new Project folder.

Finally

You should now be able to use Logic Pro to record, edit and otherwise manipulate MIDI and audio data. The next chapter deals with using the Score editor in Logic to print out music for those non-MIDI equipped beings amongst us!

Warning

If the file or region is used in another song, editing it will also affect that song too. If in doubt, make the region into a new file using the Arrange window menu item Audio>Convert regions to individual Audio Files.

Score editor

As you would expect from the creators of 'Notator' for the Atari ST, the Score editor in Logic is a sophisticated tool perhaps worthy of a book of its own. The Score Editor allows you to edit MIDI data in a similar way to the other editors, but also allows you to edit the appearance of traditional notation, based on that MIDI data. You can if you wish leave the original MIDI data unaltered or change it as in any other editor. You may want to use the Score Editor if:

- you want to produce a print out of a score
- you want to view and/or edit several sequences at the same time.
- you want to edit MIDI data as traditional notation
- you want to enter MIDI data in step-time directly into the Score Editor

You don't have to be an expert with the Score editor to use Logic. All editing of MIDI data can be performed in the Matrix, Event List and Hyper editors. However, most of us have at sometime wanted to produce a print out of a musical part, perhaps for a wind player or guitarist. Consequently, this chapter will deal with the basics of the Score editor, and tips on how to make the output of the Score Editor useful to other musicians.

The problem with computer based scoring
You can't expect to record into Logic in the normal way, open up the Score Editor and see a perfect score displayed that you can print out and get an orchestra to play. A lot of people dabble with the Score Editor and give up quickly when they present the finished score to the musicians, who start to play something in the mold of Stockhausen after a long night! The MIDI protocol stores notes with a start position, a length and a velocity. When you open the Score Editor, Logic tries to interpret your playing, and converts it into traditional notation. You'll need to do some preparation and editing to make the output from the Score Editor look presentable – and playable!

Figure 5.1 shows a simple sequence recorded into Logic and displayed in the Matrix editor.

Figure 5.1

Tip

If you want to keep the original Logic song, make a copy and use that for producing the score. Call one 'MysongMidi', the other, 'MysongSCORE'. You can keep both loaded in Logic to check the hard quantized notation version against the original.

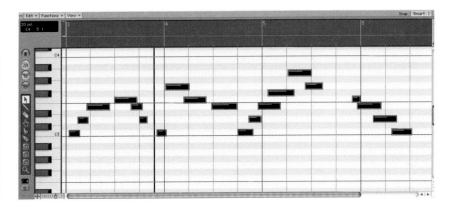

Looks simple doesn't it? You could probably write this down on a piece of notation paper, even if you aren't a maestro. Opening this sequence in the Score Editor produces Figure 5.2:

Figure 5.2

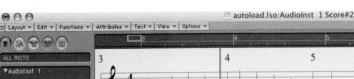

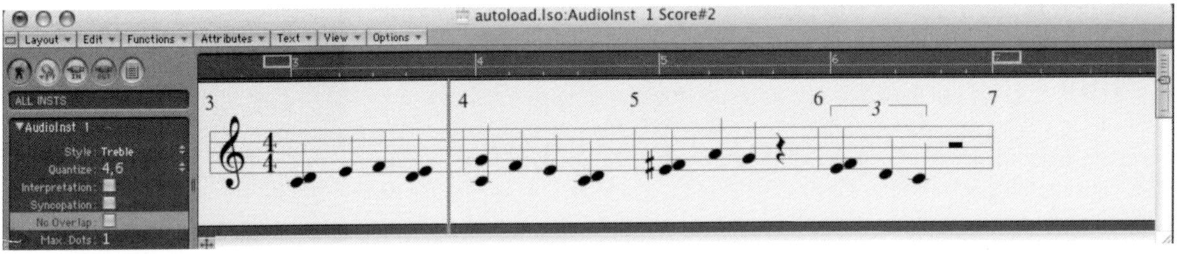

Try giving that to a Violin player! The problem with traditional notation is that it is only an approximation of the music being played. No one will hold a note exactly the length of a note in traditional notation; no one can extend that note exactly by a dot. So how do we go about solving this problem? The answer is to quantize *hard*, the parts you wish to print out.

So, if we quantize the part above to 1/8 notes and open it in the Score Editor we get Figure 5.3.

Info

It pays to reduce the number of unintentional overlaps and duplicated notes. The Matrix Editor has facilities in the Functions>Erase MIDI Events and the Functions>Note Events menus to perform these corrections.

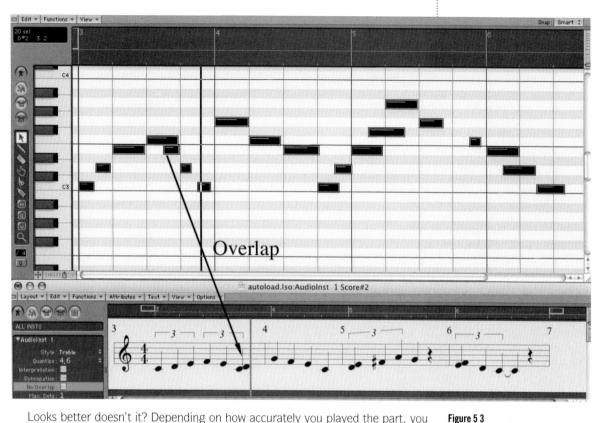

Looks better doesn't it? Depending on how accurately you played the part, you may have to drag notes around in the Matrix Editor to make sure they are pulled onto the beat you want. If you look at Figure 5.3, you will see that there is a spurious rest and an overlap still in the score. You'll need to resize the notes until they are the correct length – unless this is actually what you want!

If you actually press play and listen to this, it will sound 'wrong' to your ears. You will have played it with 'feeling', but to traditional notation this just translates into poor playing! In traditional notation, these emotional parameters are suggested by text or symbols on the score.

So the first rule of getting a decent score print out is: *quantize the parts*.

Figure 5 3

Getting around the Score Editor

When you first load the Score Editor it can look pretty daunting, but have a cup of coffee and a sit down and look again.

Figure 5.4   The Score Edit window has several of the same features as the other editor windows.

a   These are the usual running man, link, in and out icons here. The extra icon is a toggle that switches between the Score Editors two viewing modes, Page View and Linear View.

b   The Instrument Set box

c   The Display Parameter box

d   The Event Parameter box

e   The Toolbox

f   The Partbox

g   There is a zoom tool at the top of the window, along with the bar ruler which will show any cycle and drop in regions and markers.

Rather than list out all the (many!) features of the Score Edit window, the Making music way to using the Score Editor is by example. This chapter will describe how to produce readable scores for several typical applications.

Producing a piano score

Record a piano part and open up the The Score Editor. If the view is different, select the relevant View menu items to make it look like Figure 5.5.

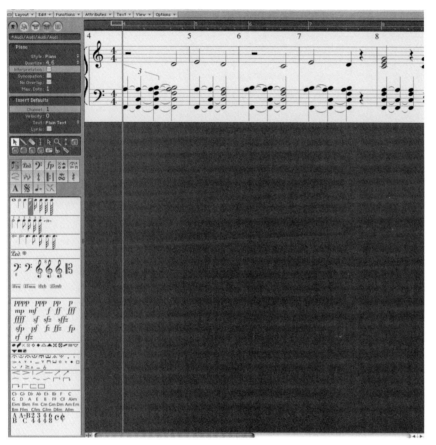

Figure 5.5
Basic piano score

The first thing to do is to make sure you haven't played any real bloopers. If you have, edit them in the Matrix Editor. Editing here and now will save much time later on. However, the score still looks a bit of a mess, even when quantized in the Matrix editor. We can do something about this later in the chapter.

NOTE: Most of the parameters described below can be used on a group of selected notes or the whole score.

Score styles

As you can see, Logic has automatically picked up the fact that we have recorded a Piano part and has split the stave into bass and treble. In fact it has chosen the default Score style 'Piano' in the display Parameter box.

If you hold and click on the Style Parameter, you can get a list of all the predefined score styles (Figure 5.6).

Figure 5.6

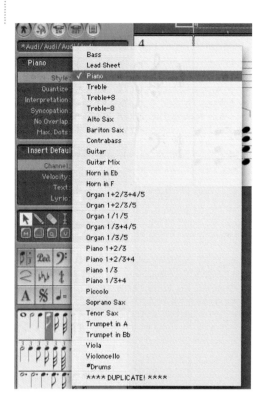

Change them and see how they affect the score display. If you want to edit a score style, double click on it in the display Parameter box; a window will open.

Figure 5.7

Here you can change the parameters of the score style. In most cases, the defaults can be left as they are, but all the parameters in the window can be edited with the mouse. You may want to change

- the SPACE between staves
- the TRP or transpose values of the staves
- the SPLIT point of the staves

Info

This quantize affects only what you see, not what you hear.

Display quantization

As well as quantizing the actual MIDI data in the Matrix Editor, you can quantize the Display of the notes in the Score Editor. The Default quantization is based on the display format from the Transport bar.

You may want to change the display quantization. There is a pop up menu displayed when you click and hold down the mouse key over the Quantize field.

There are a collection of quantization (such as 4, 8 etc.) values and hybrid (4,3 etc.) values. The hybrid and higher resolution values work best where the original part is played with accuracy.

Interpretation

One of the most powerful features in Logic is its ability to suppress rests that may occur if a note is stopped short or played a little after the beat. This is toggled on and off from the Interpretation parameter in the display Parameter box.

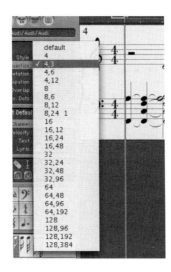

Figure 5.8

Tip

Get it right before you score! You'll find it less frustrating and less time consuming if you play accurately, quantize and correct overlaps *before* you open the Score Editor.

Here's our piano part with Interpretation set to off.

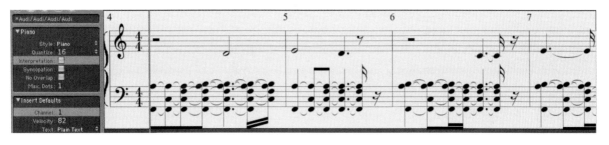

Here's our piano part with Interpretation set to on.

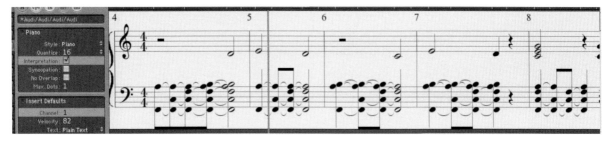

It makes a lot of difference to the readability of the score, doesn't it?

Syncopation

When it is on, the notes are displayed as actual note values.

Figure 5.11

When this parameter is off syncopations are displayed as smaller note values tied across the beat.

Figure 5.12

No overlap

When this is on, it suppresses the display of portions of notes, which overlap past the beginning of new notes. This is overlap off. Note all the spurious ties.

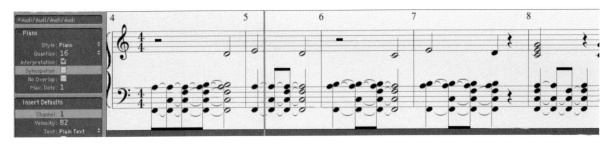

Figure 5.13

This is overlap set to on. You can normally leave this on.

Figure 5.14

Maximum dots

This sets the maximum number of dots that can be displayed after a note. The setting you choose depends on what you want your score to look like. If you don't know what to put in here, leave it set to 1.

Having edited the notes in the Matrix editor and affected the way they are displayed in the Score Editor by using the display Parameter box variables; we are now ready to prepare the part for printing.

Printing the score

Put the Score Editor in Page edit view by either clicking on the page icon (right), or using the View>Page edit menu item. Note there is also a Print View option here, which will display a WYSIWYG (What You See Is What You Get) view of the Score Logic will print.

Inserting items into the score

You may want to add text and graphical items, such as lyrics, notes and notation graphics to your score.

Inserting graphics into the score

The graphical symbols are displayed in the Part Box – If you click and hold on any of these, a pull down menu of available symbols is displayed. For example, here is the menu for the Bass Clef icon.

Notice also that various other symbols relating to this parameter are displayed in the lower part of the part box.

To use any of these symbols, select the desired symbol and drag into the score.

On the actual score sheet, symbols can be selected, deleted and moved like any other object within Logic. Some symbols can only be inserted at certain points within the score, like the tempo indicator. Logic will snap the symbol to the correct position.

Inserting text into the score

Any text that you insert into the score has properties that are set in the Text menu of the Score Editor.

Figure 5.16

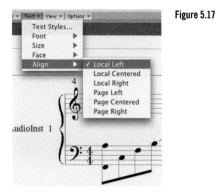

Figure 5.17

Inserting text at any point on the score

Select the text tool from the part box and select the pencil tool from the Toolbox. Click on the score. A cursor appears where you can enter text.

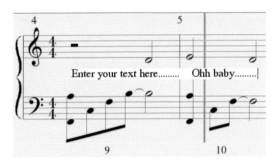

Figure 5.20

Click elsewhere to insert more text or select the Arrow tool and click on the background of the Score Editor to stop editing.

If you highlight the text with the Arrow tool, information about the text appears in the Event parameters box. These can be edited with the mouse as usual.

Figure 5.21
Choose your font

To edit the text double click on it with the Arrow tool. The text flashes and a cursor appears and you can edit the text. To delete the text click on it with the Arrow tool. The text flashes and you can delete the text with the DEL key.

Figure 5.22

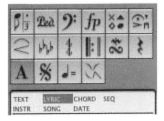

Inserting lyrics

Lyrics, in Logic, are normal text events except they are automatically centered on the notes occurring at the same time. They cause the score to space itself out to make room for the lyrics. Lyrics are usually placed above or below the stave. Here's how you enter them:

- Select the 'A' tool from the part box and select the pencil tool from the Toolbox.
- Click on the 'lyrics' field below the 'A tool.

• Click on the score. A cursor appears where you can enter lyrics.

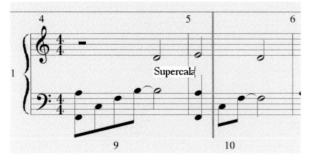

Figure 5.23

• See how the notes space themselves out to accommodate the lyrics when you press the Tab key to move onto the next note.

Figure 5.24

• You can delete and edit lyrics just like normal text.

Other automatic text objects

You'll notice in the field below the 'A' tool that, along with the 'text' and 'lyric', there are other fields. These are used in the same way as lyrics. Here's what they do:

Chord   Enter the name of a chord, e.g. C7, and it will be positioned and
        reformatted to standard chord notation.
Seq   Enters the currently displayed sequence (region) or folder.
Inst   Enters the name of the current instrument or instrument set.
Song   Enters the name of the current song.
Date   Enters the current date.

These can be inserted, edited and deleted exactly like text objects.

Global text objects

These are like the normal text objects, but are placed in special positions on the page. They then can be made to appear on every page of the score. The areas of the score where these objects will be defined as global are:

Top   The area over the top margin line
Header The area under this and the stave
Footer The area under the lower margin line
Side   The left or right margin irrespective of the ALIGN settings in the
        TEXT menu

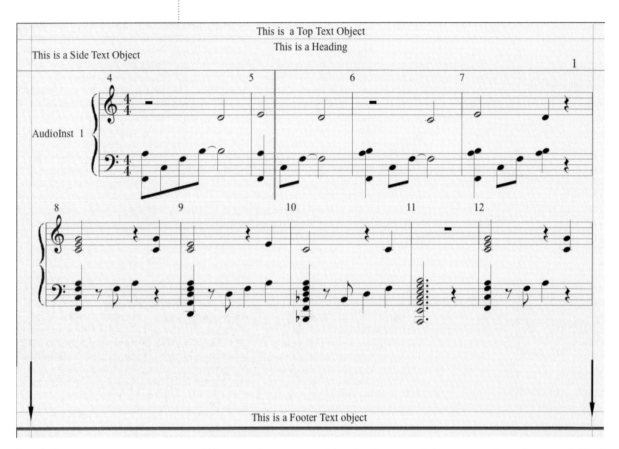

Figure 5.25
Global text objects

When you have a text object in the area of the screen where they are defined as global text objects, the event Parameters box will have the following fields shown in Figure 5.26, allowing you to change the settings of global text objects. The same is true of all the other text objects. The parameters, however, may differ.

Figure 5.26

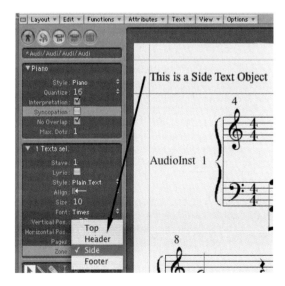

Info

All the global objects can be affected by the attributes in the Text menu.

You could, for example set the Header on every page, but the Top only on page 1 using the Pages field in the event Parameter box.

There are many other Text editing functions in the Text menu and the event part box.

Margins and general page layout

Margins can be adjusted by dragging with the mouse when you are in Print View mode (View menu). Make sure you have the arrow key selected and drag the margins to resize them.

You can edit things like bar numbers, page numbers and instrument names from the Layout>Numbers and names window.

You can change default margins, header space and other spacing parameters in the Layout>Global Format window.

Printing the score

You print the score from Logic in exactly the same way as printing from other programs. Select Print from the File menu.

Exporting the score as a graphics file

Select the Camera tool and drag it across the area of the score you wish to export while holding down the Shift key. A file dialog box opens to allow you to save the selected area as a file.

Creating a lead sheet

A lead sheet is a score that contains a melody, some chords and lyrics to provide an easy way for other musicians to learn a song. We'll use the experience gained in scoring the piano part previously to produce a lead sheet.

First record two sequences containing the chords and the melody. As stated before, you'll have less problems working on a readable score, if you quantize the parts and remove any overlaps. Double click on the Track name column and call them 'Lead' and 'Chords'. Move the 'Lead' track above the 'Chord Track'.

Select the two tracks.

Figure 5.27

- Open the Score Editor and change the style to 'Lead Sheet'. Change to Page Edit mode from the View menu.
- Adjust the parameters in the display Parameter box until you are happy with the score, as described in the Piano part above.
- Switch off the Instrument names in the Layout>Numbers & Names menu.
- Now add the lyrics
- Select the Text box
- Select the 'lyrics' field
- Select the Pencil tool

- Click under the notes and enter the lyrics. The score will change as lyrics are entered. *Don't press return after you enter each lyric!* Press Tab and all the lyrics will be spaced correctly and under the correct note. Press return when you are finished.

Figure 5.28

Info

You can highlight all the lyrics and move them by dragging with the mouse.

Tip

Use the Global Tracks Chord feature to work out Chord names. See Chapter 13 for more on Global Tracks.

Now add the chord names

- Select the Text box.
- Select the 'chords' field.
- Select the Pencil tool and click on where you want to enter the first chord. Don't press return after you enter each chord! Press Tab and all the chords will be spaced correctly and under the correct note. Press Enter when you are finished. Logic tries to make sense of what you enter, for example entering C7 produces the symbol C7.

Figure 5.29

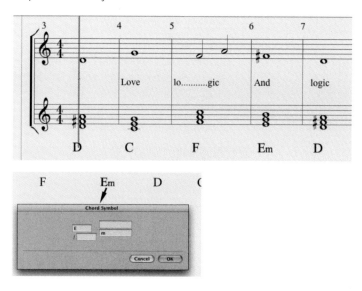

Tip

You can enter and edit individual chords by double clicking on them

Now create a title for the song, let's call it 'The Logic Blues'.

- Select the Text box
- Select the 'text' field.
- Select the Pencil tool and click on the area just under the margin – the 'header area'

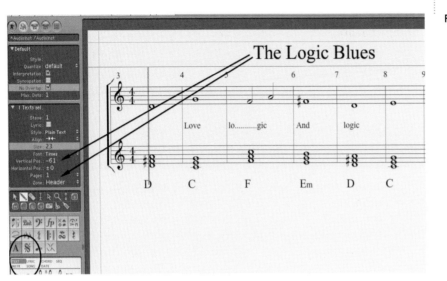

Figure 5.30

In the event Parameter box, you'll be able to change the Font and size of the Title. Now let's add some more text in the same fashion.

Select the tempo icon and drag it onto the score. The actual Tempo value is determined by the tempo setting on the Transport bar.

Figure 5.31

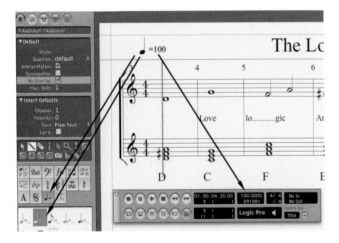

You are now ready to print out your lead sheet.

Creating a four part string section

A lot of composers aspire to writing for strings or orchestra and there is nothing more exciting than laying down a freshly printed score in front of a string quartet and having your masterpiece played correctly. Here's the PC Publishing guide to becoming an instant John Williams!

I'd suggest you record your guide sequence using sounds approximating those of a string quartet, namely two violins, viola and cello.

Figure 5 34

Remember that unlike a synthesiser, acoustic instruments have limited note ranges, and asking musicians to play one note higher than is possible on their instrument isn't the best way to start a session! I'd suggest you look up the ranges of instruments you are going to score for, in a Music Dictionary or the like.

Prepare your scoring session by quantizing the sequences and correcting for overlapped notes as in the other examples. Lay out the tracks from top to bottom.

Violin 1
Violin 2
Viola
Cello

• Select all the sequences and open the Score Editor
• Switch off the Instrument names in the Layout>Numbers & Names menu
• Turn on Page Edit mode from the View menu
• Click on each stave in turn and select the correct score style from the pull down menu. 'Treble' for the Violins, 'Viola' for the Viola and 'Bass' for the Cello. Note that the correct Clefs are created along with lines joining each stave together.

Figure 5.35

Now create a title for the song, lets call it 'String Quartet'

- Select the Text box
- Select the 'text' field
- Select the Pencil tool and click on the area just under the margin, the 'header area'. Type in the text and press Return. Change the font and font size in the event preferences box.
- Use the text tool to add the names of the instruments to the stave.
- Add other text or graphical notation items as desired

Your score could look something like this

You can then print out your score.

Other Score Editor functions

Notes can be added, edited, deleted and moved in the Score window just like other editor windows.

You can use hyperdraw in the Score Editor window, just like the Arrange page and the Matrix editor (View>Hyperdraw).

Global tracks are also available in the Score Editor.

Figure 5.36

The Arrange page

Overview

If the Environment is the heart of Logic Pro, the Arrange page is the (er … looks for a suitable organ) head! It's where you will spend most of your working day in Logic Pro and it's lucky that it's very comfortable and with a soothing decor.

Figure 6.1 shows an overview of the Arrange page. The major areas of the page are detailed below.

Figure 6.1
The Arrange page

The Region window (a)

Here you can see recorded Regions. These can contain any MIDI data (notes, program changes, controller data etc.) or Audio recordings. Each Region has a name, which can either come from the instrument track, or can be renamed, in the Parameter box (see g).

Track name column (b)

If this is switched on (View menu), double click on the track name to rename it.

Instrument name column (c)

If you move the mouse over this area and hold the key down, a list of available instruments will appear and you can select the required one. What is in this list depends on how you have set up Logic Pro in the Environment (see Appendix 1, Chapters 4 and 14).

Mute button, Record button, Freeze button, MIDI/Audio data activity level meter and Track number (d)

Clicking on the mute button will mute the whole track. Several tracks can be muted at once, as can individual Regions using the mute tool (for more on Freeze see Appendix 2).

Instrument/Track Parameter box (e)

The Instrument/Track Parameter box (Figure 6.2) shows the details of the selected Instrument or Track. It contains various parameters that affect the instrument selected. These parameters can be altered directly by the mouse, and are non-destructive. The contents of this Parameter box will vary depending on the type of Track selected. This is a MIDI Instrument track.

They are as follows:

Instrument name

Double clicking on the Instrument name opens a box where you can rename the instrument. On a MIDI track, clicking to the right of this (q) brings up a box containing the patch names of your MIDI device if you have entered these in the Environment (see Chapter 14).

Triangle

The small triangle on the box opens or closes the Parameter box.

Icon

Clicking, and holding, on the icon itself opens a list where you can change the icon assigned to the instrument. Holding Shift as you do this leaves the menu open when you let go of the mouse key, so you can use the cursor keys to choose the icon.

If the Parameter box is hidden, holding down the Shift and Alt keys and clicking on the Track column will open the icon list.

If you want to stop an instrument from appearing in the instrument list when you click on the instrument name column, deselect the X in the box next to the Icon. You might want to remove faders or MIDI ports and just make MIDI instruments available.

Figure 6.2
The Instrument/Track Parameter box

Channel

This shows the MIDI channel of the selected instrument. It can be changed here with the mouse or by double clicking on the value.

Program

An X in the box will transmit any changes made here to the MIDI device. The number on the right is the program change number. If you hold and click on this number, a pop up list appears from which you can select the program number. If you have assigned patch names to a multi instrument (see Appendix 1) their names will appear here. Clicking to the left of this number will allow you to send bank select messages. See your MIDI device handbook to see if your MIDI device uses bank select messages.

Volume

An X in the box will transmit any changes to the MIDI device. MIDI volume controller data will be sent out if you change the number in the right hand column.

Pan

This works in a similar way to the Vol parameter above. The info box (right) regarding Vol is relevant here too.

Transpose

You can transpose all regions on a Track using this parameter.

Velocity

You can adjust the overall response to Velocity for all region on a track.

Key Limiter

You can limit the range of notes played back by an instrument by setting a lower (left value) and higher (right value) note value here. All notes outside this range will not be played by the instrument.

Velocity limiter

You can limit the volume range of any instrument by setting a lower (left value) and higher (right value) value here. All notes whose velocity lies outside this range will not be played by the instrument.

No Transpose

If this is checked all Regions played by this instrument will be protected from transposition. Use this to keep drum sounds on the correct keys when you transpose a song.

No Reset

If this box is checked, no more reset messages will be sent to the instrument selected. Use this for non-musical instruments, such as MIDI controlled mixers. (See also Options>Settings>Reset messages.)

Style

Clicking on this brings up the Score styles menu. There is more on these in Chapter 5. Normally left as Auto.

Info

IF you are using Hyperdraw or the MIDI mixer leave this unchecked. Otherwise you could get unpredictable volume changes when you start and stop the sequencer.

Info

You can resize Parameter boxes by dragging the two vertical lines to the right of the box.

Figure 6.3
The Region Parameters Box

Toolbox (f)

The Toolbox can also be displayed by pressing the Esc key or using the right mouse key if you have one. A toolbox will appear at the cursor position, see Figure 7.4(a). The Toolbox is described in more detail in Chapter 4.

Region Parameters Box (g)

The Region Parameters Box (Figure 6.3) shows the details of the selected Region. If many Regions are selected some of the items will have a * next to them and can be changed for all selected items.

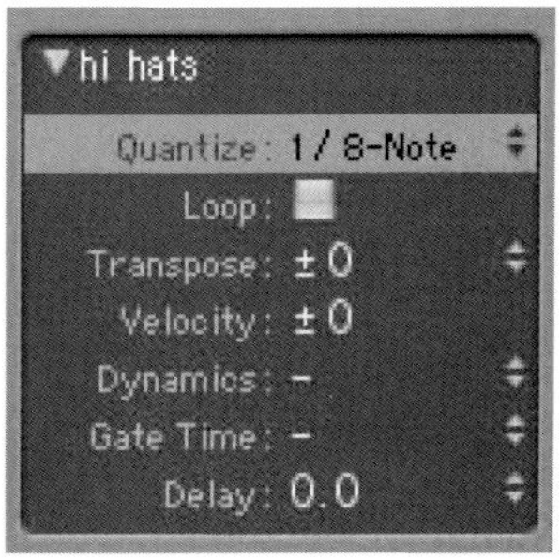

Region name

Double clicking on the Region name opens a box where you can rename it. If you have selected several Regions they will all be renamed.

Triangle

The small triangle on the box opens or closes the Parameter box.

Loop

When this is on, selected Regions will be looped until the end of the song or until another Region on the same track is encountered.

Transpose

Selected Regions can be transposed by changing the value on the right. Instruments that have No Seq Trp set, in the Instrument/Track Parameter box will not be transposed.

Velocity

This adjusts the velocity values of any selected Region(s) by the value of this parameter. Positive values are added, negative ones subtracted within the limits of MIDI velocity values (1–127).

Dynamics

This is a sort of 'compressor' for MIDI data. Hold the mouse key down to change the values from a pop up menu. This parameter changes the differences between the softest and loudest velocity values in a Region. Values over 100% expand the dynamic range of the values, increasing the difference between the softest and loudest velocity values, while those less than 100% decrease the difference, or compress, the values.

Gate time

The gate of a note refers to the time between pressing and releasing a key. The values Logic Pro uses fall somewhere between staccato (short sharp notes) and legato (long notes). The 'Fix' value means extreme staccato, values below 100% shorten the note length, values above lengthen it. The 'Leg' value produces completely joined up playing.

Delay

Alters the time delay of selected Regions in ticks or milliseconds depending on the setting in the View menu.

Transport buttons (h) and transport display (i)

The transport bar on the Arrange page has many of the functions of the main Transport bar (Chapter 10).

Resize cross (j)

This becomes visible if you hold the cursor over the position shown in Figure 6.1. Holding the mouse key down allows you to drag the position rulers down, thus enlarging them and making the transport bar visible. Dragging to the right makes the instrument name box visible.

Folders

Folders in Logic Pro are analogous to folders on your computer, except they contain Regions. You can use them to group together Regions for convenience. Their contents are shown below. Or you could put whole songs in a separate folder for live work. There is more on folders in Chapter 4.

Figure 6.4

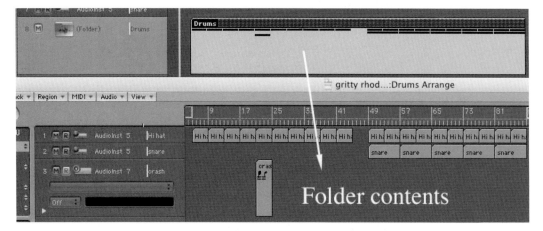

The Channel Strip (k)

The selected Track's Environment object will appear here. What is visible depends on the Track selected. Channel strips stop you having to go to the Track mixer or Environment to change volume, pan or insert effects every time you select a new track. The Track parameter box will reflect the parameters that can be adjusted for that specific track.

Audio Channel Strip

Shown in Figure 6.5.

Virtual Instrument Channel Strip

These are exactly like the familiar Audio objects from the Environment (Figure 6.6).

MIDI Channel Strip

These are exactly like the familiar MIDI objects from the Environment (Figure 6.7).

Figures 6.5, 6.6 and 6.7
Audio Channel Strip, Virtual Instrument
Channel Strip and MIDI Channel Strip

Other major areas of the Arrange page

Cycle, left and right locators, Autodrop area, Song Position Line, Zoom Controls, Running man and Link are covered fully in Chapter 4, which also deals with the use of markers, for defining positions in a song or making notes, and HyperDraw – draw directly on Regions to control volume, pan etc. The Global Track (Figure 6.1 – k) is covered in Chapter 13.

The Matrix editor

Overview

The Matrix editor is a 'piano roll' style editor, where you can edit, add or delete note events. Figure 7.1 shows note data displayed in the Matrix editor from the 'Piano' selected region. Note that the Matrix editor is used primarily to edit note data, but other data can also be processed using the Hyperdraw function.

See Chapter 4 for more on Hyperdraw. See Chapter 6 for more on the Arrange page, which has many features in common, such as Zoom controls and the Snap menu.

Figure 7.1
The Matrix Editor

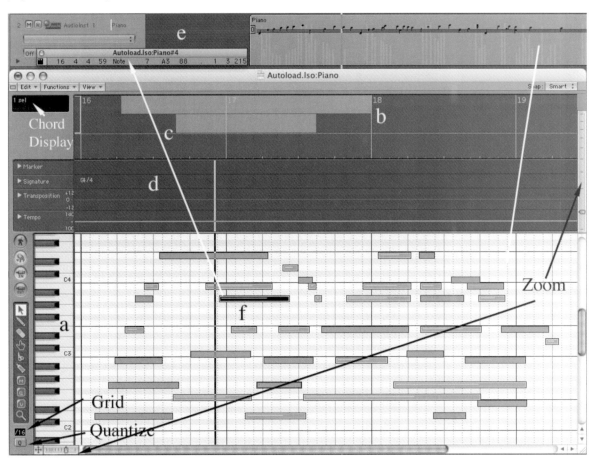

Info

The running man and link icon are covered in Chapter 4

Of course, as the sequencer runs, the notes will scroll across the Matrix editor screen. The zoom controls in the top right of the screen control the size of the note objects, just like they do for regions in the Arrange window.

You can also see from Figure 7.1 that the cycle region set by the left and right locators is visible in the Matrix editor (b) as is the autodrop region (c). The notes are displayed as rectangular blocks (f). Their length represents the length of the note, their color, or grayness, their velocity. The keyboard down the left (a) represents note pitches. If the Out icon is ON, the keyboard can be used to play notes too. If overlapping notes are selected, the resultant chord is displayed in the window in the upper top left of the window (pic left).

The functions of the icons in the Matrix editor window are pretty obvious. The IN icon, when clicked, allows MIDI data to be added via an external MIDI device. When the MIDI OUT icon is on, clicking on a note outputs its MIDI information to your MIDI devices

Using the Matrix Editor

Select a region and open the editor (Windows>Open Matrix Edit).

To change notes

Notes can be selected in the usual ways (clicking, shift/clicking, rubber banding and so on). The following affects all selected notes. The usual Logic Pro modifier keys can be used when moving and modifying note data (see Chapter 4). The toolbox is also described in Chapter 4.

Moving notes and changing their lengths

- Selected notes can be dragged up and down to change their pitches
- Selected notes can be dragged to the left or right to change their positions in time
- Selected notes can be lengthened by clicking an holding the mouse over the bottom right part of a note. Dragging to the left and right changes the length of the note.
- You can move notes in both pitch and time simultaneously, or allow movement in only one direction. This is set in the Logic Pro>Preferences>Global>Editing.
- Double clicking on a note opens up the Event list editor.

Changing note velocities

Click on the velocity tool in the tool box Hold the mouse key down and move the mouse up or down to increase or decrease the velocity of selected notes. If you have selected several notes, they will all be changed relative to each other.

Quantizing notes

Quantizing in Logic Pro is covered fully in Chapter 4. Select the notes you wish to quantize. Choose the quantize value using the Q button. All selected notes will be quantized. Or, use the quantize tool on the toolbar and click on selected notes to quantize them.

Deleting notes

Select the notes you want to delete and press the delete key, or use the eraser tool.

Cutting notes

Select the scissors tool. Place the tool over the selected note. Click on the note to cut it at the desired point. You can select several notes this way and cut them all at once.

Gluing notes together

Rubber band or select the desired notes. Select the glue tool. Notes of the same pitch will be glued together.

Other Matrix Editor functions

Functions menu

The Functions menu is similar to that in the Event list editor (Chapter 8).

View menu

This has the following sub-menus.

Scroll in Play

With this set, the SPL stays still and the noted flow past. When it's unclicked, the SPL moves.

Hide > Show SMPTE time ruler

When this is ON it displays the time in SMPTE format along with the usual beats, bars and ticks.

Parameters

You can hide the parameters if you need more screen space. Assign this command to a key command for rapid switching on and off.

White background

Change the useful grid on white background, to a less useful, wallpaper-style-but-nice-looking background.

Region colors

This colors all the notes in the region to the color set in the region from the Options>Colors main menu item.

Show selected regions only

Only shows notes in selected regions when viewing multiple regions. See Chapter 3 for more on Multi region editing.

Scroll to selection

Moves the song position line to notes selected in the window if it's not visible.

Global Tracks

See Chapter 13 for more on Global Tracks.

Event float

Opens a little float window that contains all the MIDI information for just one high-lighted note (Figure 7.1(e)).

Matrix colors

This opens a window where you can change the look of various Matrix window components.

Hyperdraw

Hyperdraw can be used in the Matrix editor in a similar way to its use in the Arrange window. Choosing Function>Hyperdraw>Volume will open a resizable Hyperdraw window where you can draw volume information. All the usual Hyperdraw functions can be used. See Chapter 4 for more on Hyperdraw. Figure 7.2 shows the Hyperdraw window being used to draw Pitch bend information, along with the various other options available.

Figure 7.2
The Hyperdraw window being used to draw Pitch bend information

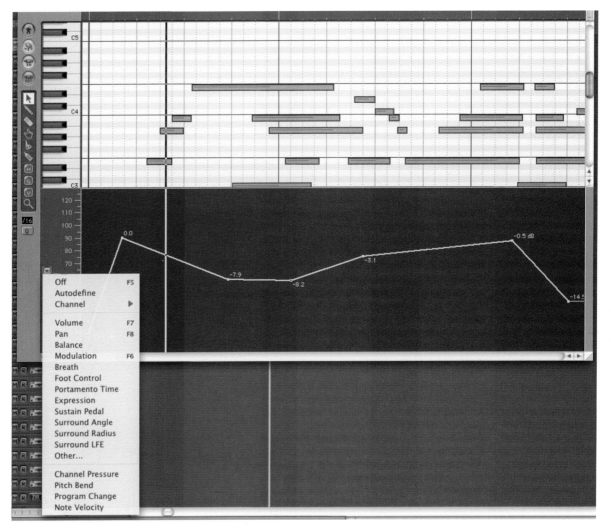

The Event List editor

Overview

The Event List editor is the only place in Logic Pro where you can edit all of the MIDI data recorded into the Region. Figure 8.1 shows the types of data Logic Pro can record, display and edit. Time is represented vertically (earliest events at the top), and the leftmost column shows the position of events.

Figure 8.1
The Event List editor

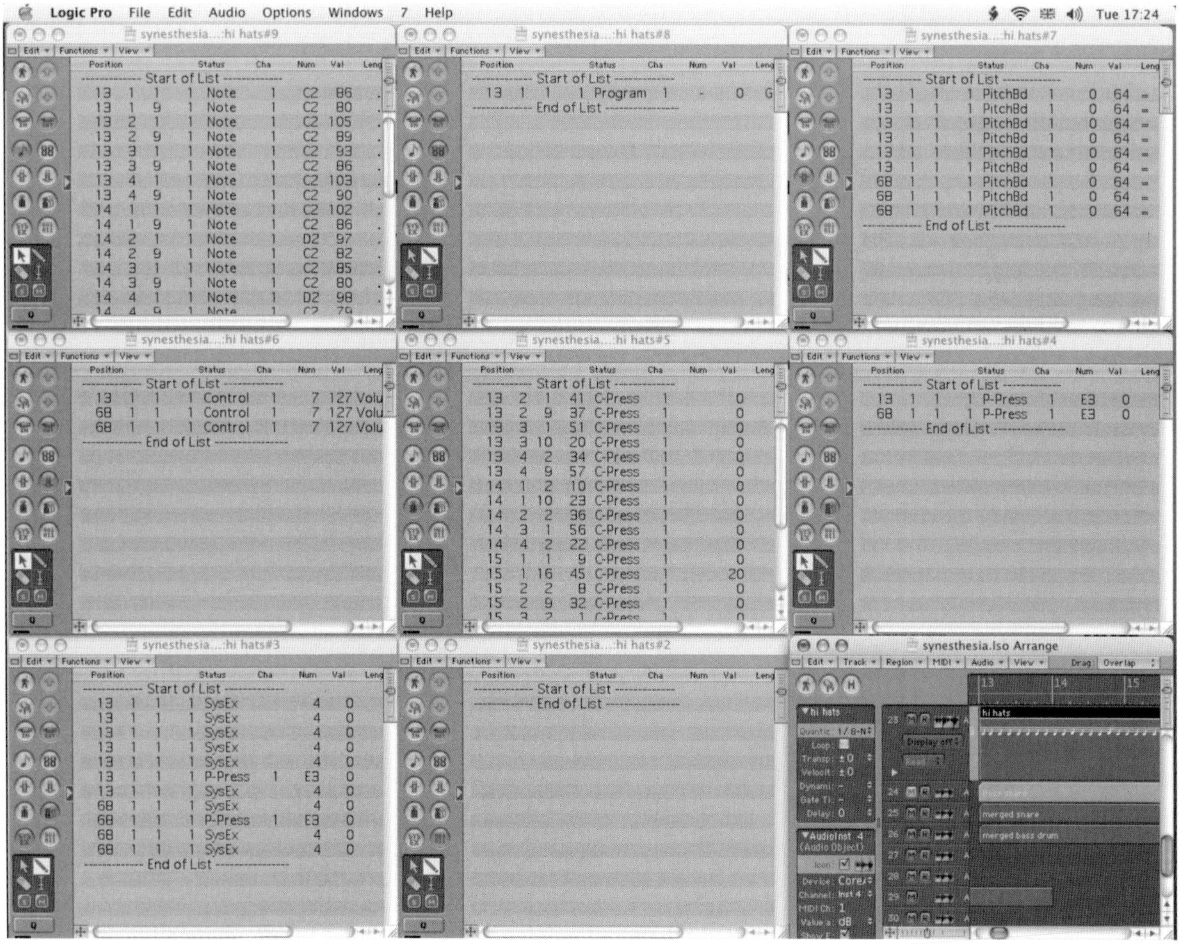

Events can be selected in the usual ways, except for rubber banding. The functions of the icons on the Event list editor are not immediately obvious. Except, perhaps for the 'note' Icon! Here is a handy reference to their functions.

 Scroll upwards through the list.

Scroll downwards through the list.

 When on, allows MIDI data to be input via an external MIDI device.

 When on, clicking on an event outputs it to your MIDI devices.

View, edit and add note data.

 View, edit and add program changes.

 View, edit and add Pitchbend data.

 View, edit and add Controller data.

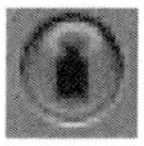

 View, edit and add channel pressure – channel aftertouch.

 View, edit and add polyphonic pressure – polyphonic aftertouch.

 View, edit and add Systems exclusive data.

 View, edit and add Meta events.

Figure 8.1 shows the data displayed when each of these buttons is pressed – for example Figure 8.2 shows the data displayed when the Note icon is ON. Of course, you can have any number of icons depressed to view different data simultaneously. Or you can, for clarity, open many Event edit windows and display different data in each. Whatever you edit in one will be reflected in all the open windows.

Info

The running man and link icons are covered in Chapter 4

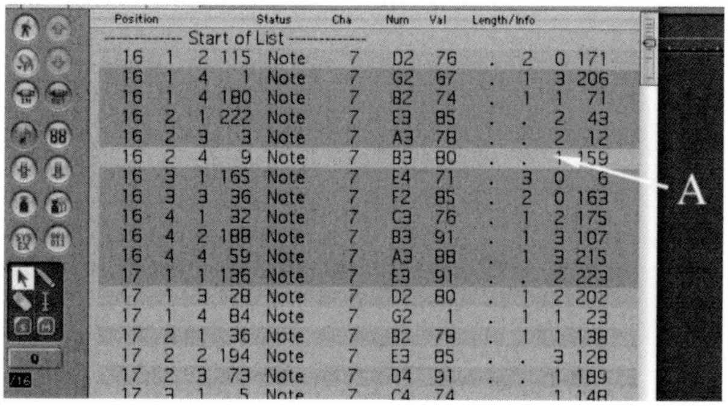

Figure 8.2
Data displayed when note icon is on

Using the Event List editor

Select a Region in the Arrange page and open the Event list editor (Windows>Open Event list).

To change a data value

As is usual in Logic Pro, there are several ways to change the data in the Event list editor. For example, you can double click on the 'position' value and enter directly a new number (Figure 8.3). Or you can use the mouse with the mouse key held down directly on the data. Some of the data values, when changed this way, will bring up a menu with available options, like the names of sounds in your synthesiser, controller names or system exclusive manufacturer names. Remember, if you have the MIDI OUT button switched on, any changes you make to the data will be output to your MIDI devices.

Figure 8.3

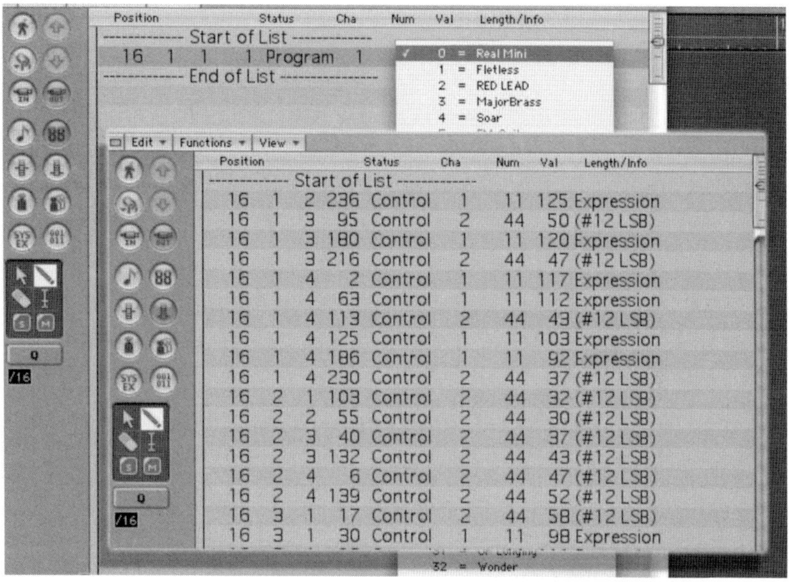

Data can also be pasted from the clipboard. If you change position data in an event, the list is updated accordingly.

To add data

Select the pencil tool. Click on the button for the type of data you want, then click on the Event list window. A data item is created at the current Song position line. You can then edit the data as needed.

To delete data

Highlight the data you want to delete and either press the delete key, or use Cut in the Edit menu.

Using the Edit menu to select data

The Edit menus in Logic Pro's editors contain many functions that are useful when selecting data to delete or edit. Most of the Edit commands are self evident.

Toggle selection is the opposite of the original selection. For example if you highlight an event and choose the Edit menu function 'Select equal objects', all the notes that are the same will be highlighted. You can see this might be a quick way for, say, deleting a bass drum note in a Region. If you then choose 'Toggle selection' all unequal notes will be selected. In the same fashion you can select muted noted, overlapping notes and so on.

Info

You can, if you wish get the event list editor to open when you double click on a sequence>make it a default by selecting it in the Logic Pro>Preferences>Global>Editing menu.

Of course, all these Edit functions will work on all data types. So you could, for example, select all program changes that are the same or all the Channel pressure data in a Region.

The Functions menu

Using this menu, you can perform various functions on selected highlighted data. You can:

- Set the locators by highlighted objects
- Quantize and de-quantize
- Erase MIDI events – most of these functions are self-evident. Unselected, within selection will delete an unselected MIDI event within a selection. So in Figure 8.2, this will delete the event depicted by A
- Copy MIDI events. This opens a window with parameters you wish to use when copying events
- Unlock SMPTE position
- Lock SMPTE position – you can lock the SMPTE position of an event or events, so that whatever you do, change tempo, time signature etc., the events will always stay at the same SMPTE time. Unlock SMPTE position returns the events to normal.

Transform

See Chapter 4 for more information on transform.

The View menu

Here you can:

- Change the position and length of the MIDI events from bars and beats to SMPTE units and vice versa
- Show the lengths of events with reference either to the whole song or just the selected sequence
- Show the position data with reference either to the whole song or just the selected sequence
- Hide the toolbox and other parameters
- Show Sysex information in hexadecimal format
- Scroll the song position line in the edit window to the first of the selected events

Transport

9

Most of the functions of the Transport bar are discussed in a real life situation in Chapter 4, 'Using Logic'.

Overview

Figure 9.1 shows all the on screen variations possible with the Transport bar. The Transport bar is opened using the Windows>Open transport menu.

Figure 9.1

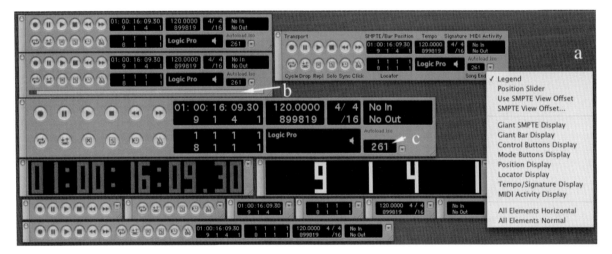

The Transport bar is particularly flexible in Logic. It can be configured, sized and positioned in many ways, as you can see from Figure 9.1. All these different variations are obtained by opening a new Transport window and using the choices in the menu (Figure 9.1(a)).

There is no limit to how many Transport bars you can open (apart from screen size and memory limitations of course!). Like every Logic window, all the Transports are linked (you can see in Figure 9.1 that they all show the same values) and can be stored as part of a screenset for instant recall. Most of the controls on the Transport bar (start, stop, pause etc.) can also be assigned to Key commands. The Transport bar is a 'float' window and is always on top of other windows.

Figure 9.1(b) shows the position display (the white line at the bottom of the Transport). You can grab this with the mouse and drag it left to right to rapidly move through a song. This marker on the indicator also moves as the song plays so you get a rough visual indication of the position within the song.

Figure 9.1(a) is the menu produced when you click on the small down arrow to the right of the No In and No Out on the Transport bar. Figure 9.1(c) is the number of bars in the song.

The Transport bar controls in more detail

Mode controls

These controls (Figure 9.2) switch various functions on and off.

(a) Cycle

Logic will loop around the positions set in the Left and Right locator window (see later in this chapter).

(b) Autodrop

When this is set, Logic will, when set to record, 'Punch in' automatically at the left autodrop value, and drop out of record at the right one.

(c) Erase

When this is set, Logic replaces any MIDI data or audio recording on the track Logic is recording onto. When it is off, Logic creates a new region or merges the data into an existing region, if you are recording in cycle or loop mode.

(d) Solo and solo lock

In Solo mode (one click on the solo button), all selected regions are played, everything else is muted. In Solo lock mode (double click on the solo button, the button inverts in colour) Non-highlighted regions can be edited without affecting the solo status of selected regions.

(e) Sync

Forces Logic to run in synchronization to an external timecode (MTC, SMPTE etc.).

(f) Metronome

This button switches the audible click on and off.

- Logic can be made to repeat one beat indefinitely until it receives a MIDI message. This is set in using the File>Song settings>Recording window. Set the 'When Beginning' parameter to 'Wait for Note'.
- Logic can be made to automatically switch the sync mode button on when it receives external sync (see page 147).

Sequencer controls

These are like the familiar tape recorder functions.

(a) Record

When on, puts Logic into record mode, then pressing the play icon starts recording. How Logic records depends on whether you have set a count in, or a cycle region, as well as other preferences. See Chapter 4 for more details.

(b) Pause
Holds Logic in record or play mode. Pressing pause again or play, continues in the same mode.

(c) Play
Starts Logic from the song position pointer or from the left locator in cycle mode. Pressing play twice in rapid succession has the same effect as pressing stop twice, but of course starts Logic playing from that position.

(d) Stop
Drops Logic out of record or play and stops the sequencer. If you press it twice quickly in rapid succession Logic moves the song position line to the beginning of the song, or the left locator in cycle mode.

(e) and (f) Rewind and Fast forward
The Rewind and Fast forward buttons have different effects depending on the state of play:

* If Logic is stopped they move forward or back bars for as long as they are held down
* If Logic is running, moving the mouse to the left or right will cause the MIDI and Audio events to be output faster, sort of like a tape recorder in fast wind mode.

Position display
These show the current Song position line values.

(a) Song position line in SMPTE time
The way this field is displayed can be changed from the Logic Pro>Preferences>Display>Display SMPTE menu item.

(b) Bar position
This is given in bars : beats : divisions :ticks. The way this field is displayed can be changed from the Logic Pro>Preferences>Display>Display Clock Format menu item.

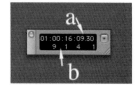

Figure 9.4
Position display

Tempo/signature display
This display (Figure 9.5) has the following components.

(a) Song tempo
Defines the tempo for the whole song, unless you have variable tempi – in which case it displays the tempo at the SPL. The tempo can be directly edited by clicking on the display and holding the mouse key down while moving the mouse up or down to increment or decrement the value. Alternatively, double clicking on the tempo display opens a box where you can type in the value directly. If you have a tempo list set up, this box will display the tempo at the point of the song position line.

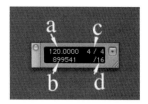

Figure 9.5
Tempo/signature display

(b) Memory

The amount of memory remaining for use by Logic. If you double click on this memory display, a dialog box opens allowing you to reorganize the memory. This can increase the amount of data your Logic song can hold.

(c) Time signature

Time signatures can be changed in a similar fashion to tempo. Changing the time signature directly has an effect at the song position the SPL is set to.

(d) Division

The division is the 'grid' setting for all position displays. If you open the Matrix editor, you can see the effect of changing the division on the background grid. This affects the 'snap to' of notes and how they are quantized.

Locator display

Figure 9.6
Locator display

The locator positions can be entered directly here, or with the mouse on the Arrange page (See Chapter 4, 'Using Logic'). These locators define the positions which Logic loops around in cycle mode and, in conjunction with the Key command 'Go to left locator', an easy way to get back to a known part of the song. (a) is the Left locator, (b) is Right locator.

Drop in/out points

These only appear when the cycle and autodrop buttons are switched on. They can be edited directly here or with the mouse on the Arrange page (see Chapter 6). You could, for example, set a loop using the left and right locators and the auto-drop in and out points within this loop. So you can concentrate on the twiddly bits rather than the shock of the record button.

MIDI indicator display

Figure 9.7
MIDI indicator display. Double click on this area to stop all MIDI flow out of Logic (Panic Button)

This display gives information about the MIDI information flowing into and out of Logic. It displays note or controller information. For more detailed MIDI monitoring see Chapter 14 – the Environment.

Other bits and bobs

There are other menus hidden in the Transport bar (Figure 9.8).

- Pressing the *Record* button and holding the mouse key down brings up menu 'a' in Figure 9.3. As usual most of these functions can be assigned to Key commands. The *Recording Options....* menu opens the relevant Song Settings menu
- Pressing and holding the mouse key over the synchronization button brings up menu 'b' in Figure 9.3
- *Internal Sync* forces Logic to be the timing master
- *SMPTE Sync (MTC)* forces Logic to follow incoming SMPTE or MIDI Time Code
- *MIDI Clock sync* forces logic to follow incoming MIDI clock

Figure 9.8

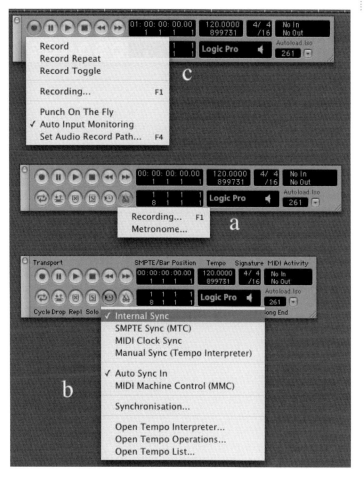

- *Manual sync (tempo interpreter)* forces Logic to follow tempo interpreter information. The tempo interpreter allows you to use, say the computer keyboard or an external percussive signal to set the tempo.
- When *Auto sync In* is checked, Logic automatically sets itself up to respond to incoming time code. For example, you have SMPTE time code coming in at 25 frames per second, Logic will automatically set itself to receive it
- With *MIDI Machine Control* Logic can send and receive MIDI machine control
- *Synchronization...* Opens the synchronization panel where you can set various options
- Tempo and synchronization are dealt with in Chapter 4
- The menu (Figure 9.8 a) allows you to find the MIDI set up for your click, or opens up the *Recording Options...* page to set count-ins etc.

Figure 9.9

Chord display

The MIDI IN and OUT section of the transport bar (Figure 9.9) displays the chord played on a MIDI controller.

And some extras

A short click on the fast forward or rewind will move to the next marker. If you haven't any markers, the SPL will move to the next bar. Long clicks fast forward or rewind and moving the mouse left or right while doing this changes the rewind speed. You can also use two Key Commands Shuttle forwards and Shuttle backwards, moving the SPL along in chunks.

The Hyper editor

Overview

The Hyper editor tends to get overlooked in Logic Pro, as much of its simpler functions, such as MIDI mixing and controller editing, can be reproduced by Hyperdraw and Automation in the Arrange and Matrix windows. However, the Hyper editor can be useful if you need to graphically edit several MIDI controllers simultaneously, or you want to set up a 'Drum Editor'.

Figure 10.1
The Hyper Editor

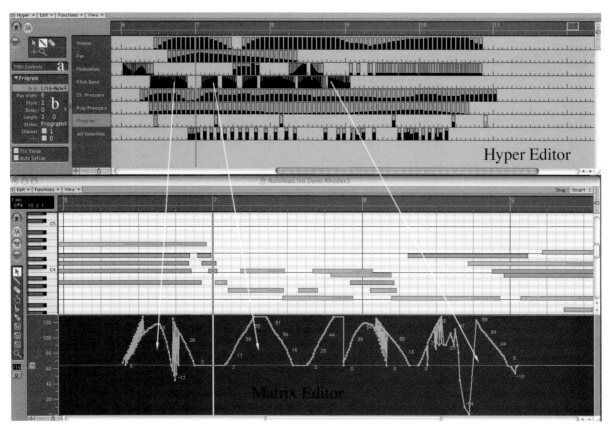

The Hyper editor deals with MIDI 'events' or data. These can be notes, MIDI controllers, program changes and so on.

Figure 10.1 shows a typical Hyper edit window. Data can be freely drawn, deleted and modified, and any changes made in other editor windows, are reflected here. In this figure, you can see that the volume information in the Hyperdraw window of the Matrix editor is reflected in the Volume area of the Hyper edit window. As you can see, the Hyper editor looks very like the Arrange page and Matrix editors. The bar ruler at the top can display and modify the cycle region and the autodrop region, as in those windows. The link, running man and out icons work as in the Arrange page (see Chapter 6). You can also utilize Global Tracks in the Hyper editor (Chapter 13).

If you look at Figure 10.1, you can see MIDI controller data displayed in horizontal fields. These are known as Event Definitions, and can be created, deleted and modified within the Hyper editor.

Editing the controller data

Open the Hyper editor by selecting a region and selecting the Windows>Hyper Edit menu item. The toolbox can be used to draw and erase event data.

The pencil tool

The pencil tool is used to draw controller data directly onto the screen.

The crosshairs tool

Use the crosshairs tool to draw linear fades. Click on a point within the event definition display window and drag the line which appears, to where you want it. Click again, and a linear series of data is drawn. When using these tools, the Parameter box has the following modifiers. You can add new events, or modify existing ones. Data is drawn according to the values in the Parameter box.

Parameter box (Figure 10.1 (b))

Figure 10.2

Name
You can change the name of the event definition by double clicking on its name (Figure 10.2).

Grid
Defines the quantization of the controller events.

Delay
Delays or advances all the controller events in ticks.

Penwidth
Defines the width of the pencil. A small value is a thin pencil, fatter produces less controller data.

Style
There are four different display types for the data. Types 5 – 8 are the same as 1 – 4 but flash. You can delay the controller information on a track wide basis. The values are in ticks and musical divisions.

Length

Defines the length of notes. Useful if Hyper edit is used as a drum editor. Make sure that note off events are not transmitted at the same time as note on events, for optimum timing. Use a value of 100 ticks as a default. The left value is divisions, the right, ticks.

Status

Clicking and holding the mouse button down brings up a menu where you can define the type of MIDI data you want to edit.

Channel

You can set the MIDI channel of the data to be sent. If this is unchecked, MIDI data is sent on the same channel as it was received on.

-1-

This parameter, with a pull down menu, defines which controller value is set, or which note is played. If the instrument playing the region is a Mapped instrument (see Chapters 3, 4 and Appendix 1) the menu will contain a list of the sounds mapped.

Fix value

If this is checked, you cannot change the height of any events drawn. This is useful if you want to add many events with the same value, or for those with wobbly drawing hands. Individual events, such as notes and program changes, can edited be grabbing the events with the pencil tool and dragging them. When you select several events, hold down the SHIFT key as you do so.

If you are altering several events at the same time, you can change all the values proportionally to each other. When the highest event hits the top or bottom, the other events cannot be changed any further. However, if you hold the Option/Alt key down when you are altering an event, all selected events can be moved to the top or bottom.

Auto Define

If checked, the Hyper>Create Event Definition function will create an event based on selected events in another editor window.

Moving and copying events

Select the events to be edited. Hold down the Alt key and click on the events. A hand appears. Drag the events to a new location. Selected events can also be cut and pasted using the Edit menu items as for other windows.

Hypersets

When you first open the Hyper editor it will show the data in the selected region (Figure 10.1). This grouping of controller types is called a hyperset. You can create your own hypersets. Figure 10.1 shows the hyperset 'MIDI Controls', the default set, containing the basic MIDI controller data.

Choosing a hyperset

Click and hold on the button Figure 10.1(a), to select hypersets from the pull down menu.

Working with hypersets

Hyper sets consist of several event definitions. For example, the event definitions in Figure 10.1 are:

* Volume
* Pan
* Modulation
* Pitch bend
* Cha. Pressure
* Poly Pressure
* Program
* All velocities

Creating a hyperset

Select Hyper>Create hyperset. A set is created with a preset Volume event definition.

Naming a hyperset

Double click on the hyperset button (Figure 10.1(a)).

Deleting a hyperset

Select Hyper>Clear hyperset.

Selecting event definition

Click on the name of the event definition. It will be highlighted. You can only select one definition at a time. When selected, the definition's parameters appear in the Parameter box (Figure 10.1(b)).

Creating an event definition

Select Hyper>Create event definition. If you select a region then choose Hyper>Create event definition, Logic Pro will create definitions for either all the events in the region or just the selected events, depending on your response to the dialog box Logic Pro presents you with.

You can also, from the Hyper menu, copy event definitions between hypersets. Convert event definitions opens a box where you can change one event type to another. For example, you could change Volume (Controller 7) to Balance (Controller 8). All the values in the Parameter box can be changed here, as can the quantize values of the data.

Auto define

If you have another editor window open and you select an event in it (note or controller etc.) and Auto define is on, an event definition is automatically created in the Hyper editor. If the event definition already exists, it is not duplicated. Several event definitions can be auto created at the same time.

Figure 10.3

Using the Hyper editor as a drum editor

Logic Pro does not have a dedicated drum editor. As it is sometimes useful when editing drum parts to see the notes on a grid, you can use the Hyper editor to perform this function.

The easiest way to set up a hyperset as a drum editor is as follows:

- Create a mapped instrument of your drum and percussion sounds (See Appendix 1)
- Record a short sequence using all the sounds assigned to keys. Just click on the pause and record button on the transport bar (or select record via a key

Figure 10.4

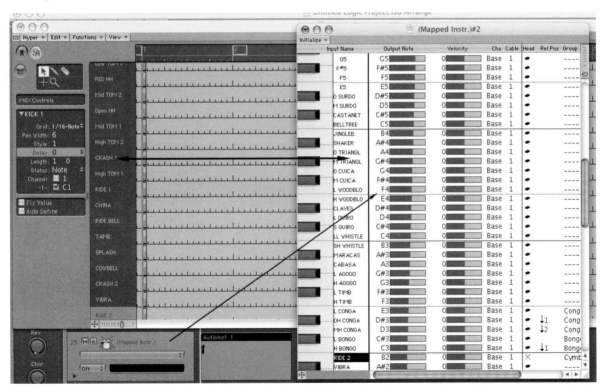

command) and play each note in turn. No need to press play. Then stop recording. Don't press play!

- Make sure the sequence is selected and then open the Hyper editor.
- Select Hyper> Hyper Hyper Set menu item. Double click on 'set initialized' and enter a useful name, Like 'Korg Drums'
- Click on the volume event definition and select the Hyper>Delete event Definition menu item.
- Select the Hyper >Multi Hyper Event Definition menu item. In the Dialog box which appears, select All (all events in current sequence).
- You will see something like Figure 10.4
- The names of the drums down the left of the window are imported from your Mapped instrument.
- Select the Edit>Select all menu item.
- Press the delete key to delete the drum events, i.e. the notes you played in.
- Adjust the zoom of the window as desired.

You can now enter drum data directly with the pencil tool or by recording as usual from the MIDI keyboard (you may want to switch the File>Song settings> Recording>Merge new recordings with selected regions menu item to On, if you want to loop around and add new notes at each pass. Step time input (Chapter 13) is also useful when writing drum parts.

You can delete notes with the eraser tool and drag them around as with any events in Logic Pro. You can also change the grid values for each event definition.

If you want to adjust the grid value of several event definitions, just Shift click on them to select them all. Grid values are changed in the Parameter box. You may want the bass drum (Kick 1) to default to 1/8th note, the Open HH to 1/16, so select these individually and edit the Grid parameter.

Figure 10.5

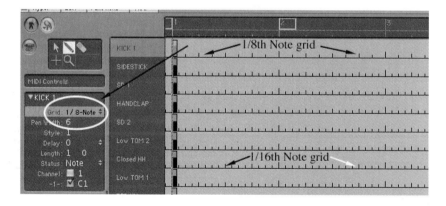

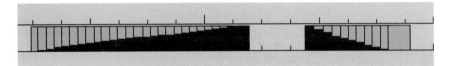

Tip

The Grid value defines where new notes will appear on the Hyper edit window when you create them with the pencil tool. It's a sort of pre-quantize effect. For example, if you want to add a bass drum on every bar, change the grid value to 1:1. You can then only pencil in notes on the first beat of the bar. If you want to create hi-hats on every 16th beat, set the grid value to 1/16. Now, dragging the pencil across the Hyper editor, will create a hi-hat note on every 16th beat. You can, of course, change the grid value after you have drawn events. Grid values are changed in the Parameter box.

The velocities of the notes are shown as the dark areas of the note columns. These can be edited with the pencil tool. Note how easy it is to draw a variable velocity on the 'Tite HH' in Figure 10.3. Also notice the rise in the GatedSnare toward bar 9.

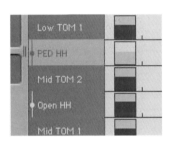

Figure 10.6

Speaking of Hi Hats, next to the Hi Hats in the 'Drum Editor' (Figure 10.7) are some little dots with lines through them. These mean that these channel definitions are in 'Hi Hat mode' (just click to the left of the name to switch it on or off). What this means is that only one event can be output at the same time when in this mode. You may want this to happen if you are trying to emulate a human drummer more closely – only closed or open hi-hats can be played on one set at a time.

Of course, you can group any instruments like this. You may want a monophonic bass line for example. The Hyper editor isn't just for drum notes!

Figure 10.7

Other Hyper editor data

The Edit menu has similar facilities to the Event list editor (Chapter 8). The Functions menu has similar facilities to the Event list editor. The View menu has similar facilities to the Matrix editor (Chapter 7), but obviously with the omission of the HyperDraw items!

Key commands

Overview

Almost every function within Logic can be assigned a Key command. In fact, some of Logic's features can be accessed only by Key commands, so it's easy to miss them! Key commands are assigned in the Key Commands window. You can open it from the Logic Pro>Preferences>Key Commands menu.

The Key commands window is also where you set remote control via MIDI. This allows you to use an external MIDI controller (keyboard, mixer surface, switchbox etc.) to control Logic Pro's functions. Some ideas on how to use this feature are outlined below:

- Use the low keys on an 88 note master keyboard to control Logic's transport functions, go to the locators or open various editing windows.
- Use a footswitch connected to a synthesiser to put Logic into record for punch in and out. To do this, set your keyboard to generate a MIDI controller when the footswitch is depressed and then assign that controller in the Key Commands window to put Logic in record.
- Use your drum pads to change screensets and confuse your drummer. I'm sure you can think of many more uses for this function!

The Key commands window

Figure 11.1 shows the Key commands window. The window is divided into several columns.

Command

This column show the keys assigned to a certain function in Logic Pro. For example in Figure 11.1, the 'F1' key is assigned to the Logic command 'Recording Options'. The capital 'I' key is assigned to the 'Import File...' feature. A dot next to a command means that it is not available in any of Logic Pro's menus, i.e. it is only available as a Key command.

As you can imagine, it isn't always easy to find the Logic Pro commands which you may want to assign a key to. You may have the same problem finding out which keys you have already assigned to which command! Fortunately Logic Pro has several features to help you out.

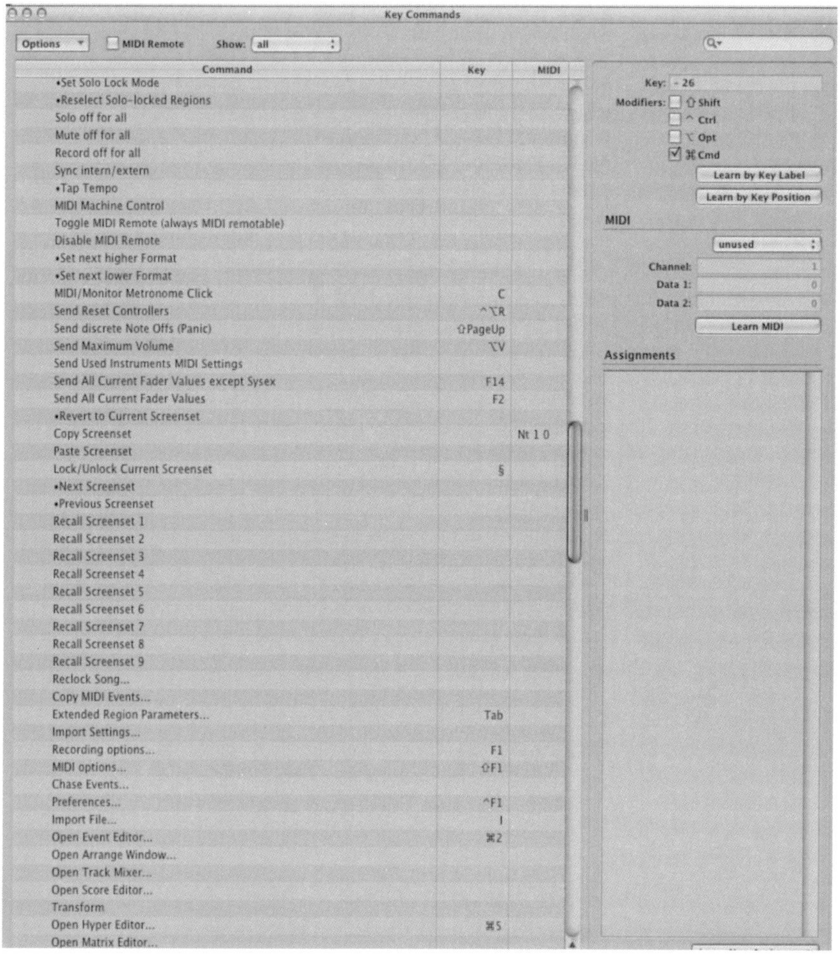

Figure 11.1
The Key commands window

Referring again to Figure 11.1, you can hide the unused Key commands, or only display the ones you have already assigned using 'Show' pull down menu – the options are 'All', 'unused' and 'used'. You can also find a particular Key command. Figure 11.2 shows a search for the word 'goto' and all the Key commands relating to this are displayed along with their assignments.

If you want to find which Logic Pro command a particular key has been assigned to, make sure the 'Learn by Key Label' and 'Learn by Key Position' buttons are not set to ON. Then type the key on the computer keyboard. Logic Pro will highlight the relevant assignment. Figure 11.3 shows the result when you press the 'p' key.

You can also see in Figure 11.1(a), that Logic Pro displays the information about a key assignment at the top right of the window in a Parameter box. This information can be modified directly here. So you could change the computer key or MIDI channel assigned, for example.

Info

You'll note that some of the commands are assigned to numbers. For example 'Goto left locator' is assigned the number - 83. This is the ASCII code for the number 1 on the numeric keypad, and allows you to define the numeric keys and the number keys separately.

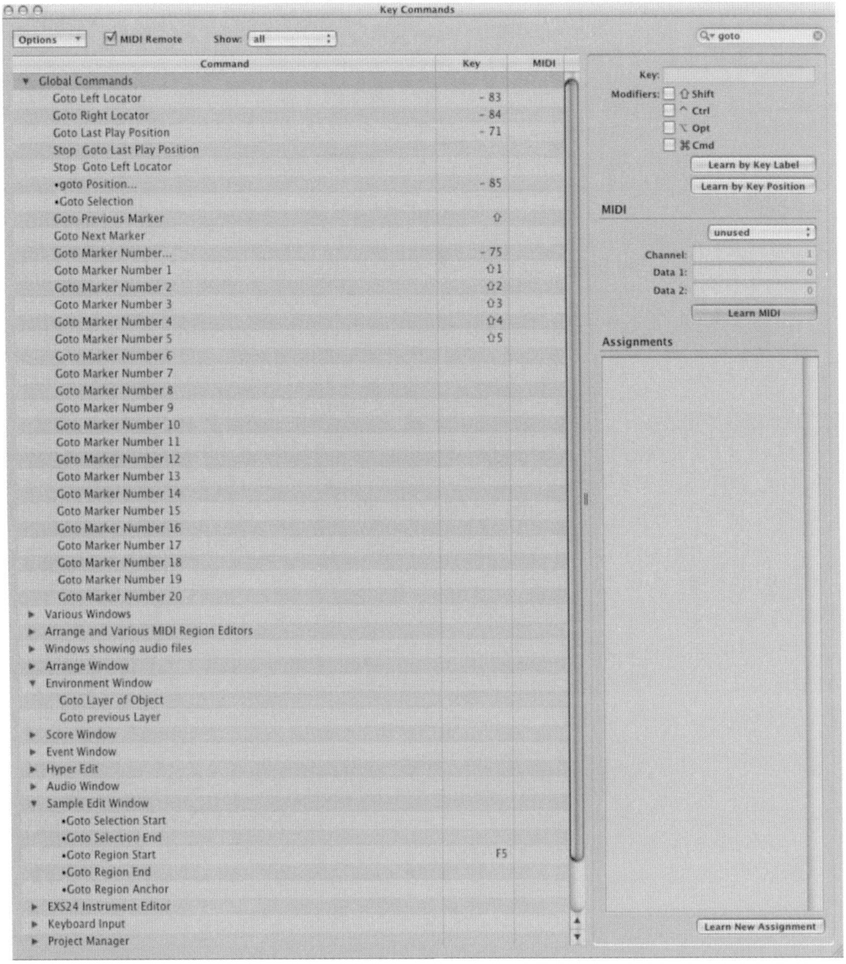

Key Commands
Options
MIDI Remote
Show: all
goto
Command
Key
MIDI
Global Commands
Goto Left Locator - 83
Goto Right Locator - 84
Goto Last Play Position - 71
Stop Goto Last Play Position
Stop Goto Left Locator
•goto Position... - 85
•Goto Selection
Goto Previous Marker ⇧
Goto Next Marker
Goto Marker Number... - 75
Goto Marker Number 1 ⇧1
Goto Marker Number 2 ⇧2
Goto Marker Number 3 ⇧3
Goto Marker Number 4 ⇧4
Goto Marker Number 5 ⇧5
Goto Marker Number 6
Goto Marker Number 7
Goto Marker Number 8
Goto Marker Number 9
Goto Marker Number 10
Goto Marker Number 11
Goto Marker Number 12
Goto Marker Number 13
Goto Marker Number 14
Goto Marker Number 15
Goto Marker Number 16
Goto Marker Number 17
Goto Marker Number 18
Goto Marker Number 19
Goto Marker Number 20
Various Windows
Arrange and Various MIDI Region Editors
Windows showing audio files
Arrange Window
Environment Window
Goto Layer of Object
Goto previous Layer
Score Window
Event Window
Hyper Edit
Audio Window
Sample Edit Window
•Goto Selection Start
•Goto Selection End
•Goto Region Start F5
•Goto Region End
•Goto Region Anchor
EXS24 Instrument Editor
Keyboard Input
Project Manager
Key:
Modifiers: ⇧ Shift
^ Ctrl
⌥ Opt
⌘ Cmd
Learn by Key Label
Learn by Key Position
MIDI
unused
Channel: 1
Data 1: 0
Data 2: 0
Learn MIDI
Assignments
Learn New Assignment

Figure 11.2

Page Left-most
Page Right-most
Hide/Show Transport
Hide/Show Parameters P
Hide/Show Toolbox
Grid
Plain Background

Figure 11.3

Modifier keys

Some of they keys cannot be reassigned, as they have special functions within Logic Pro. These are the so-called 'modifier keys'.

- Shift
- Control (CTRL)
- Alt (Option)
- The Apple key (shown right)
- The backspace key can only be used in conjunction with modifier keys, i.e. Shift and backspace.

⌘

- Most of the other keys can be redefined.

Some Key commands are pre-set within Logic Pro. These are the default Key commands for the following functions:

- Record Ready (i.e. record and pause) key is the space bar
- Play is the '0' (zero) key on the numeric keypad
- Stop is the Enter key on the numeric keypad
- Record is the * key on the numeric keypad

Tip

Redefine the most common sequencer functions to the keys you are used to using if you are coming to Logic from another sequencer.

There are some other pre-defined keys, including those for entering notes when Step editing (see Chapter 17 for more details).

MIDI remote settings

In Figure 11.4, the first column (a) shows the MIDI messages. It consists of 4 columns. The first refers to the type of MIDI data i.e. note, controller, program, pressure etc.

The next column (b) shows the MIDI channel on which the MIDI data is received. The next two columns (c and d) show values for note on or note off, if that is relevant to the incoming MIDI data.

In Figure 11.5 you can see that 'Record Toggle' is assigned to a MIDI controller, on channel 7 with an on value of 65. This is actually responding to the footswitch on a Roland D50.

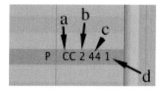

Figure 11.4

Figure 11.5

Record		*
•Record Repeat		⇧*
•Record Toggle		- 82	CC 7 65 1
•Capture Last Take as Recording		H
•Capture Last Take as Recording & Play		

Quick reference

To assign a Key Command

- Switch on the 'Learn by key label' or 'Learn by key position' button. The difference is that while 'Learn by key label' learns the reference to an ASCII code, 'Learn by key position' assigns the actual ASCII data to a command. So Learn by key label' would display 'Space', or 'F11' for example, "Learn by key position' would display an actual ASCII number, allowing two different keys with the same letter or number to be used as they will have two different ASCII values.
- Highlight a Logic command you wish to assign to a key.
- Press the computer keyboard key you wish to assign.
- If the key is already assigned, Logic will tell you.
- Turn off the 'Learn…' buttons.

To assign a MIDI Remote Control Command

- Switch the 'Learn MIDI' button on
- Highlight the Logic function you wish to assign to the MIDI command
- Send the MIDI command (press the key, move the slider, press the button).
  Note If you want to assign a MIDI note on message, switch off 'Learn MIDI' before you release the MIDI key
- Switch the 'Learn MIDI' button off
- MIDI remote control can be switched on and off with the MIDI remote checkbox. This is useful when, say, you need to use those extra keys to make music!

To find an already assigned key command

- Click on the box to the right of the standard OSX search box (11.7)
- Enter the command to be found
- Press enter
- To see all the commands again, put a space in the find box

To check the function of a computer keyboard key

- Make sure the 'Learn key' buttons are switched off
- Press the computer keyboard key you wish to check
- Logic highlights the relevant assignment

To print a key command

- Use the menu Options>Copy key commands to clipboard
- Open a word processor
- Paste the command into the word processor

Other functions

The menu item Options>Import Key commands allows you to import a Key command set up from another Logic Pro preferences file. So you could, for example, load in your Key commands into someone else's Logic Pro set-up, or load an emulation of another sequencer package for a user unfamiliar with Logic Pro. In the Options menu you can also initialize or reset various aspects of the Key commands.

Controller assignments

For more on these see Chapter 17.

Tip

Print out your Key commands and stick them under a transparent mouse mat.

Info

Key commands are stored in the Logic Preferences file in the /Library/preferences folder. Its a good idea to make copies of these files in case they get corrupted or overwritten.

The Audio window and Sample editor

Logic Pro provides many tools for the editing, archiving, adding, deleting and manipulation of audio files. Apart from the obvious cutting and pasting, resizing and dragging of audio regions in the Arrange page, Logic Pro has two main tools for dealing with the audio files it generates. This chapter details the Audio window and the Sample editor.

The Audio window

The Audio window is opened from the Audio menu, or from a key command you have set up in the Key command window. The figure shows a typical Audio window. The window has the usual Zoom settings and Link icons.

The Audio window is split into several columns. Column A is a list of all the audio files either recorded or imported into Logic Pro. The display shows complete audio files and any regions created in the Arrange page or Sample editor. Regions or files can be renamed by double clicking on their names. If you try and rename a file, rather than a region, Logic Pro will warn you that changing the actual name of the file may have an impact on any other Logic Pro song using that file.

Column B shows the details of the files along with a graphical display of the files themselves. These file details are displayed only if the View>Show file info menu item is checked. The graphical file displays are either shown or hidden by clicking on the little triangles to the left of the window. When the files are displayed, you can open the Sample editor by double clicking on the waveform. Column B has the following 'sub' columns.

Srate

Logic Pro can use various sample rates simultaneously, depending on the Audio hardware installed. The sample rate for the Audio file is displayed here.

Bit

This is the bit depth of the file. Again, depending on the audio hardware installed, Logic Pro can support different bit rates simultaneously.

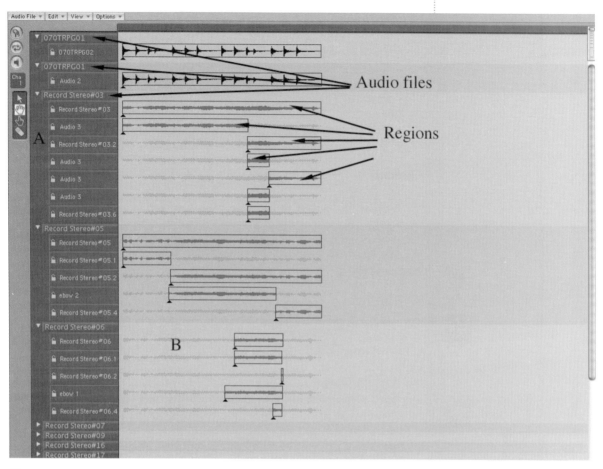

Audio files

Regions

Figure 12.1
The Audio window

Cha
This icon shows whether the file is stereo or mono.

Stereo file
Mono file

Figure 12.2

Size
This gives the size of the file in Kb.

Location
This shows the disk and directory where the file is stored.

The Cycle, Speaker, Cha, Dev and toolbox icons

The Cycle icon
When this is On, the audio region is looped continuously.

The Speaker icon

Clicking on this plays file or region from the start. You can play the region from any point by clicking on the waveform using the Arrow tool.

The Cha icon

This is the Audio channel, which the file will play back on when auditioned. Stereo files play back in stereo by default. If you highlight one side of a file or region, hold down the Shift key and then click the Speaker icon, the file will play back the selected audio in mono.

The Toolbox

The arrow tool

Selecting this tool allows you to audition files from any part of the file or region by clicking and holding the mouse on the waveform.

The hand tool

Selecting this tool allows you to drag files and regions to the Arrange page.

The finger tool

Selecting this tool allows you to alter the start and endpoint of a region or file. Clicking and holding the mouse over a region allows you to 'drag' the region to a different position within a file. You can also adjust the Anchor point here.

The eraser tool

Selecting this tool and clicking on a region deletes it. Alternatively, you can select a region and press the delete key.

The Audio file menu

This menu contains several functions for looking after the files used in your Logic Pro song.

Add Audio file

This opens up a dialog box that allows you to add audio files created in another song, by another program or copied or 'ripped' from an audio CD.

Add Region

As above, but allows you to add a region created within an audio file. This region could have been created within another program.

Set Audio Record path

This opens a dialog box that allows you to set the folder where audio recorded within Logic Pro will be stored. Each audio interface installed can have different record paths. You can select other options such as:

Maximum recording time.

It's recommended that this option is kept checked, otherwise files recorded in Logic Pro may become fragmented.

The Song Recording Path

This setting ensures that audio recorded is stored in the same folder as the Logic Pro song (Figure 12.3).

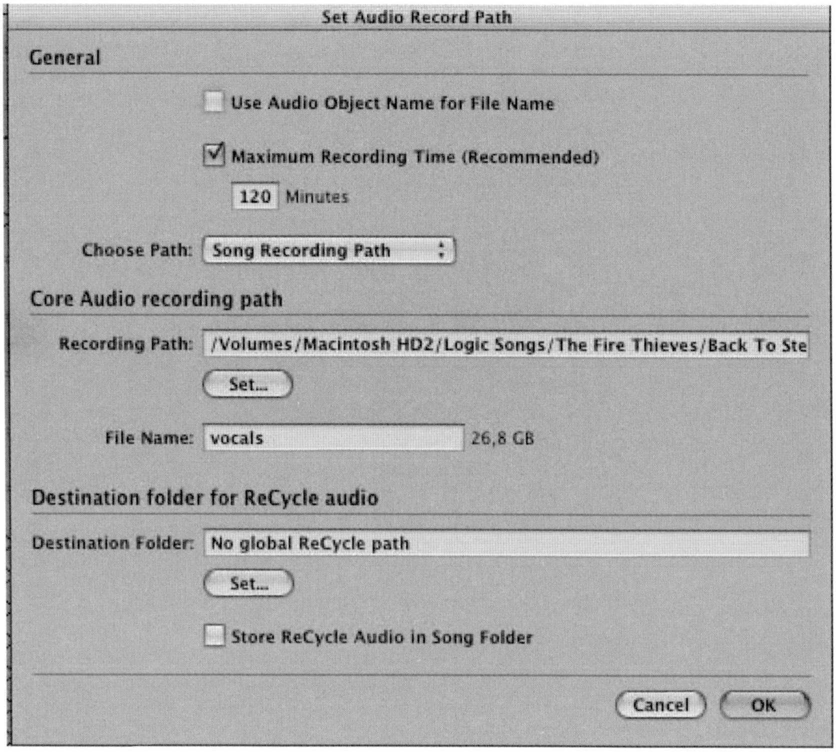

Figure 12.3
The Song Recording Path

Other useful Audio file menu items

Optimize File(s)

This will delete any fragments of any selected audio files not used in a Logic Pro song. This will free up disk space.

Save region(s) as

This will save any selected regions as separate audio files. You may want to do this if you want to perform destructive editing in the sample editor.

Delete fade file(s)

This will delete the temporary fade files created in the generation of fades in the Arrange page.

You can also copy, delete, make backups, move and convert audio files and regions here.

The Edit menu

Apart from the usual Undo, Cut, Copy, Paste and selection items, the Edit menu contains some special items.

Info

This gives various information on selected files.

Search zero crossings

When selected, Logic Pro looks for the best point to start an audio region when the start or end of a region is changed. This is also true in the Arrange window. If a region or file doesn't start playing at a zero crossing point, you may hear a click.

Disconnect/reconnect split stereo pairs

Normally, Logic Pro treats stereo pairs together for editing. You can override this here. You may want to just edit the left side of a recording (say by destructively changing the EQ in the Sample editor).

The View menu

The items in this menu allow you to change which files or regions are displayed, in what order (i.e. by date, time, name etc.) and whether the file info is displayed on the Audio Window. You can also color the audio objects here. These colors will be reflected in the Arrange page.

The Options menu

This menu allows you access to the hardware set-up of the various audio interfaces you may have. You can also set the sample rate for the files here, if your hardware allows it.

Strip Silence

This function allows you to create audio regions automatically. It 'cuts' up audio files into regions depending on the loud and soft passages and gaps, within a file. The Strip Silence window has the following functions.

Figure 12.4
Strip silence

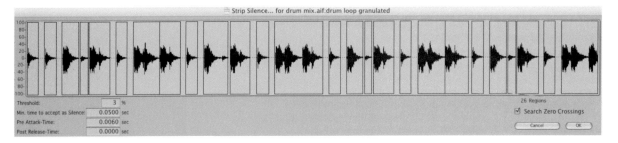

Threshold

This defines the amplitude threshold that the a passage has to be greater than to be defined as a region. The higher the threshold the more short regions produced.

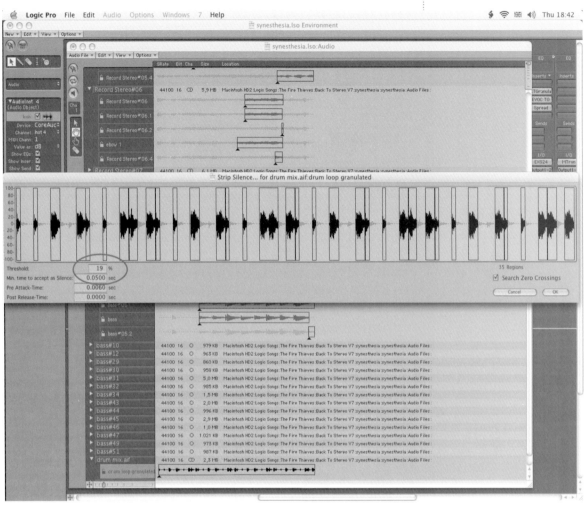

Minimum time to accept as silence

Figure 12.5

You can adjust the Minimum time to accept as silence. This defines the length of a
gap in the audio that is defined as silence and therefore where the cuts are made.

Pre and Post release times

The Pre and Post release times can be adjusted to prevent strip silence from 'chopping' off slow attack times at the start and end of regions created. Clicking on OK will generate regions based on the settings.

Figure 12.6

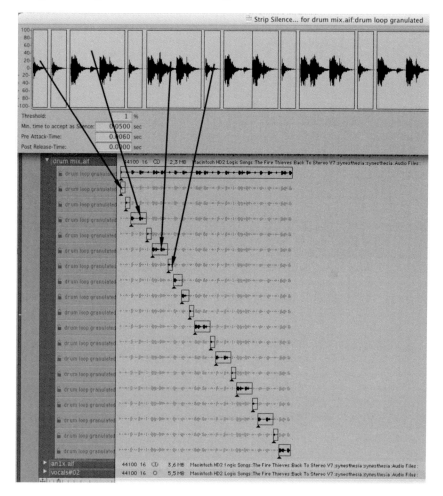

Folders

In a complex song, you may have hundreds of audio files in the Audio window. This can make tracking down individually files a nightmare. Fortunately, you can sort audio files into groups, just like folders in OSX. To group files, highlight the files you want.

Figure 12.7

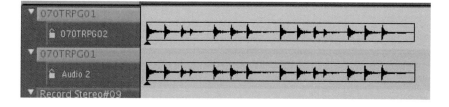

Then use the menu item View>Create Group. You'll be asked to name the group.

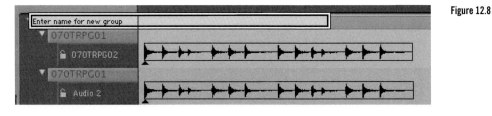

Figure 12.8

Figure 12.9

You can see the files within the group.

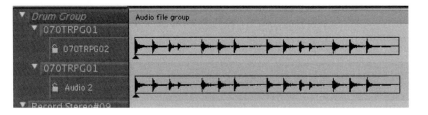

Figure 12.10

The Sample editor

Important

A lot of the processing in the Sample editor is 'destructive'. This means it will change the audio files stored on hard disk. If you are working on a region you have copied, you must first convert it to an individual audio file using the Audio file>Save Selection as in the Sample editor window or the Audi>Convert regions to New audio files on the Arrange page.

The Sample editor is where all fine editing and various kinds of processing of audio files within Logic Pro is performed. It is opened either by double clicking on a region or file in the Arrange page or Audio window, or by highlighting the region or file and using the main Audio>Sample editor menu item. All processing within the sample editor is done in non real-time, and the faster the computer, the faster the processing.

The Sample editor will allow you to:

- Fine edit the start and end points of an audio region
- Draw on the waveform directly to edit out clicks etc.
- Perform destructive editing of a region such as Normalization, fading, gain changing and sample rate conversion.
- Use the Digital Factory to Change the pitch and tempo of audio files, amongst other things.

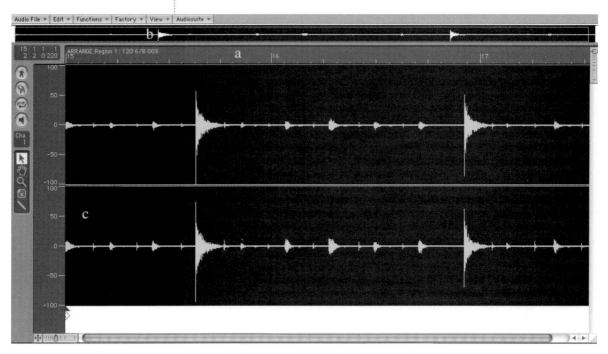

Figure 12.11

In Figure 12.11, a is the timeline. This can be set to display various time units, such as bars/beats or SMPTE time. These are set in the View menu. If the Running man icon and the Link icons are On, the Song Position Line will move in synchronisation with the rest of Logic Pro if you start the sequencer. The timeline will show the position of the audio region in the song if the Sample editor is opened from the Arrange page, and the position of the audio region in the Audio file if the Sample editor is opened from the Audio window.

b shows the waveform of the whole audio file. This is called the Overview. If you have double clicked on a region the region will be displayed in the Sample window, and its position highlighted on the Overview.

The waveform can be enlarged or reduced in size using the Zoom tools. The S and E (a and b in the figure above) are the start and end point of the region. These can be edited directly with the Arrow tool.

c in Figure 12.11 shows various data about the region. The top value is the start point of the region, the lower one the length.

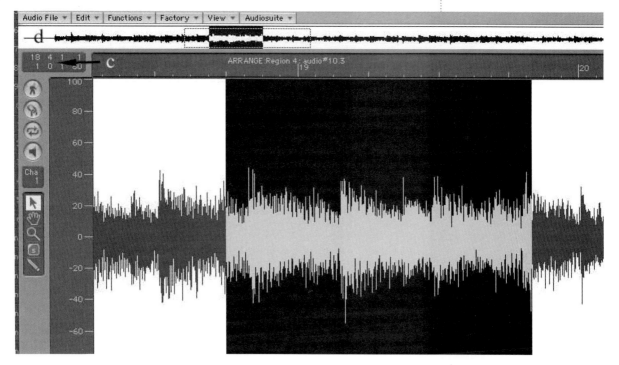

The Cycle, Speaker and Cha icons and the toolbox

Figure 12.12

The Cycle icon

When this is On, the audio region shown within the Sample window is looped continuously. This is particularly useful for selecting regions you want to loop.

The Speaker icon

Cicking on this plays a region, or section highlighted. You can play the original file from any point by clicking and holding on the overview (d) when using the Arrow tool.

The Cha icon

This is the Audio channel which the file will play back on when auditioned. Stereo files play back in stereo by default. If you highlight one side of a file or region, hold down the Shift key and then click the Speaker icon, the file will play back the selected audio in mono.

The Toolbox

The arrow tool

Selecting this tool allows you to audition files from any part of the file or region by clicking and holding the mouse on the waveform.

The hand tool

Selecting this tool allows you to drag highlighted audio in the Sample window.

The magnifying glass tool

Using this tool, you can drag a box across the waveform in the Sample window to magnify the waveform. If you magnify it so you can see the actual waveform as samples.

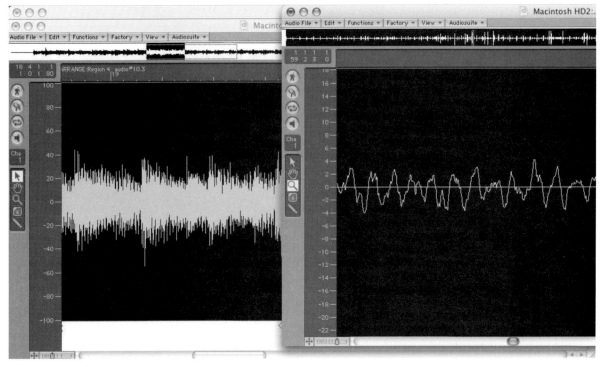

Figure 12.13

The Pencil tool

Use this to edit the actual waveform to remove clicks etc.

The Solo tool

If you drag this tool across the Sample window, the audio will 'scrub', allowing you to locate a specific point in an audio file or region.

Using the Sample editor

Processing the audio file

The Sample editor is a fully functional stereo sample editor, similar to 'stand alone' editors. The following outlines a typical use for the editor.

Record a guitar part in stereo. Don't worry about making noises before you start playing or in between parts. Just concentrate on getting a good performance (Figure 12.14).

You may want to cut it up into individual regions in the Arrange page, and name the regions. Note the 'Noisy' and 'quiet' regions (Figure 12.15).

First convert each region to individual Audio files. Select all the regions in the Arrange page then use the menu item Audio>Convert regions to New audio

---

Tip

All destructive processing takes time. The speed of the processing is dependant on the power of your computer. Logic Pro shows the number of samples processed in the menu part of the Sample editor as processing progresses.

Figure 12.14

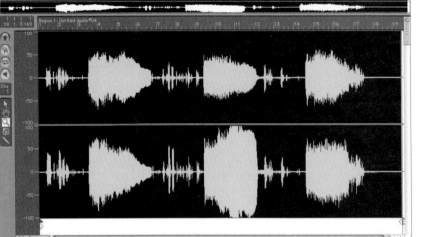

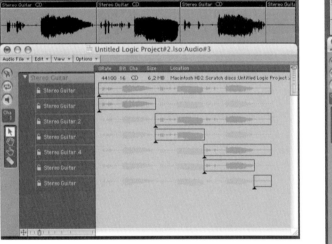

Figure 12.15 (above)   **Figure 12.16 (right)**

files.Logic Pro will ask you where to store the new files it creates (Figure 12.16

Remember: the original recording will now be untouched. All processing done now will be on the new files created.

Now what might we want to do with the guitar part? First we can remove any unwanted noise from the beginning of the part.

Double click on the first 'Stereo Guitar' region, either in the Audio window or the Arrange page. It will open in the Sample editor. Use the zoom and window size controls to bring the waveform into the centre of the window.

You could create a backup of the file using the Audio file>create backup menu item. You can see the noise at the start of the region.

Highlight the noise. Select the Functions>Silence menu item. The highlighted area is silenced.

Figure 12.17

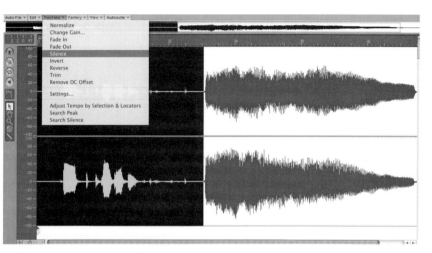

Figure 12.18

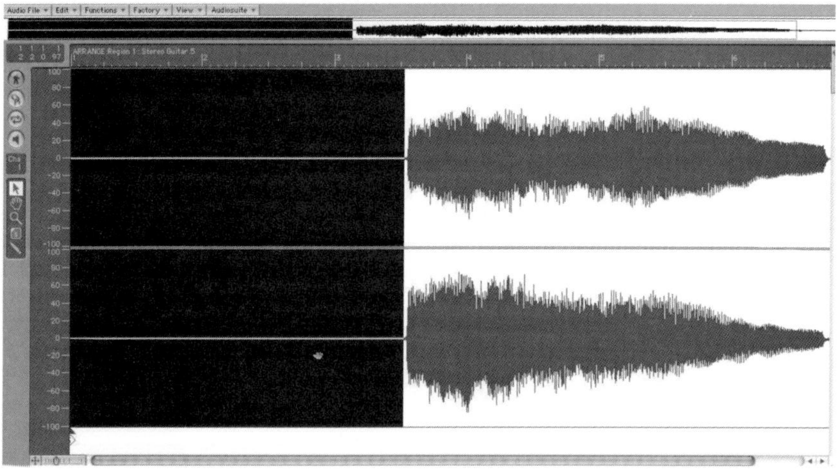

Now let's fade out the part. First choose the type of fade from the window opened up from the Functions>settings menu. Here you can select the fade types (either S-shaped or curved) using the boxes next to the (S) and the slope of the curve using the Curve parameter. Highlight where the fade is to start and stop.

Figure 12.19

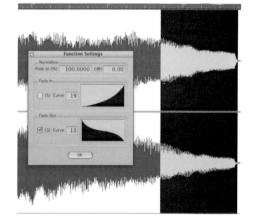

Select the Functions>Fade out menu item. The fade out is performed (Figures 12.20 and 12.21).

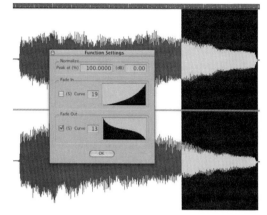

Figure 12.20

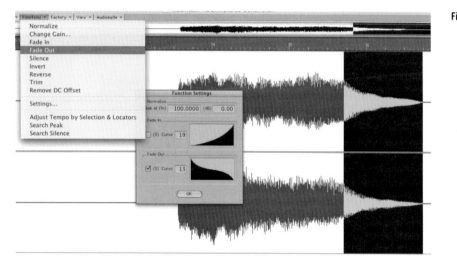

Figure 12.21

Now close the window. Use the standard window close box for your computer. Logic Pro will ask you weather you want to Make the last edit permanent or to Undo the edits, which will leave the audio file untouched.

Repeat this function with all the regions, so that any extraneous noise is removed. If you look at this section of audio, you'll see that middle section is too quiet compared with the beginning and end (Figure 12.22).

So let's correct that. Highlight the quiet region and select the Function>Change gain menu item. Select a value – you may need to try out this function several times. Click on OK to change the gain (Figure 12.23).

Using this technique you could perform the other processing in the Functions menu. Of course, performing some of the functions outlined above could add noise to the audio. This can be removed, along with many other types of processing by using the Digital Factory.

Figure 12.22

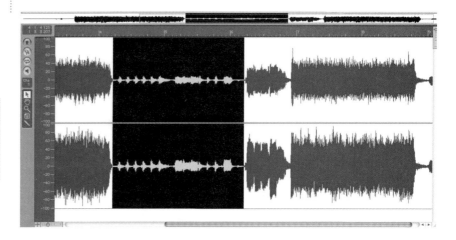

Tip

Use the 'Search maximum' function to determine the maximum level of adjacent regions and change the gain accordingly.

Figure 12.23

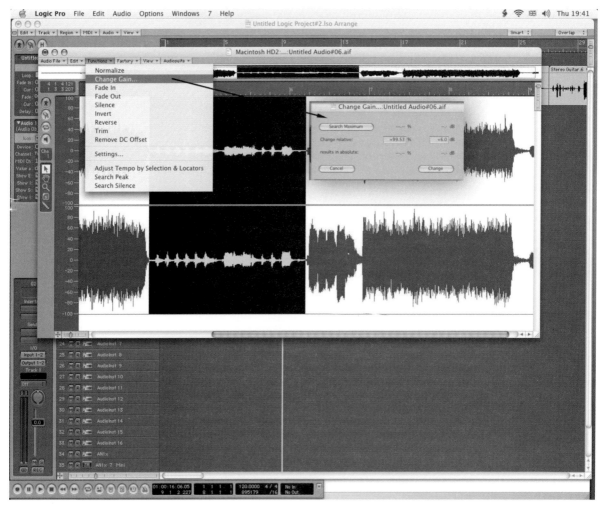

The Digital Factory

The Digital Factory is a suite of programs that destructively manipulate the audio in a variety of ways. The following section describes each of the Factory's features with a demonstration of their use. Like all the Sample editor functions, the Digital Factory should be used on audio files especially created for their use by converting regions to files as described previously. The effects of some of the Time Machine's features are not entirely predictable – it's another case of try it and see what happens. Don't be afraid to experiment (Figure 12.24).

Tip

Use a copy of a file if you are not sure what effect your processing will have so you can easily get back to the original.

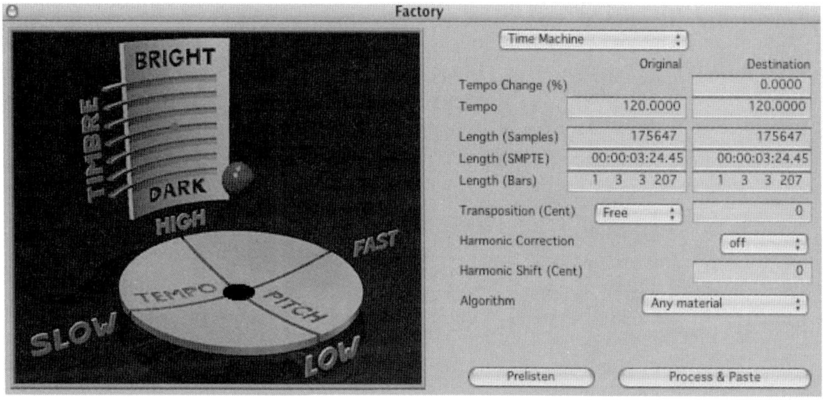

Figure 12.24

Each Digital Factory item can be selected from the Factory menu in the Sample editor, or from the pull down menu on the Factory window itself.

Time Machine

The Time Machine can be used to increase or decrease the pitch of an audio recording, with or without changing its duration. Conversely it can be used to change the duration of a recording without changing the pitch. The Harmonic correction and shift parameters can be used to change, for example, a male voice into a female voice, and to reduce the 'chipmunk' effect common to transposition.

You could use The Time Machine, for example, to create a vocal or guitar harmony without recording a new performance. Note: Not all the parameters need to be changed at the same time.

Tempo Change (%)

Use this to increase or decrease the tempo of a recording in percent.

Tempo

Set a tempo change here. It's essential that the correct number of bars are set in the fields below for the original tempo to show here. You can also set the original length of the region in samples or SMPTE time.

Transpose

Choose a value to transpose here. With some audio interfaces you can use the Prelisten button to check the pitch change.

Tip

Prelisten only works on the transpose feature of the Time machine , not the others.

Free transpose means that the tempo of the recording does not change during transposition. In most cases this is what you would need to create harmonies and so on. Classic transpose means that the tempo will increase or decrease as the pitch changes. It's very like the speeding up of a tape recorder.

Harmonic correction and Harmonic shift

These work in conjunction with the Transpose setting. The Harmonic correction attempts to change the formants which define the timbre of a sound. The upshot of this is that transpositions will sound more natural with Harmonic correction However, using it in conjunction with Harmonic shift, it can provide further effects. These are detailed below.

Harmonic correction must be On.

- Transpose set to a value other than zero and Harmonic shift set to zero – the formants are left unchanged as pitch changes, creating a more 'natural' transposition.
- Transpose set to zero and Harmonic shift set to a value other than zero. This will change the formants in the recording but not the pitch. This could be use, for example, to add harmonics to a guitar or to convert a male voice to a female voice or vice versa. Positive Harmonic shift values to make females, negative to make males.

Note: The Time Machine's functions can be used independently or simultaneously.

The Groove Machine

Logic Pro can allow you to alter the 'feel' of an audio recording using the Groove Machine. This is especially useful on percussion parts, but could be used with bass or guitar, or even vocals.

Figure 12.26

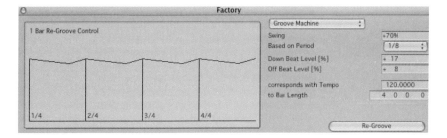

To use the Groove Machine the tempo of the audio file must match the Logic Pro song. You can either change the tempo of the recording using the Time Machine as detailed above, or change the tempo of the Logic Pro song as described in Chapter 4. The parameters are as follows.

- Swing – this adjusts the amount of 'swing' imposed on the audio. 50% is no swing. Start with values between 55% and 65%.
- Based on period – sets the swing to 16th or 1/8th note swing.
- Down beat level and Off beat level – these parameters change the levels of the down beats and Off beats of the rhythmic part. There is a visual display that

reflects these changes. Raising the levels can cause clipping, and Logic Audio will inform you if this happens.

- Correspond with tempo and bar length – these values are automatically transferred from the Arrange page to the Groove machine.

The Audio Energizer

The Audio Energizer increases the perceived level of the recording without changing the quality of the sound. It is similar to the Normalize function in the Sample editor, but it 'squashes' the occasional high peak allowing a recording to sound louder overall. Factor increases the effect. Attack and decay can be used to reduce the 'digital' feel of any processing.

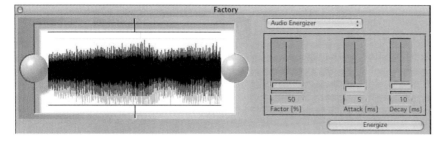

Figure 12.27

The Sample Rate Converter

The Sample Rate Converter is a simple facility to provide high quality sample rate conversion. This may be useful if you record digitally from a DAT that was recorded at 44.8kHz but want to convert to 44.1kHz for CD burning.

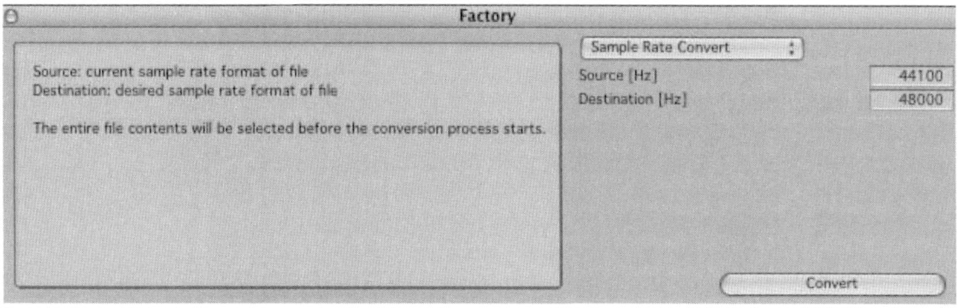

Figure 12.28

The Silencer

This feature provides a simple noise reduction facility alongside a spike reduction program. The Silencer simply has buttons that select the degree of noise reduction. The Spike reduction aims to identify and reduce spikes or pops in a recording. There are two parameters:

- Sensitivity – the higher the sensitivity the lower the peaks detected as spikes.
- Method – controls the intensity of the smoothing of the peaks. Gentle is the weakest smoothing and Aggressive is the strongest. Re-Build replaces the peak with a 'synthetic' replacement. This could be attempted where the other methods have failed

Figure 12.29

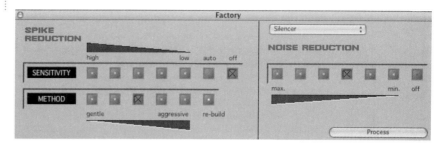

Other Digital Factory features

The following Digital Factory features attempt to treat audio data in a similar fashion to MIDI regarding Groove templates and Score production from audio recordings and Quantization of audio files.

Audio to MIDI Groove template

Logic Pro can create Groove templates from audio files (the concept of Groove templates was covered in Chapter 4). Say you have a recording of a drum part that has a particular feel that you like. You can use this audio file to create a groove template that you can then impose on your own MIDI drum parts. Of course, you can use groove templates on other audio parts too.

Figure 12.30

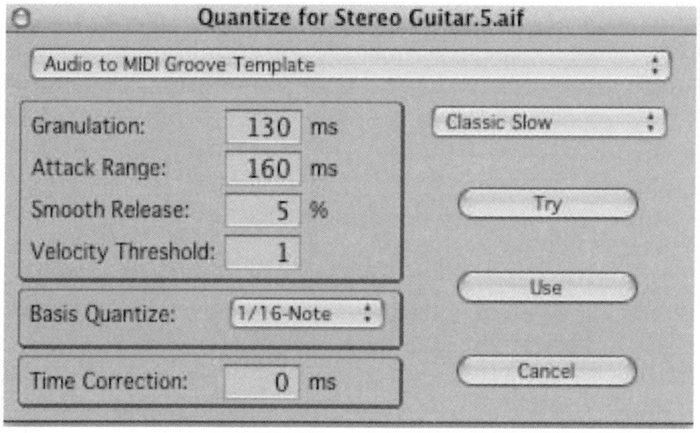

> **Tip**
>
> Switch off the Edit>Search zero crossings item in the Sample editor when using the Audio to MIDI Groove feature.

Here is an example of the use of groove templates. Choose a suitable audio file. For example chose a one or two bar drum loop. Open the sample editor. Select Factory>Audio to MIDI groove template. The parameters are as follows.

*   Instrument type (A) – these are presets you can try on your audio to produce groove templates. These are made up of the following parameters. Any edits are stored in the Logic Pro Preferences file.
*   Granulation – start with values between 50 to 200 ms. This parameter determines the time span of the louder parts to determine the 'velocity points' to be used in the groove template. These define the actual groove.
*   Attack range – this defines the attack range of the sounds in the audio material used in the groove template. Percussive sounds have short attack times. Try values between 4 and 40ms.
*   Smooth release – use this parameter when the audio files you are using has a long release time. Try values between 0 and 5%.

- Velocity threshold – sets a velocity threshold below which individual sounds in a file are ignored. Usually set to 1. If the file contains very loud material, you could try changing this parameter.
- Basis quantize – if the audio file you have has few easily definable velocity points to use in the groove template, you can use this parameter to impose new velocity points. This doesn't affect the velocity points derived from the audio file.
- Time correction – you can use this parameter to compensate for delays created by external MIDI devices. If you play an external MIDI device using the groove template at the same time as the audio file the template was derived from and the MIDI device is not exactly in time, this parameter will compensate for that.

If you look at the Sample editor, you can see the velocity points that will be used in the groove template displayed (A) below.

Figure 12.31

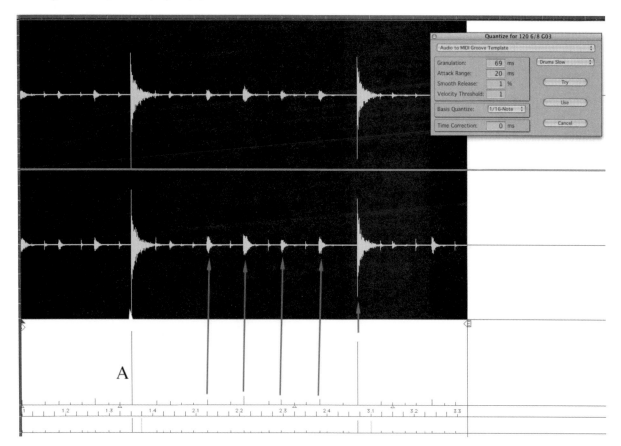

- Audio points – these are the quantization points Logic Pro has created from the audio file based on the parameters you have set.
- Quantize – this is the Basis quantize value result.
- Result – this is the combination of the above two quantize values. Clicking on any Audio point will remove it from the groove template.
- Try – this will impose the groove template on any selected region.

When you are happy with the groove template, click on Use to install it in the current song. The template appears in the quantize flip menus in Logic Pro under the name of the audio region or file that defined it.

Audio to Score

Logic Pro can produce musical notation from monophonic lines. These should be cleanly recorded for this feature to work properly. This could be useful for producing a violin score from a guitar solo, or a score for solo instrument from a recorded voice. Try using it on complex material and you'll get instant Frank Zappa.

Tip

To use the Audio to Score, first open the Sample editor, then go to the Arrange page. Select the MIDI instrument you wish the sequence generated to be played back on.

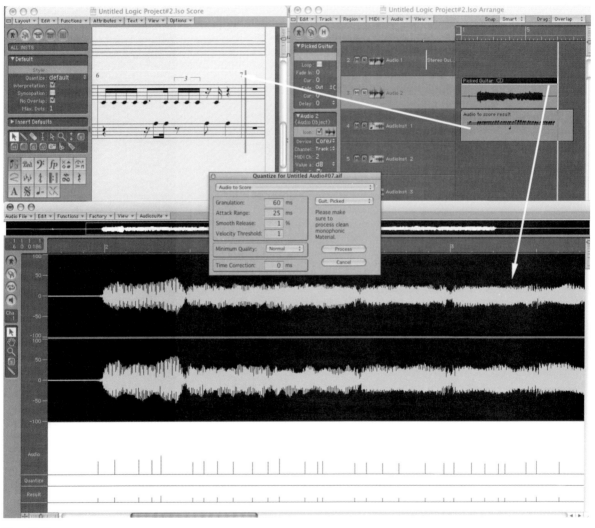

Figure 12.32

As you can see, most of the parameters are the same as for the groove template creator described above. The presets are a good place to start. The only extra parameter is Minimum quality. When set to High only clearly defined trigger points are converted to score. The Normal setting is more tolerant of sloppy playing but will generate more spurious notes.

The Staves contain the following information.

Stave 1

Contains the notes as identified by Logic Pro from the audio file. Clearly recognised notes are on MIDI channel 1.

Stave 2

Contains notes that were not clearly identified by Logic. Notes are on MIDI channel 2.

Stave 3

All other notes picked up by Logic. Detuned pitches will be here alongside notes derived from noisy material. These notes are on MIDI channel 3.

Quantize Engine

Logic Pro can quantize an audio recording in a similar fashion to quantizing MIDI recordings. The parameters are the same for Audio to MIDI Groove template. It can be seen as the converse of that feature.

Again, the presets are a good place to start. The extra parameters are as follows.

Quantize by

These are the standard quantize values used in Logic. The flip down menu will contain any groove templates you have created.

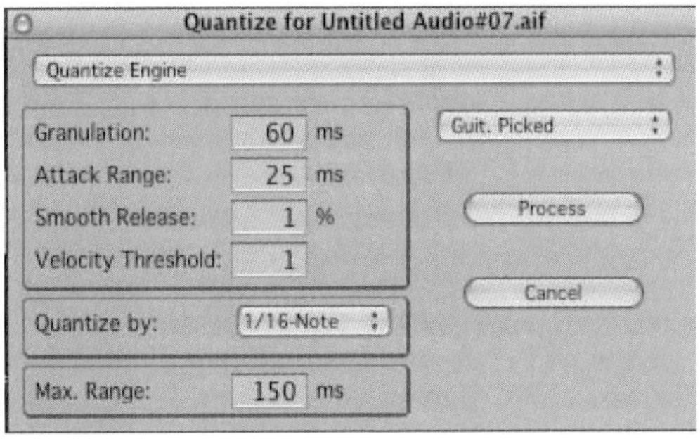

Figure 12.33

Max range

The maximum time by which a loud peak in the audio material can deviate from the quantize value set above. Small values provide good results when the audio material is similar to the quantization groove. Large values should be used when the audio deviates greatly from the Groove template.

Conclusion and some advice

The Digital Factory is not a miracle worker. Sometimes the results may not be exactly as you predicted. But don't be despondent – serendipity is an important part of music creation. You may find that the incorrect results are more 'musical' than you expected – and more innovative. As with much in Logic Pro, it's best to 'try it and see'.

Global tracks

Overview

Global tracks are specialized tracks that run alongside your other tracks in the Arrange page Matrix, Score or Hyper edit windows. You can view or hide Global tracks from the View menu.

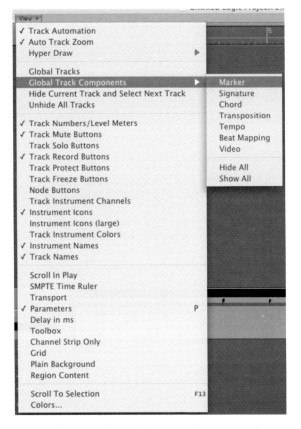

Figure 13.1

Using Global tracks you can easily place time and tempo changes, markers or Global transposition in the timeline of a song. You can also place video in Global tracks if you are editing audio to video.

Global tracks can be of several types, which can be selected from the Global Track Components menu.

Tip

Set up Key commands to hide and show various Global Track components as and when you require them.

All Global tracks can have the following editing functions.

- Use the pencil tool to draw events (such as Markers or Time signatures).
- Use the Arrow tool to drag events in time or to change their values or durations.
- Double click on an event to change its value or edit its content.
- Delete an event using the Erase tool.

Global tracks in more detail

Marker

As well as creating Markers as described in Chapter 4, you can create and manipulate Markers in a Global track. The easiest way is to create them from the 'From regions' button (select regions first). Alternatively, use the Pencil tool or the 'Create Markers' Key Command to Create a Marker at the current SPL.

Figure 13.2

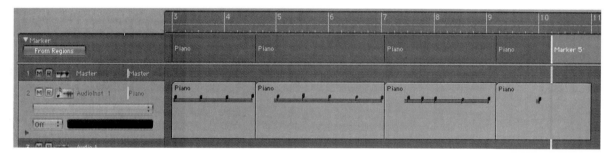

Figure 13.3
The Marker window

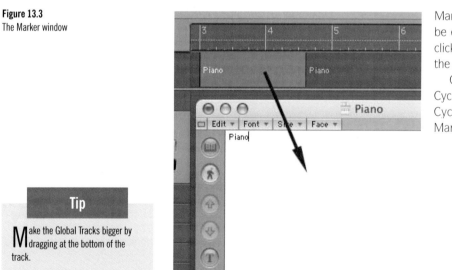

Markers thus created can then be dragged or resized. Double clicking on a Marker will open the Marker window.

    Create a marker from a Cycle region by dragging the Cycle region down to the Marker track.

Tip

Make the Global Tracks bigger by dragging at the bottom of the track.

Signature
Time and Key signatures.

Time signatures
You can place Time Signature information on this track. Click on the top half of the Signature Global Track using the pencil tool. A window opens where you can select the desire Time Signature.

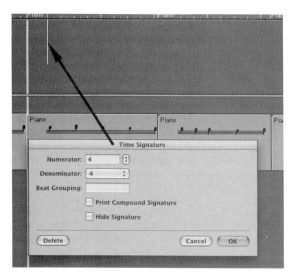

Figure 13.4

You can reposition the Time Signature event using the Arrow tool.

Key signatures
Clicking on the lower half of the Signature Global Track with the pencil tool allows you to insert a Key Signature.

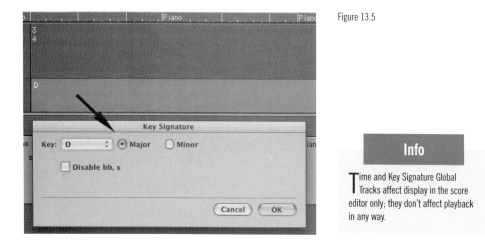

Figure 13.5

Info

Time and Key Signature Global Tracks affect display in the score editor only; they don't affect playback in any way.

Chord

You can display the chords in a region by selecting the region and clicking on Analyze. The chord names appear in the Chord Global track. The 'Change display only' function is switched on automatically when doing this so you don't accidentally transpose your tracks.

Figure 13.6

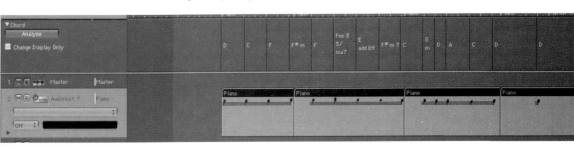

If you insert a Chord using the pencil tool a window opens allowing the Chord to be entered.

Figure 13.7

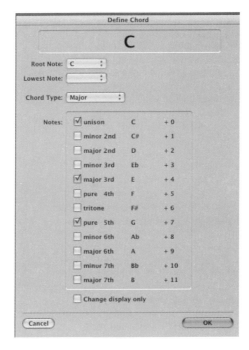

What happens next depends on the status on the 'Change display only' parameter.

- 'Change display only' selected – the Chord name is just added and does not affect the actual pitch of any tracks.
- 'Change display only' not selected – the whole song is transposed in pitch based on the chord. (Except for those Audio or MIDI Instruments, which have their 'No Trp' checked in the Track parameter box. Normal audio files are not always affected, but Apple Loops will be transposed. See Chapter 17 for more on Apple Loops.)

Transposition

This is a Global transposition – all of your tracks in a song will be transposed. MIDI and Audio Instruments will be transposed, as will Apple Loops with a key setting.

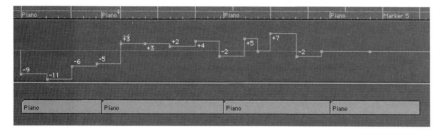

Figure 13.8

You add transposition points with the Pencil tool. You can then edit these using the Arrow tool.

Tip

Hold down the Ctrl + Alt + Apple key while clicking to open a text box for direct entry of a transposition value.

Tempo

Tempo changes are added using the pencil tool.

Figure 13.9

This makes it really easy to insert variable Tempo into a song. You can use the Global Tempo track alongside more traditional Tempo manipulation. See Chapter 4 for more on Tempo.

If you want to create transitions between Tempi (i.e. speed up and slow down a song) grab the node just under the second Tempo node and drag. The cursor becomes a finger and you can then drag the Tempo curve.

Figure 13.10

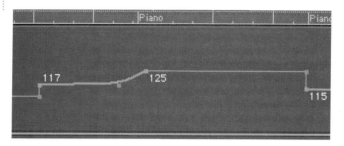

The number of Tempo events per quarter note are set using the pull down menu.

Figure 13.11

You can select between nine different Tempo tracks from the pull down menu.

Figure 13.12

Tip

To copy a complete Tempo track to an alternative track, hold down the Option key while selecting a new Tempo alternative.

Double clicking on the Tempo track while holding the Shift key down, opens the Tempo event editor window (See above). You can cut and paste Tempo events here. The Tempo track is intimately connected to the Beat mapping track.

Beat mapping

This is similar to the Reclock function as described in Chapter 3, but does it in a more graphic way. It allows you to set the tempi of a song after recording, allowing you to play freely and worry about the tempo afterwards. Once you have 'beat mapped' the recording, you'll get all the advantages of recording with a metronome, such as;

- The metronome click will be in time
- You can quantize regions
- MIDI and Apple loops will automatically adjust to the tempo of the song.
- It helps with interpretation in the Score editor.
- When using beat mapping you connect the beats present in your recording to the bar positions on the Beat mapping Track window. Here are a couple of examples.

MIDI or Virtual instrument regions

Record a region without using the Metronome. Note that the initial tempo set in Logic is 120 bpm (beats per minute). If you open the Matrix editor, you can see where the beats actually lie in the performance.

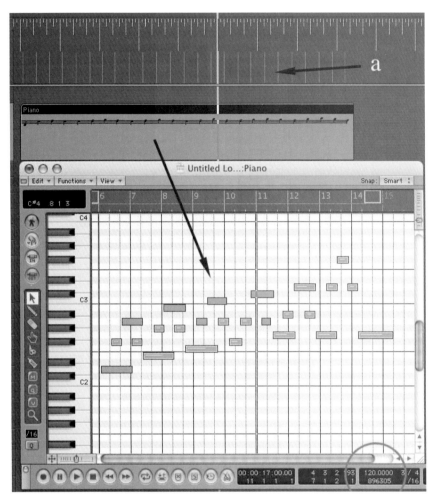

Figure 13.13

You can see where Logic has displayed the actual notes in the part on the Beat Mapping Global track.(a)

The next part can be performed in either the Matrix editor or Arrange page (or Hyper editor, for that matter).

- Select the first note in the region (Figure 13.14).
- Click and hold on the first beat in the Beat mapping track.
- You'll see that the line will turn yellow and that 'Set Beat' will appear in a small window.

Figure 13.14

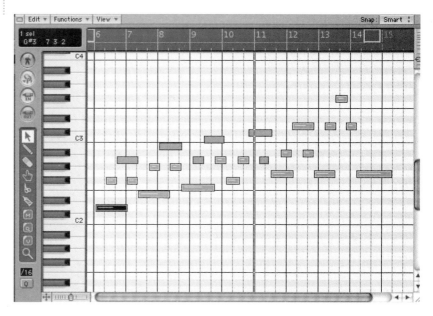

- Drag the mouse (while still holding down the mouse key to the first note in the region.) (Figure 13,15).

Figure 13.15

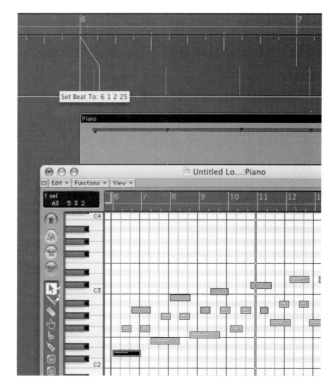

- Release the mouse key. You'll see that the first note in the region is aligned to the first note of the bar in the Beat mapping track.

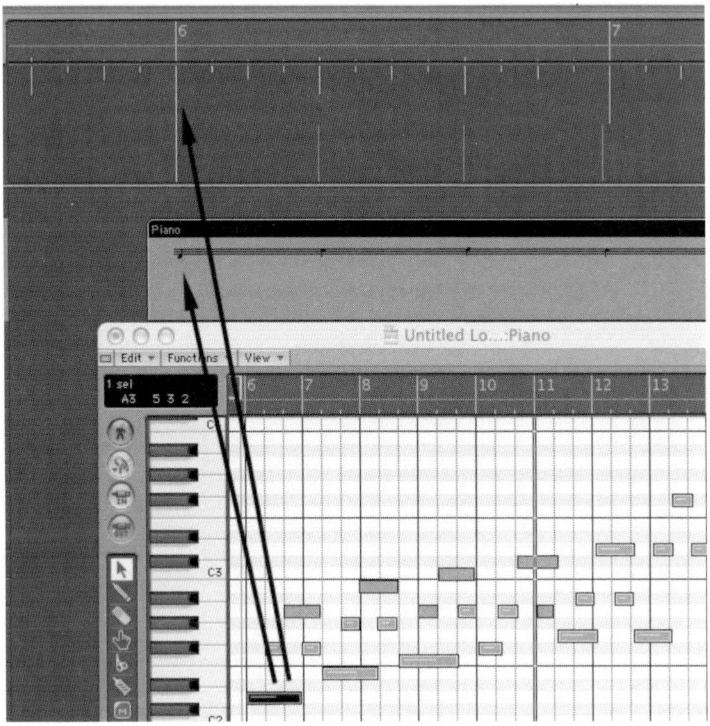

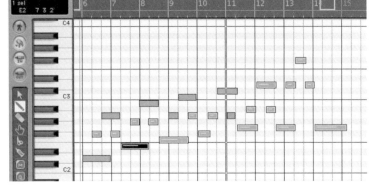

Figure 13.16

- Now select the note that you consider to be the first in the next bar.

Figure 13.17

Figure 13.18

- Click and drag the yellow line from the bar line to the note in the same way as for the first bar (Figure 13.18).
- Release the mouse key. You'll see that the second note selected in the region is aligned to the second bar of Beat mapping track.

Figure 13.19

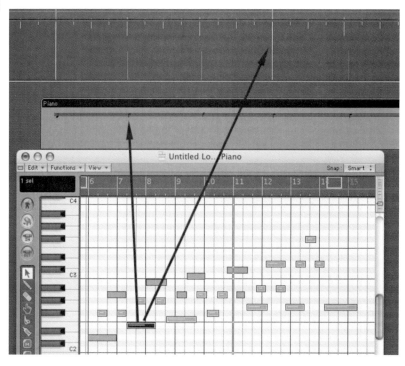

- Repeat for all the bars in the region (this region has four bars of playing)

Figure 13.20

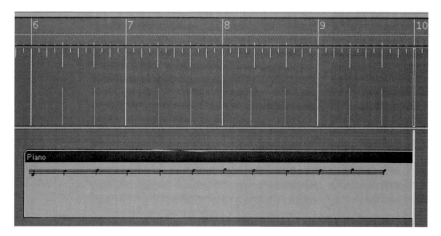

- Now repeat for any notes within the bar if needed.
- Logic will create tempo changes for each bar – you can see these if you open the Tempo Global Track.

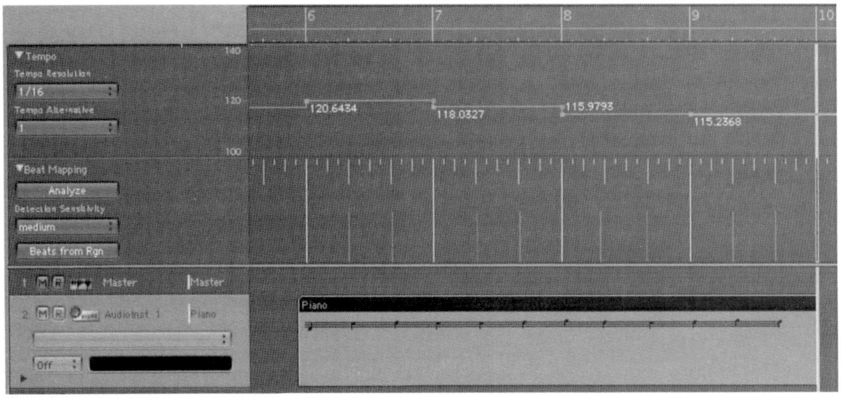

Figure 13.21

Audio regions

To map an audio region. Logic must determine rhythmically significant spots in the recording. For a drum snippet, this could be the bass drum or hi-hat part. These spots are usually louder or more prominent and Logic can use this to analyse the recording.

> **Tip**
>
> If you just set the tempo for the first bar or a region, you can then quantize the entire region using this tempo value as a guide.

> **Info**
>
> To delete set tempo points, click using the erase tool.

• Select an audio region. This is a four bar drum loop.

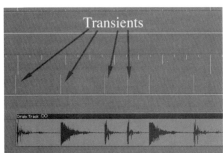

Figure 13.22

• Click on Analyze to detect the transients in the Audio file.

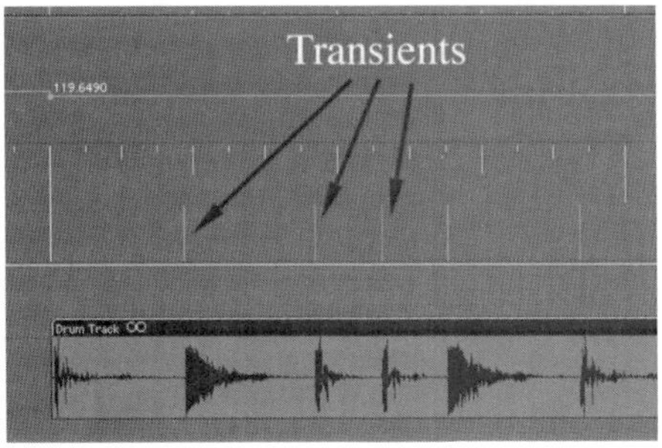

Figure 13.23

There are a couple of parameters you may like to consider when trying to use Beat mapping with audio regions.

Detection sensitivity

A high detection sensitivity will detect more transients and give you more points in which to use for beat mapping. This may or may not be a good thing, depending on the audio region – you may detect transients that are not really there. Like a lot of things in Logic, you can always undo the beat detection and retry at any time.

Once you have detected the transients, you can beat map the tempo in exactly the same way as for MIDI regions.

Figure 13.24

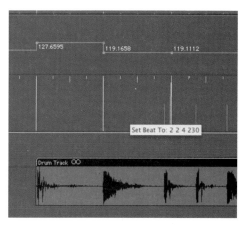

Tip

Start with a low detection sensitivity and increase the value until you get the results you require.

If you record a MIDI region (using an external sound source or Virtual instrument) with a Metronome, you can use the Beats from Region button to 'map' the tempo from this MIDI region to the song.

Record a region with a fixed tempo close to the one of the audio file. Edit the beats in the region until they sync with the audio file beats. Then click the Beats from Region button. Logic will create tempo changes to preserve the timing.

Figure 13.25

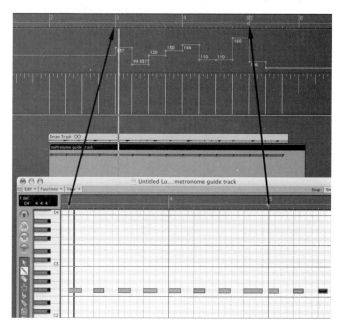

Video

You can load a movie into the Video track using the Open movie button or clicking in the Video track with the pencil tool. You'll see the movie opened out in thumbnails. You'll use this track if you want to write music or other audio to picture.

There are a few things you can do with the Video track.

- Double click on the thumbnails to open the movie in its own window.

Figure 13.26

- Clicking on the Detect Cuts button will detect scene changes. These are inserted as Movie markers, which you can then use with Beat Mapping as detailed previously in the Chapter.

While the Global Tracks features are duplicated elsewhere in Logic, their overall view is useful in complex arrangements. If you work to movies, they are invaluable.

The Environment

The Environment is the heart of Logic Pro, and it can seem as complicated as a coronary operation if you want to use it to its full potential. However we'll concentrate on what you actually need to know to get the best from the program.

You don't need to use the Environment to use Logic. However, if you want to get the most from the program and create editors, use MIDI modifiers, such as Arpeggiators and Transformers, you'll need to delve into the Environment.

The Environment is the place where the 'object orientated' nature of Logic Pro is most apparent.

Figure 14.1 shows all the objects you can create in Logic Pro. Of course in a normal Environment set up, most of these would be wired to something! The following objects are available from the New menu. The objects can be highlighted and moved or deleted, cut and pasted. Some can also be resized in the usual way.

Figure 14.1
Environment objects

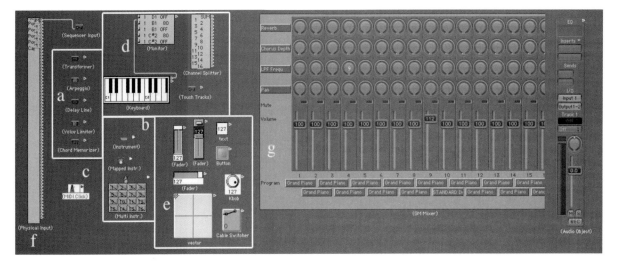

Objects are connected together by cables. Just drag the cable from the small arrow on the top right of an object to another object. Delete cables with the erase tool.

The Environment also has a Parameter box (i) in Figure 14.2, that displays certain variables of selected Environment objects.

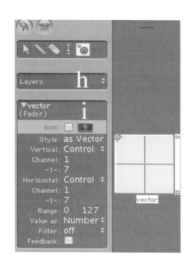

Figure 14.2

Layers

Environment objects exist in layers. These are like separate pages within the Environment and are accessed by clicking and holding over the box in Figure 14.2 (h).

Layers can be created and deleted. Objects on different layers can be connected via cables. Layers are useful in keeping the Environment tidy. You could, for example, have on one layer all your MIDI instruments, on another faders controlling the parameters on a synthesiser, on another a MIDI mixer and so on. Figure 14.3 shows various layers in a typical Environment.

Info

You can have many Environment windows open with different layers visible

Figure 14.3
Layers in a typical Environment

The Environment toolbox

The Arrow tool

This tool is used to highlight and move objects. If you hold down the Alt key while you drag, a new object is created with cabling intact. This is useful for making multiple copies rapidly.

The Pencil tool

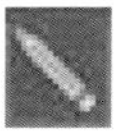

This tool creates a standard Instrument wherever it is clicked in the Environment window.

The Erase tool

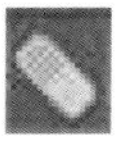

This deletes objects and cables when it is clicked on them or rubbed over them.

The Text tool

When selected, clicking on a text field, such as the name under an object, opens a box where you can rename it. Highlighting an object and clicking on the name in the Parameter box also does the same.

The MIDI tool

When selected, clicking on an object in the Environment causes that object to be selected in the Arrange window.

Objects and their parameters

When you click on an object, a Parameter box opens for you to enter or change various values. Here is the Parameter box for the MIDI click object.

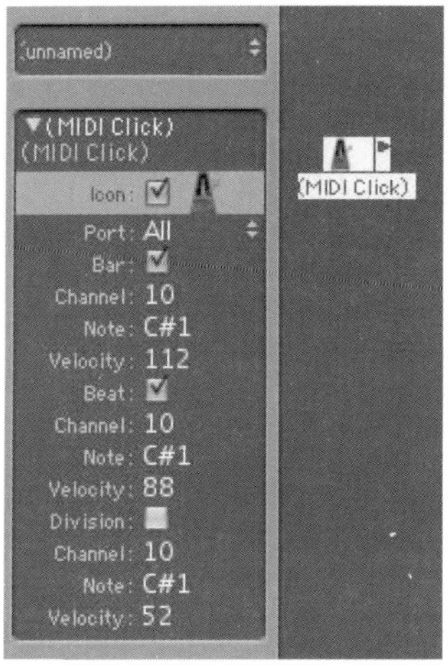

Each Parameter box has a box for a tick next to the icon. When unchecked, it stops the instrument from being displayed in the Instrument list in the Arrange page. In general, you will want to hide these icons. One obvious exception being Instrument and Audio, Audio instrument, Auxes and Buss objects themselves – you'll want to use these to make music!

As usual, the little down arrow hides or shows the Parameter box. Also as usual, you can rename an object by double clicking on the name to the right of the little arrow.

Info

You may want to refer to Figure 14.1 when reading this section – the letters in brackets refer to the different sections of the figure.

Figure 14.4

Physical input and sequencer input

The Physical input and sequencer input, Figure 14.1 (f), is where the input of the MIDI interface connects to the input of the sequencer. Just one each of these is needed in your Environment. Normally, the physical input is connected directly to the sequencer input. However, you can place objects (Transposer, Transformer etc.) between these if you want to change the MIDI data before it reaches Logic Pro

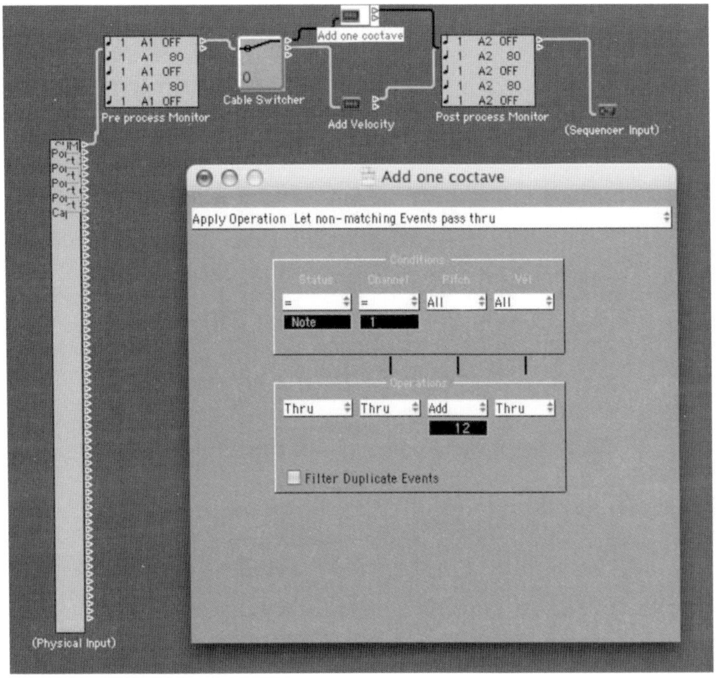

Figure 14.5

Multi Instrument, Instrument and Mapped instrument

Instruments, Figure 14.1 (b), are the objects that become the virtual analogues of your external MIDI devices (synthesisers, modules, effects, MIDI mixers etc.) You can assign patch names to your MIDI devices here too. These are the objects you usually will choose in the Arrange window to actually record music into Logic Pro. There is more on Instruments in Chapter 4.

Monitor

This is used to monitor MIDI data passing through Logic Pro, Figure 14 (d). Figure 14.5 shows the monitor measuring data before it reaches Logic Pro and after it's been modified by a transformer, the pre and post process view objects.

Channel splitter

Use the channel splitter, Figure 14.1 (d), to route MIDI data to various places depending on their MIDI channel number. MIDI events arriving at the input of the channel splitter are re-routed out of the connected output. All non re-routed channels come out of the Sum output. Figure 14.6 shows a typical example. MIDI data on channel 16 is sent to the delay line. Data on channels 1 – 15 are sent to the arpeggiator.

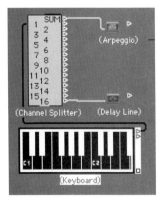

Figure 14.6

Keyboard

The keyboard (Figure 14.1 (d)) can be connected anywhere in Environment. Use it for checking the effects of transformers or other objects if your MIDI keyboard/guitar or MIDI'd nose flute are too far away. Keyboard has the following parameters:

• Cha – the MIDI channel that the keyboard sends its data out on
• Vel – the velocity value of the data
• Lowest – the C note of the lowest key on this keyboard

Transformer

The Transformer object, Figure 14.1 (a), converts one type of MIDI information into another. Double clicking on the transformer brings up a window where you can modify various parameters. Its operation is very similar to the Transformer window (Chapter 4), but its operations are carried out in real time.

The Transformer object checks for a Condition you set up. If the data meets this condition, then Operations set by you are carried out on the data. The pull down menu lets you select various internal signal path conditions.

You could use the Transformer object to:

• Transpose in real time any incoming MIDI notes
• Increase the velocity values of incoming MIDI notes if, for example, your keyboard has a maximum velocity output value of 100, you could increase this to 127
• Convert modulation data to aftertouch
• Convert a sustain pedal press into a note value. How about converting the pedal press into a bass drum sound on your synthesiser?

Voice limiter

This object (Figure 14.1 (a)) limits the number of simultaneously played notes in a MIDI data stream. Voice limiter has the following parameters:

• Voices – sets the number of voices or notes to be played simultaneously
• Priority – defines which notes are let through if the voice limiter receives more notes that that set in the voices field. If the value is 'Last', the most recently received notes are played. Similarly, 'Top' plays the highest notes and 'Bot' the lowest.

Delay line

This object (Figure 14.1 (a)) acts as a delay line, in a similar way to an echo unit, except it works with MIDI events. Remember though, the sequencer must be running for it to work, and if you are using it to delay notes, each repeat will eat into your MIDI modules' polyphony. Delay line has the following parameters:

• Thru original – if checked, the original notes are heard, if not you just hear the delayed ones.
• Repeats – the number of repeats
• Del – sets the delay time between individual repeats. the left value is in divisions, the right in ticks

- Trp – this value sets the transpose pitch of the repeats
- Vel – the change in velocity of the repeats. A negative number makes the repeats fade out in volume, a positive value makes the delays fade up.

Arpeggiator

This object (Figure 14.1 (a)) creates an arpeggio of a chord played. The sequencer must be running for this to work and the speed of the arpeggio is defined by the tempo of Logic Pro. Arpeggiator has the following parameters:

- Direction – defines the direction of the notes. A pull down menu has the following values referring to the direction of the notes in the arpeggiated chords.
- Up – upwards
- Down – downwards
- UpDn – up and down. Top and Bottom notes played twice
- Auto – direction depends on which key you press first
- UpD2 – up and down. Top & Bottom notes played once
- Rand – notes played randomly
- All – the whole chord is repeated
- Velocity – can be left at the original velocity, a random value, or any set value
- Lim – defines the note range where notes are arpeggiated. Those outside this range are unaffected
- Res – defines the rhythmic note value of the arpeggio. A value of 'None' switches the arpeggio off.
- Length – defines the length of the arpeggiated notes
- Snap to – the grid value of the arpeggiated notes. Normally this is set to the bar denominator. So for 4/4 set it to '1/4'
- Repeat – 'On' creates continuous arpeggios, 'Off' just arpeggiates once
- Octaves – you can spread the arpeggio over 1 to 10 octaves
- Crescendo – positive values cause the arpeggio to increase in volume, negative ones cause them to diminish.
- Controller – with this, you can adjust the parameter values above using MIDI controllers

Chord memorizer

Double clicking on the chord memorizer object (Figure 14.1 (a)) opens a window where you can define a chord to be played whenever you hit a single note on the MIDI controller. You can do this in two ways:

Click on a note on the top keyboard in the chord memorizer window. This will be the note that plays the chord being memorized.

With 'Listen' unclicked, click on the notes you want the chord to consist of on the bottom keyboard on the screen. Or, with 'Listen' clicked, play the chord on your keyboard. Next, Click on 'OK'. Now cable the

Figure 14.7

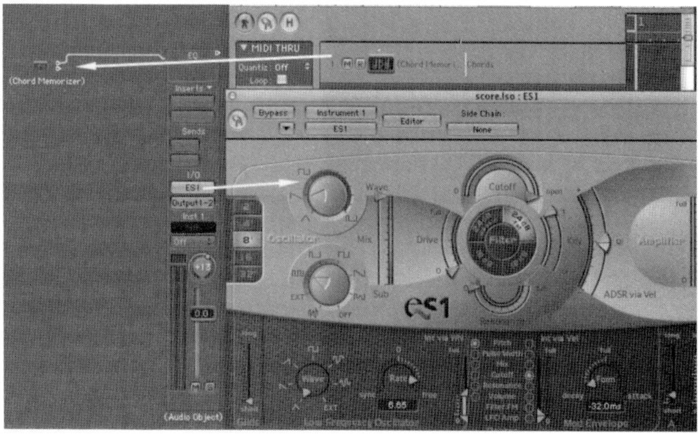

chord memorizer as shown below. Select the chord memorizer as the instrument in the Arrange page (make sure the icon cross is clicked in the Parameter box). When you play the defined note, the chord will play.

You might want to rename the chord memorizer object to something more useful like 'Amazingly big hands!' for those 20 note chords!

Various faders

Faders (Figure 14.1 (e)) can be used to generate all types of MIDI data. At their most simple, they can be used to control the volume, pan, chorus etc. of a connected MIDI device. Fader movements can be recorded into Logic Pro. Of course faders include, buttons, knobs and switches in the Logic Pro universe.

Other more complex uses of faders

If your MIDI device can accept them, you can use faders to send MIDI controller data to adjust filter cut-off or other parameters.

You could send out SysEx (Systems Exclusive information) to control parameters on your MIDI devices. In this way, an on-screen representation can be set up in a Logic Pro Environment of a MIDI device, and you can use this to program the device or adjust the device's parameters in real time. Figure 14.8 is an editor for a Korg MS2000 synthesiser.

Figure 14.8

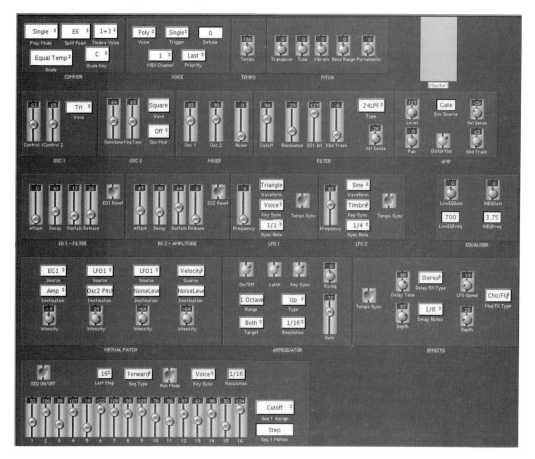

GM Mixer

The GM Mixer object (Figure 14.1 (g)) is an 'already set up' mixer for controlling a GM (General MIDI) module.

Touch tracks

Touch tracks (Figure 14.1 (d)) allow you to assign different MIDI notes to regions. These regions can then be played from a keyboard or other MIDI controller. See Chapter 3 for more on Touch Tracks.

Working with cables and objects

Objects and cables can be deleted by selecting, and then using, the delete key or the erase tool. You can drag cables from one object to another.

In the Options menu there are various commands for sending the values of faders to your MIDI instruments.

Send all fader values except SysEx

Use this command to send controller information to your MIDI devices to reset volumes, pan etc. Sending SysEx information can send out a large amount of MIDI data, especially if you have a lot of 'front panel' – type set ups for your instruments. Using this command and excluding SysEx, will prevent MIDI overload and song playback problems. You can also overcome this problem by putting each of your 'front panels' on a different Environment layer, swapping to each layer in turn, 'selecting all' faders and using the command 'Send selected fader values'.

Send all fader values

As above but sends SysEx information too. The rest of the Options menu deals with positioning of objects.

Other Environment lovelies

Colouring objects

Objects can be coloured by highlighting them and selecting View>Object. If you use an object to record in the Arrange page (an instrument, for example) the regions generated with the object will be the same colour as that object.

Mixer automation

Once you have set up your faders and switches to control your MIDI devices, you can record their movements into Logic Pro. There is more on mixer automation in Chapter 4.

Importing environments

Environments can be imported from other songs. Either part of or a whole Environment can be imported and this can be merged with an existing one. As you use Logic Pro, you will find that you are often adding to or tweaking your Environment. Perhaps you have added a synthesiser and want to create a new instrument and 'front panel' for it? Use this feature to keep old songs up to date.

Here is how you do it. Let's, for the sake of this example, import an Environment from the 'Autoload song' into the 'Old Logic song'

*   Close the Autoload song if it's open.
*   Load the 'Old Logic Song.'
*   Open the Environment window.
*   The Options for importing Environments are in the Options>Import Environment menu

Figure 14.9

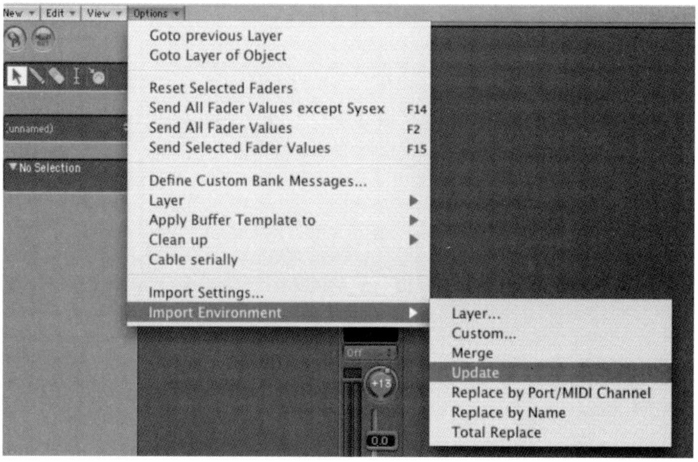

*   Select Options>Import Environment>Update
*   Logic Pro will open a file box. Select the Environment you want to update from. In our example, select the Autoload song.
*   The Environment from the 'Old Logic Song' will be updated to the one in the Autoload song. This cannot be undone. If you want to get back to the previous 'Old Logic Song' use the File>Revert to Saved menu item right away.

As you can see from the figure opposite, there are various other options for importing Environments. The Replace by port/MIDI channel is useful if you want to import your standard Environment into a loaded MIDI file, for example.

Audio objects in more detail

Audio objects are also covered in more general detail in Chapter 3 and Appendix 1

EQ

Double clicking on the EQ box opens the Channel EQ. EQ is short for Equalisation. EQ is used to change the tonal quality of anything it's applied to. Think of it as a sophisticated version of the bass and treble controls on your hi-fi.

The Channel EQ is a Parametric EQ with several different types of shelving. You can open several Channel EQs on the same Audio or Instrument object (Figure 14.10).

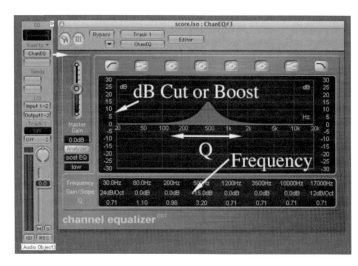

Figure 14.10

There are other EQs available from the Plug-in pull down menu.

- Hi Shelf – choose a frequency to be cut or boosted. There is no bandwidth parameter.
- Low Shelf – choose a frequency to be cut or boosted. There is no bandwidth parameter
- High Cut – this is a high pass filter allowing only frequencies over the chosen frequency to be allowed to pass through.
- Low Cut - this is a low pass filter allowing only frequencies below the chosen frequency to be allowed to pass through.

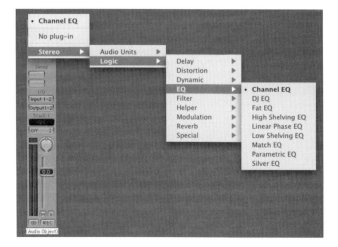

Figure 14.11

> ### Info
>
> Parametric – Parametric EQ is probably the most useful type in most cases. With a Parametric EQ you select the frequency to be boost or cut using the Hz parameter and then use the dB (or volume) parameter to actually boost or cut at that frequency. The Q control adjusts the width of the EQ curve. Use a small value for fine EQ - ing and a larger one for a broad adjustment.

You can have as many EQs in an Audio object as you want. You can turn each EQ off with the bypass button.

Inserts

Inserts are where the plug-in effects within Logic Pro are utilised. Plug-ins are discussed in Chapter 15. Logic Pro has an ever-expanding range of these supplied, including such stalwarts as reverb, compression and delay along with more esoteric effects such as autofilter and overdrive. In addition Logic Pro can use Audio Unit plug-ins and Virtual instruments. You can have as many Inserts per Audio object as your computer processor or external audio hardware will allow.

Figure 14.12

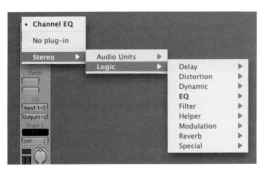

Figure 14.13

Sends

These allow you to route the Audio object signal to another part of Logic Pro. Depending on your audio hardware you can use Sends to send to a Buss Audio object, to an external output of the audio interface, or to Effects on an Audio interface card (Figure 14.13).

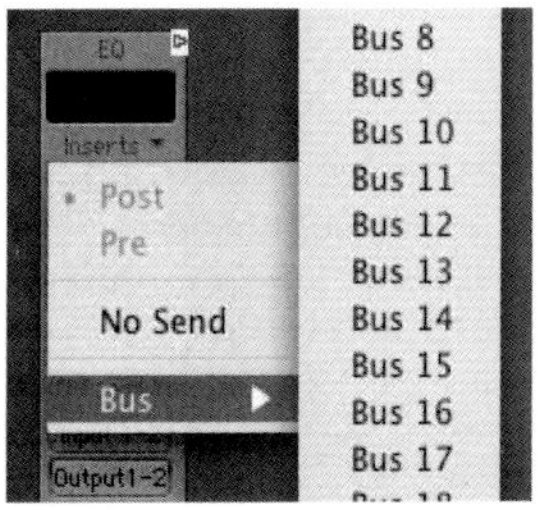

Send to a Buss Audio object

This can be useful in two ways. If the Send is set to pre-fade, you could mute all the channels and use the Send knob to route audio to a Buss Audio object. The overall level of the 'sent' audio can then be controlled by the Buss Audio object slider.

Figure 14.14

> **Info**
>
> Sending many signals to a Buss Audio object with Plug-ins is much less demanding on computer processing than using a Plug-in on each Audio object. Say for example you want the same reverb on a set of backing vocals. Use a send to send all these to a Buss Audio object and apply the Reverb to that instead. Send them pre fader and you can control their levels together too.

If you insert some plug-ins on the Buss Audio object, you can then add these effects to all the signals sent to that object – rather like an external effects unit. Of course you can combine these two features.

Figure 14.15

I/O
Here you can chose the input to use for recording (Figure 14.16). The number of inputs shown depends on your Audio interface.

Output
Here you can choose the output of the Audio object (Figure 14.17). The number of outputs shown depends on your Audio interface. If you use a Buss Audio object as the output you can use the buss in exactly the same way as described under the Send section above, except the levels sent to the Buss are set by the Audio objects fader itself.

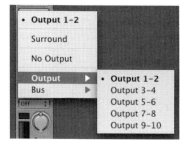

Figure 14.17

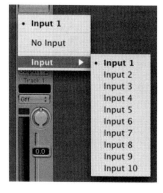

Figure 14.16

Pan
This moves the signal across the stereo field. On a stereo Audio object it changes the balance of the left and right channels.

Fader
This sets the level of the audio that the Audio object controls.

Audio object Parameter Box

When an Audio object is selected the Parameter box shows the parameters relating to that object. These are as follows:

Figure 14.18
The Parameter box shows the parameters relating to the object

- Audio object name (a). Double clicking here allows you to rename the Audio object. This new name will appear in the Arrange window Track name column.
- Icon (b). Clicking and holding here allows you to change the icon relating to the Audio object.
- Dev (c). Clicking and holding here allows you to chose which of the available installed devices, which the output of the Audio object can be routed. What appears here depends on the installed audio interfaces in your computer and the computer type.
- Channel (d). Clicking and holding here allows you to chose which available track the Audio object relates to. The number of tracks available here depends on the audio interface installed on your computer. You can also select the type of Audio object here, such as Instruments, Busses, Auxes etc. (Figure 14.19).
- MIDI Ch (e). This sets the MIDI channel the Audio object sends and receives MIDI data on. It defaults to the same MIDI channel as the track number.
- Val as (f). Clicking and holding here allows you to chose weather the value display on the Audio object is numerical or in dB. 0dB equals 90.
- Show EQs, Inserts, Sends, I/O. Allows you to show or hide these parameters.

Figure 14.19

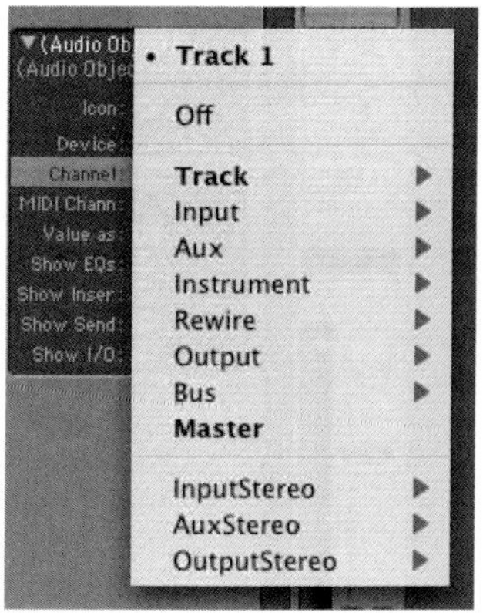

You can adjust most of the numeric values on the Audio objects and their Plug-ins and EQ by double clicking on the number and entering the data directly. To set the Audio faders to 90 or 0dB, hold down the Option key and click on the fader.

Plug-ins 15

What are plug-ins?

Plug-ins are the software equivalents of external effects units, such as reverbs, compressors, delays and so on. Most external effects units are just software running on dedicated DSP chips. Plug-ins use the DSP power of the computer to run software analogues of effects – so called 'native' DSP. There are two types of plug-in: 'real time' or 'non real time'. Real time plug-ins are the true counterparts of external effects units as they process the audio as it is playing back. Non real time destructive plug-ins actually change the audio file permanently. The advantage of this is that the computer only uses its DSP power as the file is being processed. You could for example use a non real time compressor to compress a guitar part, and free up DSP power for reverb on vocals. You can, of course, keep a copy of the original guitar audio file if you change your mind later!

The advantages of native processing is that it moves us further in the direction of the 'studio in a box' and that updates are as easy to provide as those of any software. Also you often get these plug-ins 'free' with software. Logic comes with with many types. In the case of plug-ins using AU technology, there are hundreds of free or inexpensive plug-ins available thanks to the open nature of the format. The plug-in parameters can be easily automated within Logic Pro, so that you could, for example, vary the reverb or compression in real time as a song plays. Presets can be created and stored for use in other songs. The main disadvantage is that the computer must be very powerful to emulate the quality and stability of external units. However, modern computers are powerful enough to replace all your external MIDI and effects hardware if you desire. The plug-in formats that Logic Pro can use are detailed below. Logic Pro can use many plug-in types simultaneously – another example of the flexibility of the software.

Virtual effects

Logic Pro 'native' plug-ins

Depending on what version of Logic you have, the software provides a variety of plug-ins. Figure 15.1 shows some of the range of plug-ins currently supplied with Logic Pro.

As you can see there are traditional effects such as reverb, EQ, delay, expander, noise gate, compressor, modulation (flanger, phaser) and so on. There are also some more esoteric plug-ins in the Special section, such as Spectral gate and Bitcrusher.

Figure 15.1

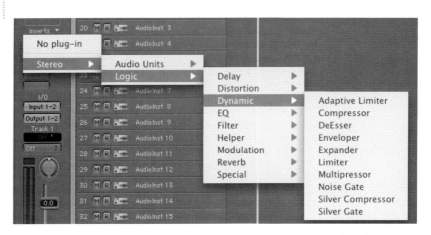

The reason Apple provides several types of the same plug-in, (for example, PlatinumVerb, GoldVerb and EnVerb are all reverbs,) is that they all use different amounts of DSP processing power. The less power required, the less powerful computer you need, or, more importantly, more effects can be used at once. You don't always need the best quality effects. For example the reverb on a backing guitar could be of lower quality than on lead vocals. Or you could use low quality plug-ins as an effect. Logic gives you a choice.

Figure 15.2

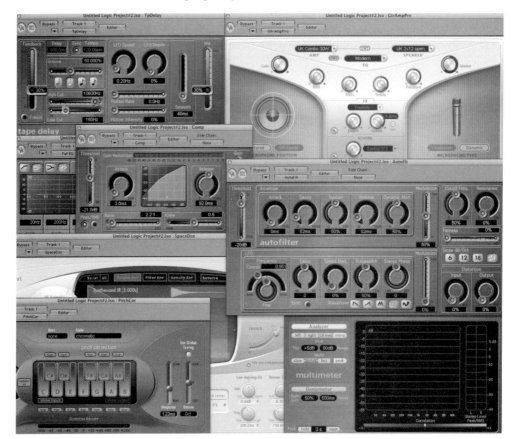

As you can see from Figure 15.2, the plug-ins have similar parameters to the hardware based effects you may be used to. But they are much easier to edit as they are all displayed simultaneously. This is obviously a better way to edit than the often 'painting a room through a letter box' style of parameter access of hardware units.

Audio Unit (AU) plug-ins

AU plug-ins are similar to Logic Pro native plug-ins, but it's an 'open' format. AU is a very popular Macintosh format and many people have written plug-ins. Some are traditional, some are weird and many are free and available on the Internet. AU plug-ins appear in the plug-in menu alongside Logic Pro's native plug-ins. VST plug-ins are stored in a folder within the \Library\Audio\Plug-ins\Components folder

Digidesign plug-ins

If you use DAE and Digidesign hardware there are several plug-in formats available. You can use TDM and Audiosuite and non-real-time destructive plug-ins with a TDM system.

TDM plug-ins

These are real time plug-ins that utilise the DSP power of Digidesign ProTools audio interface system. ProTools uses DSP chips on internal cards that fit into the Mac's PCI slots so the computer itself need not be as powerful as with native systems.

Virtual instruments

The next step to replacing external effects units with native counterparts, is replacing all those synthesisers and samplers with 'virtual' instruments. Logic Pro has several virtual instruments included, and many more can be used with AU plug-ins. As you can imagine, virtual instruments put even more demands on a computer's processing power.

Advantages of virtual instruments:

- Easier to program – you can have 100 on screen 'knobs' if your virtual instrument demands it.
- Flexibility – you could have several 'instances' of the same virtual instrument. Imagine how much five analog monophonic synthesisers would cost!
- Manipulation – you could record the parameter changes you make into Logic Pro. For example, you could record filter sweeps on a virtual polysynth.

Disadvantages are

- Require huge computer resources- especially if you use them alongside audio recording and effects plug-ins.
- Don't look as sexy in your studio!

Logic Pro's ES1 Virtual Synthesiser

As an example of a virtual instrument, we'll look the ES1 Virtual Synthesiser. First of all you need to select or create an Audio object using the Track>Create Multiple menu item. Then click and hold on Cha and select an Instrument from the pull down menu.

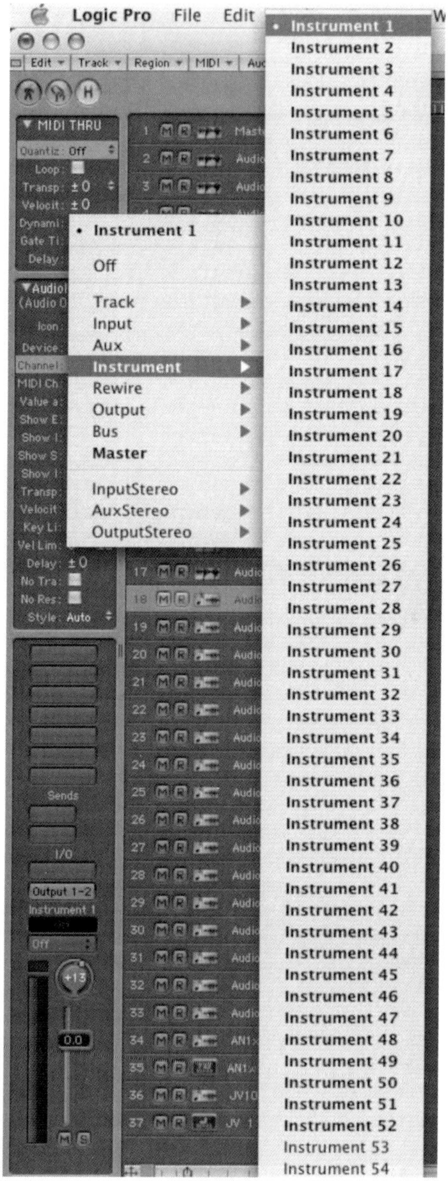

Figure 15.3
Virtual instrument pull-down menu

If you click and hold the mouse over the top insert box you will see the ES1 listed. Select it (Figure 15.4).

Then double click on the insert box. The ES1 window will open (Figure 15.5).

As you can see the ES1 is a fully functional synthesiser. The outputs of the ES1 are routed through the audio interface outputs and the parameters can be recorded into Logic Pro like any plug-in.

Any virtual instrument conforming to the AU standard can be used with Logic Pro. The Internet is a good place to search for shareware instruments, and there are more and more commercial ones appearing. The 'Studio in a box' is beginning to become a reality.

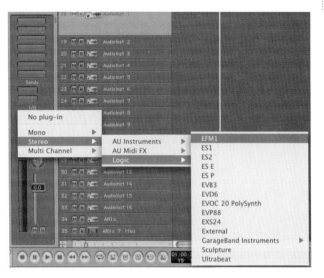

Figure 15.4
Select the instrument you want

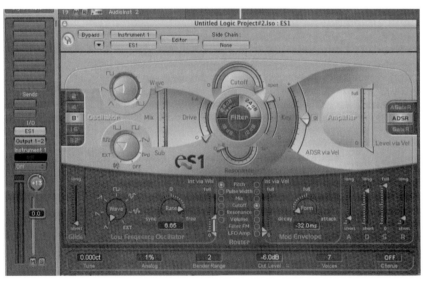

Figure 15.5

Aux inputs and Multiple output (multi channel) Virtual Instruments

Multiple virtual outputs

These behave something like a hardware synthesiser with separate, physical, audio outputs. Some of Logic's own virtual instruments have this feature along with many AU format plug-ins. The advantages of these outputs are that, for example, a single EXS24 sample instrument can send different samples to different virtual outputs for separate processing. You may have, for example, a drum kit with several instruments such as hi hats, snare and bass drum spread across the keyboard for easy playing. You may also want to process these samples in different way. You may want, for example, reverb only on the snare, compression on the bass drum and so on.

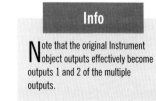

Info

Note that the original Instrument object outputs effectively become outputs 1 and 2 of the multiple outputs.

Figure 15.6

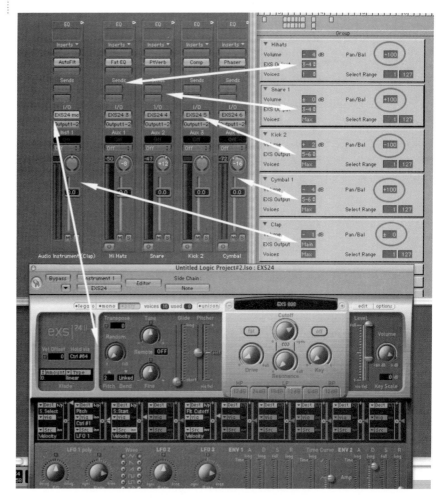

In Logic, you send the different samples to a specialised Audio object– The Aux (or Auxiliary) object. You can create Auxs in two ways:

- Create an Audio Instrument object from the New>Audio object Environment menu item and select Aux from the Cha parameter menu.
- Create them from the Arrange page Track>Create multiple tracks menu item. More Auxes are created in the Channel menu as needed.

Figure 15.7

If you have any multiple output instruments, you can select them here in the I/O menus. They are called 'Multi Channel' in Logic Pro.

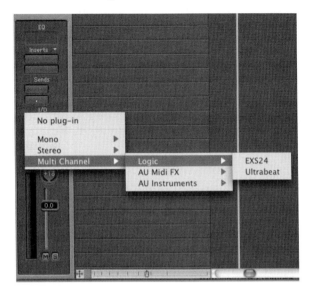

Figure 15.8

Select an output channel in the Virtual instruments editor screen. This example is for the EXS sampler – your Virtual instrument may have a different assignment method. Note that the outputs are shown as stereo. To route, for example to output 3 only, pan hard to the left. To output   4, pan to the right. Note that the claps are being sent to the original instrument object which are, effectively, outputs 1 and 2.

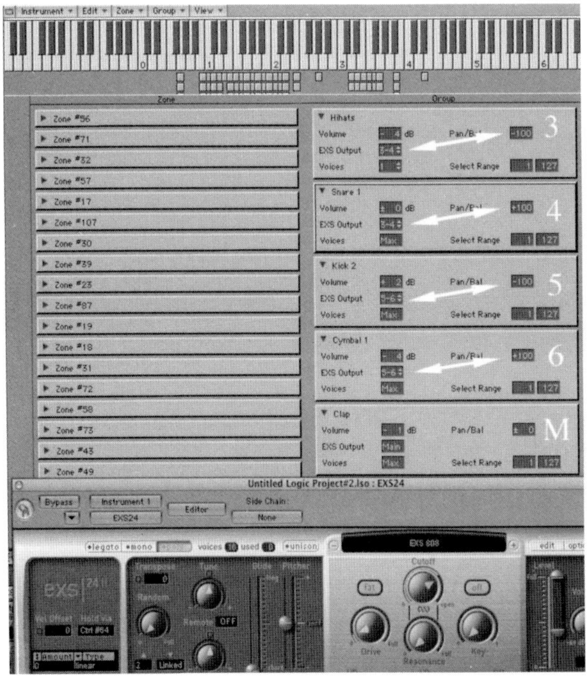

Figure 15.9

In Figure 15.9, the numbers refer to the outputs from the EXS24. 'M' is the main output, which is routed through the original Virtual instrument Audio object. The pan for this is at '0' as it's a stereo out. Here's how to set it up.

- Create an audio object from the New>Audio object Environment menu item. Make sure it's selected.
- Select Aux from the channel menu (Figure 15.10).

Figure 15.10

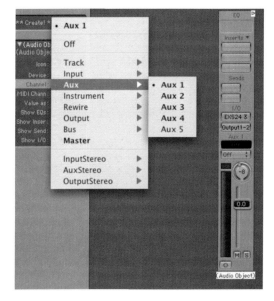

- If you click and hold on the I/O section of the Aux object, you will see the inputs from the Multi Channel instrument. You need to have a different Aux object for each output. You can then add EQ, Reverb or any other Plug-ins as per usual on an Audio object.

Figure 15.11

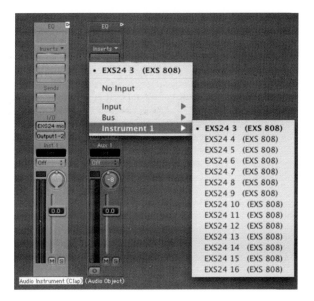

Live Inputs and External instruments

If you have a soundcard or interface with multiple inputs, you can route the outputs from an external synthesiser or mixing desk back into Logic Pro. These inputs can then be incorporated with audio tracks and virtual instruments when bouncing down, eliminating the use of an external mastering machine, such as DAT or Tape. Live inputs are just another Audio object.

Create one from the Environment page New>Audio object menu item or from the Arrange page Track>Create multiple.... .menu item.

Now choose a mono or stereo input via the channel parameter. These inputs represent the physical inputs on your interface. The examples here are inputs 5 and 6. You could rename this object to 'FX return' or 'JX3P input' for example (Figure 15.12).

If you are returning the sound from an effects unit, such as a reverb, you'll obviously need to send the audio to the unit from somewhere within Logic Pro. The best way to do this is to use a Bus Audio object.

First create an Audio object from the New>Audio object Environment menu item. Now select a Bus object from the Channel parameter list. Make sure it's a stereo bus if you have a stereo FX unit. Rename the object 'Bus FX send' (Figure 15.13).

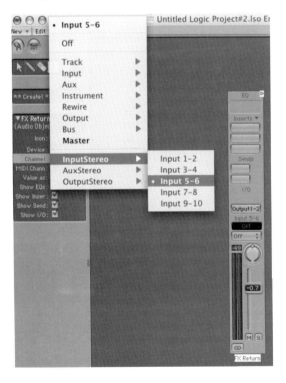

Figures 15.12 and 15.13

Select the outputs you have the external FX unit connected to. Say outputs 5 and 6 as previously (Figure 15.14).

Now, if you send to this bus from an audio track, the Bus acts as a send to the external FX, while the live inputs are a return.

Figures 15.14 and 15.15

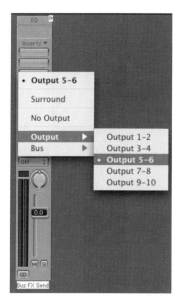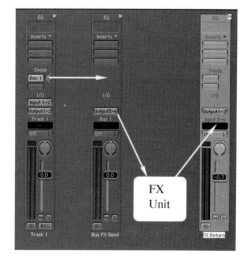

• Select the View menu item > I/O labels.

Figure 15.16

• You can now rename the various sends, inputs and outputs.

Figure 15.17

• You can also name any input, outputs or busses on your system.
• You can also send directly to outputs and return to inputs on a channel using the I/O plug-in (Figure 15.18).

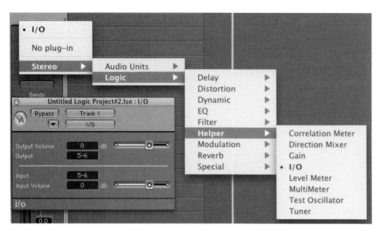

Figure 15.18

External instruments

These are specialized versions of Live inputs. You can route the outputs from your external hardware (Synthesisers etc) to the inputs of your Audio interface and then onto the Arrange page in Logic. The advantage of the External Instrument is that the sound from the hardware device can be easily bounced down during a real-time mix along with Virtual instruments and Audio tracks. You could also return hardware effects units through an External instruments track. Here's how you set them up.

- Select or create an Audio Instrument object (Figure 15.19).
- Instance the External plug-in from the pull down menu (Figure 15.20).

Figure 15.20

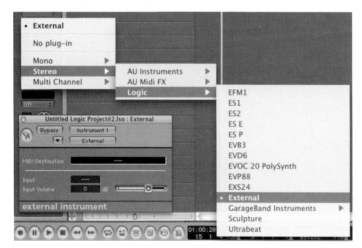

Figure 15.19 (above)

Figure 15.20 (left)

• Select a MIDI instrument from the pull down menu.

Figure 15.21

Tip

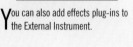

You can also add effects plug-ins to the External Instrument.

Figure 15.22

• You can see that the External Instrument looks exactly like a Virtual instrument track.

Channel Strips

Logic can store whole Audio or Instrument objects complete with plug-ins and parameters as Channel strips. You could, for example, store a favorite combination of compressor, delay and EQ for processing vocals. Logic also ships with a plethora of pre-set Channel strips to get you started. Channel strips are loaded and saved from the pop up menu that appears when you click on the little arrow to the right of the Inserts label on a track.

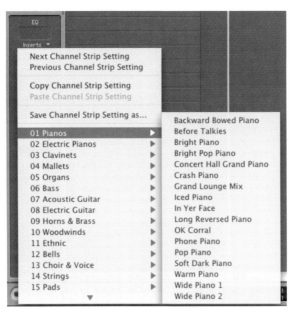

Figure 15.23

Automation, mixing and mastering

This chapter gives you some tips on using Logic Pro for mixing your recordings, and then mastering the resulting mixes.

Here are some definitions, with reference to Logic Pro.

Mixing

Mixing is the process where all the elements of a Logic Pro song are blended into a stereo recording, called the 'Mixdown master'. Not just stereo either – these days you may want to mix down to Dolby 5:1 or other Surround formats. These elements could contain audio recordings within Logic Pro that may have plug-ins processing them in real-time and an external mixer, or multiple input audio interfaces, bringing in the audio outputs of external MIDI devices. Remember that the sounds produced by external MIDI modules and the like are not produced from the computer itself. If you intend to run these devices 'Live' during mixdown (so you can make changes up to the last moment), you will need to use an external mixer to 'sub-mix' them – see Figure 16.1. You can also use Logic's 'Live input' audio objects to bring in the MIDI device's outputs directly.

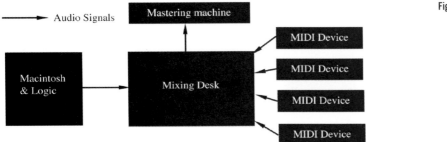

Figure 16.1

There is, of course, nothing stopping you recording MIDI devices as audio files into Logic Pro, and mixing down the whole lot within the program. Of course, the beauty of using a sequencer like Logic Pro is that, depending on the extra equipment you are using, the whole process can be automated. So throughout a song, you can precisely define the level of each part, the plug-ins used on each part, and even the parameters of external mixers and effects units, providing they can be MIDI controlled.

The Mastering machine could be a DAT, MiniDisc, cassette recorder or reel-to-reel tape machine. Alternatively, if you are using only audio tracks and plug-ins, or you can route external devices into Logic, you can master or bounce directly to an audio file. You can then process this file further and burn to CD without the audio ever leaving the computer.

Mastering

When you have your stereo mix, you may want to remove noise at the start and end, 'sweeten' it with EQ and compression, fade it out or in or perform other processing. The Sample editor in Logic Pro (see Chapter 12) is a very well specified stereo editor that can perform these tasks. If your mix was directly to a Logic Pro file, you can just re-import it using the Audio window. If you mixed to an external CD Recorder, DAT or MiniDisc, you can record the results back into Logic Pro, preferably via a digital input on your audio interface card, to maintain the quality and volume level of the recording. Or use the bounced file as described previously.

Some mixing tips

Figure 16.2

A completed song within Logic Pro could look like Figure 16.2

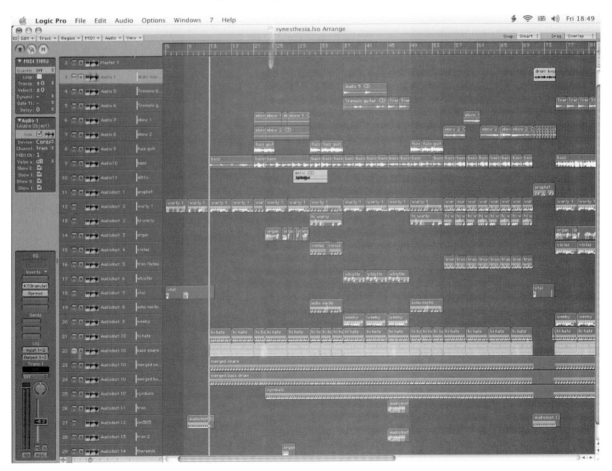

There are several parameters you might want to automate throughout a song. These include:

- The levels or volume of audio tracks
- The EQ or tone of audio tracks
- The levels of the MIDI devices, such as synthesisers and drum machines
- The parameters of the plug-ins inserted on Audio or Virtual instrument channels

All these can be controlled from within Logic Pro using MIDI controller data or the Logic Pro automation system described later. You can also use a mixture of the two methods. You could use Hyperdraw, as described in Chapter 4, to do the automation. However Logic Pro has an integrated mixer that helps you with the process – the Track Mixer.

The Track mixer

Open the Track mixer using the main page menu item Windows>Track Mixer.

As you can see from Figures 16.3 the mixer is a representation of the tracks you are using in the Arrange page, with the Track names appearing at the bottom.

Figure 16.3

Info

If you want to see your Buss an Aux objects in the Track mixer, you'll need to add them to the Arrange page first.

There are many ways to mix a song. There are also many mixing philosophies that would fill a book in themselves. However, there are several golden rules you can follow that will get you started.

Mixing tips

- Listen to music that you like through the speakers you are using to mix your Logic Pro song. This will give you a idea of what a mix 'should' sound like on your system
- Don't mix the song on the same day you record it
- Don't listen for long periods at high volume
- Check for a balance by listening to the mix from another room with the door between them open. You can really hear if the vocals are too loud or soft this way. Listening at low volume is another good check.
- Get someone else in to check the balance of the vocals in the mix if you are the singer. It's likely that you will have mixed the voice too low
- Don't be afraid to mix in sections and then 'glue' them together at the mastering stage
- Do experiment.
- Be prepared to break all the rules until it sounds right!

The Making Music guide to mixing

- Set all pan controls to the central position
- Set all the volume sliders to zero
- Set all buss knobs to zero

First of all you need to get a rough balance of the various audio tracks and MIDI tracks. How you do this depends on the type of music you are mixing. Lets assume it's a song with audio tracks containing vocals, drums, recorded bass and some keyboard pads and solos coming from MIDI devices or Virtual instruments.

You can show or hide tracks from the Arrange page View menu. This may be useful if you have objects that you wont want to use in the Mixdown (Buss returns etc). You can handily hide and unhide tracks using Key commands. You can also click on the hide icon to show or hide tracks.

- To hide a track, select it and use the View>Hide current track and select next track menu item.
- The next track is selected.
- Repeat with all the required tracks.
- Start off by setting the levels with the drums a few dB below 0. Now bring the level of the vocal up to a comfortable level.

A note on levels

When you mix, the levels of all the instruments will creep up. Eventually you will run out of headroom and distortion will occur. Remember 0dB is the MAXIMUM level in a digital system. You can't 'push the level into the red' as on an analog recorder. Excessive EQ boosting can also have the same effect.

Bring up the level of the other instrument levels. Don't be tempted to increase the levels of the drums to compensate for the loudness of other instruments. Instead, reduce the levels of the other recordings. Also keep an eye on the output level of the Track mixer master fader and the level of mix going into your mastering machine, if you're using one.

When you are happy with the overall level of the mix, you could pan some of the tracks to spread them across the stereo picture.

Groups

You may want to adjust the levels of some tracks together. You can group several objects together so that moving one of their faders will move all those in the same group and keeping the same relative levels.

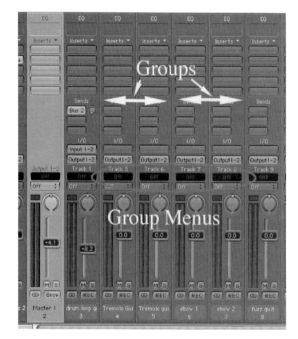

Figure 16.4

To assign a group to a Track, use the Group pull down menu.

Figure 16.5

You can see which group is selected on the Group display.

Figure 16.6

If you open the Group settings window

Figure 16.7

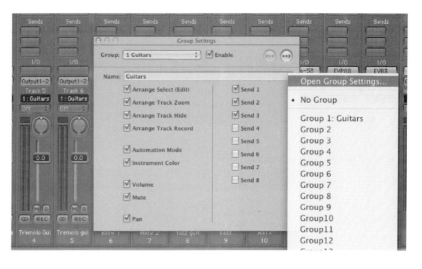

You can:

- Name the group (i.e. Drum 'Subgroup', 'Guitars' etc.)
- Choose what is to be grouped. For example, you could group sends to a bus (for reverb) or Arrange page automatic zooming as well as faders and pans.

Now we can insert EQ and plug-ins. Note in Figure 16.8 that the tracks 5 and 6 send their outputs to buss 2, which has a compressor and Emagic's PlatinumVerb Reverb as plug-ins. The volume slider of buss 2 will then control the outputs of all these tracks. Note also that tracks 7 and 8 have sends to buss 1. Buss 1 also has compression alongside a flanger. The level slider on buss 1 now acts as a return level for these effects to be blended in with Tracks 7 and 8. You can see that these sends are linked in the 'Ebows' group.

Figure 16.8

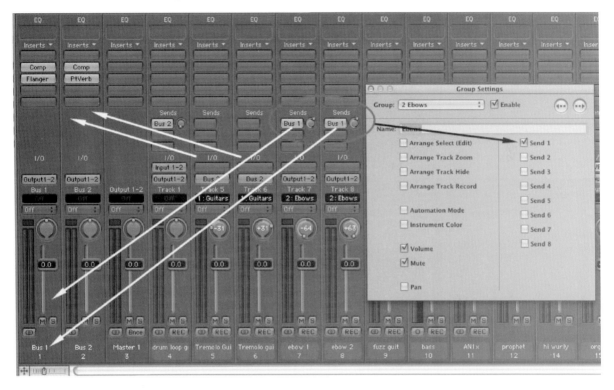

We are now ready to record Mixer automation. Logic's automation allows for the total automation of all of the softwares's parameters, such as volume and pan, as well as all those for plug-ins.

Logic automation overview

It's always been possible to automate MIDI data using Hyperdraw and Hyperedit within Logic Pro. The Track Mixer window also had a primitive automation section. However, this system was limited to automating regions themselves – the data was 'fixed' to the regions, so if you removed or deleted them, the automation was lost. Also, as the old scheme used MIDI data, you were limited to 8 bit, or 128 step, automation. This could result in noisy fade outs and limited the precision in your automation data curves.

Track based automation

In Logic Pro has a 32 bit automation system. You now record automation data directly onto the track itself, irrespective of whether there are regions there or not. You could, for example, replace a region with a new recording and the automation would remain the same. Or you could move the automation data with a copied region. We'll look at the specific parameters in more detail later, but for now let's get automating.

How to automate

Record some tracks. Then select the View>Track Automation menu item in the Arrange page. Tracks can contain either MIDI, Audio or an Audio Instrument data. Open an Arrange page and the Track Mixer window from the Windows menu. Arrange the windows as shown in Figure 16.10.

Now set the used tracks' automation to 'Latch' (Figure 16.9). Play back the track. Move the faders, pan controls – in fact anything you can grab. You may want to automate the mute state of a track, the EQ, sends or the controls of any inserted plug-ins. You can be in record or playback mode – automation will be recorded either way. You'll see the automation data being written as you move the controls. The new automation type is described in the Instrument list. You'll also see how the automation is continued between objects.

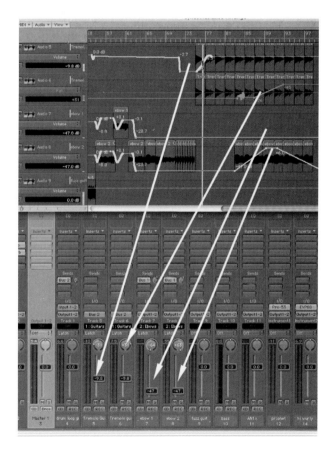

Figure 16.9 (above)

Figure 16.10 (right)

You can stop the track and start playback again. If you move the faders again, the automation data will be updated. The 'Latch' setting allows you to easily replace previously recorded data. It's an intuitive way of automating.

Figure 16.11

So where's the automation data gone? Logic stores its 32 bit automation data in 'hidden' tracks. You can show these tracks and edit the data they contain.

Select a track with some automation recorded on it.

Figure 16.12

Now select the View>Track automation menu item in the Arrange page. The track will be zoomed out and you will see the automation data on the track. You can zoom further to make the data clearer. You'll also notice that some new parameters have appeared next to the track. You'll also see the data values displayed at the nodes.

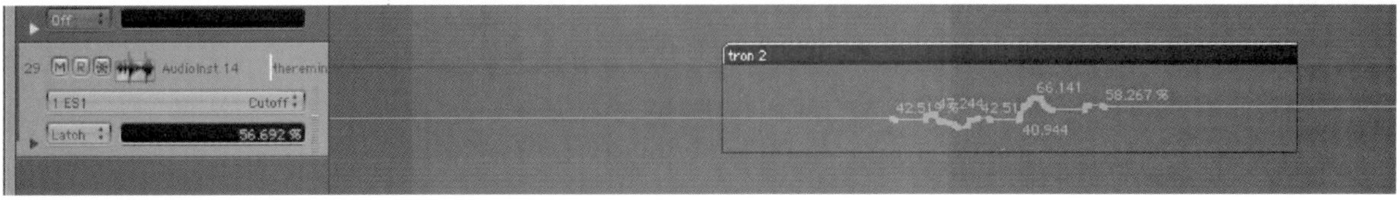

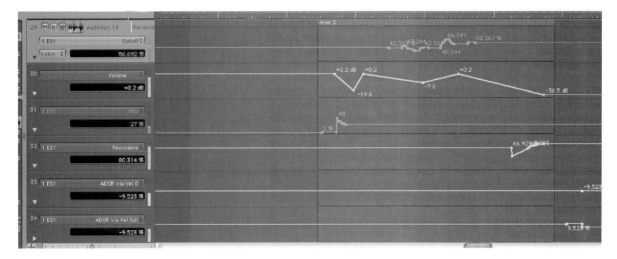

Figure 16.13

You can select the automation data to view in two ways. Click on the automation parameter. A pull down menu appears and you can choose the data that has been automated.

Figure 16.14

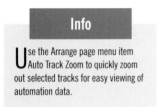

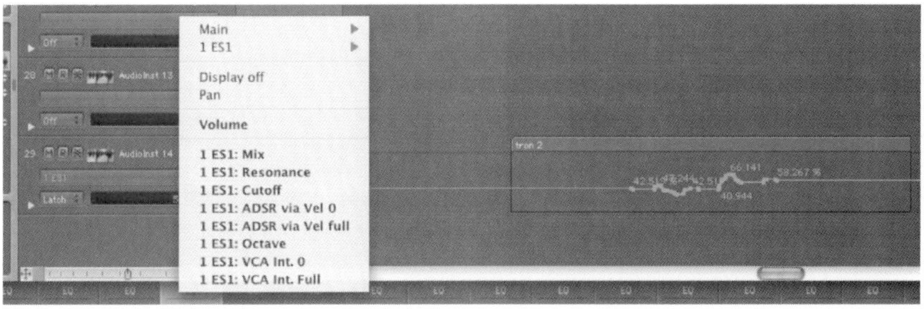

Info

Use the Arrange page menu item Auto Track Zoom to quickly zoom out selected tracks for easy viewing of automation data.

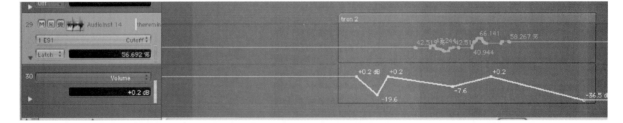

Click on the little arrow below 'Latch'. This opens another 'hidden' track containing the automation data.

Figure 16.15

You can continue to open these hidden tracks, and display all the recorded automation data.

Figure 16.16

When you change volume, pan, mute or any plug-in parameter, it's automatically recorded on these invisible automation tracks. You'll notice that all Logic plug-ins and other automation data is displayed by name. This should apply to all AU plug-ins too, assuming they have been written using the correct protocols.

If the zoom level is enough you can see all automation data on a single track, overlaid in different colours.

Editing automation data

Apart from editing the automation by moving the sliders in the Track Mixer window, you can also edit the data directly with the mouse. This can be achieved in several ways.

The curves can be edited using the arrow tool exactly as was done in earlier versions using Hyperdraw. In fact, you can see that this type of editing is a kind of track automation hyperdraw. The difference is the resolution is 32 bit and not 'real' MIDI data.

- Click on a node to delete it.
- Click on a line to add a node.
- Click and hold a node and drag to move it.
- Click and hold while holding the ALT key and you can drag all the data on a track after that point, together.

If you select the Broken Arrow tool (right) you can create various S- shaped curves if you drag data between nodes, as long as the parameter is set to Curve.

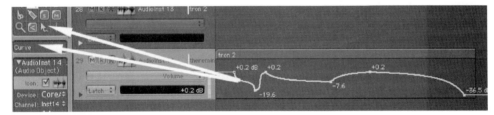

Figure 16.17

Dragging in different directions will produce different curves.

- Moving the mouse to the right produces a horizontal S curve.
- Moving the mouse to the left produces a vertical S curve.
- Moving the mouse up produces a concave curve.
- Moving the mouse up produces a convex curve.

Editing the data

When you have recorded or drawn automation data you can edit it using the mouse in various ways. Use the Arrow tool.

- A short click on a node deletes it.
- A short click on a line or anywhere off a node creates a new node and the line passes through it. If you click and hold you can drag the newly created node.

Info

You can also perform the same curve drawing with the normal Arrow tool if you hold down the Ctrl and Alt keys while dragging.

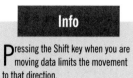

Info

Pressing the Shift key when you are moving data limits the movement to that direction.

Figure 16.18

- A long click on a line allows you to drag a line between two nodes.
- A long click on a node, line or selection while holding down the key you can copy.
- If you don't make a selection clicking with the ALT key down, will drag all the data after the current mouse position.
- A double click while holding down the ALT keys selects all the automation data.

You can also use the Automation tool with the parameter underneath set to 'select' to highlight automation data for editing.

More detailed editing is also possible. There is a key command available 'Automation event edit'. Set this to a suitable key. Highlight an automation track. Press the key. You'll see an Edit window open where you can fine tune the automation data.

The Main menu item Options>Track automation also has several useful automation settings parameters. This opens up a small window.

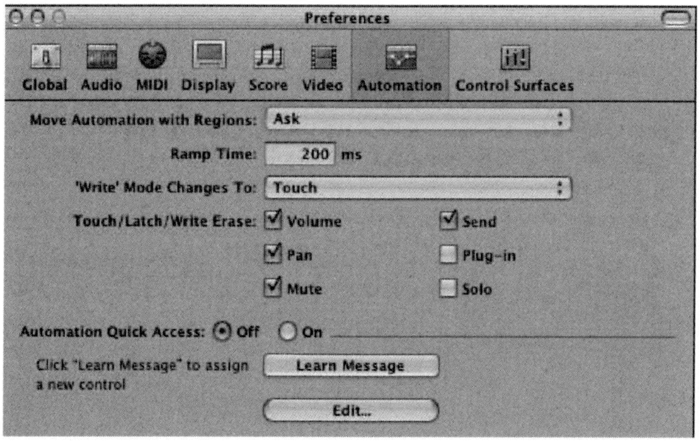

Track Automation settings

Move Automation with objects. Set this parameter to 'ASK' to get Logic to give you the choice of moving the automation data when you copy or move a region with automation data recorded.

Ramp time defines the time the automation data written in 'Touch' mode will take to return to the previous value.

The other parameters relate to the automation mode 'Write'. In Write mode, when you move a fader all data is erased as the SPL passes it. You can choose which data to erase here.

- You can use the 'Delete…' menu items to delete automation data in various ways. Most are self explanatory. 'Delete orphan data…' deletes data that has lost the actual track it was recorded on. Perhaps it was a copy that was deleted.
- The 'Write to…' menu items to make sure the last automation value you recorded remains at that level until the end of a track or to the right locator.
- The 'Move.' menu items allow you to convert automation data to MIDI data and vice versa. You may want to change old style hyperdraw and automation data to the new automation style. Or, if you are transferring data to another

sequencer or earlier version of Logic, you can change the track automation to normal MIDI data. Note: You'll lose the high resolution of the new automation system if you do this.

Automation quick access

You can quickly assign a control on a keyboard or MIDI mixer, as long as it puts out MIDI controller data when moved, to an Automation parameter.

- Turn ON Automation Quick access.
- Click on 'Learn Message'
- Slowly move your control. This could be a modulation wheel, a pedal knob or slider.

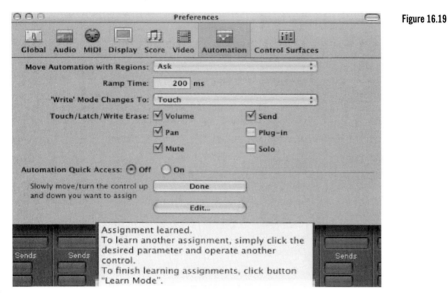

Figure 16.19

- Click on 'Done'
- If you click on 'Edit....' A window opens

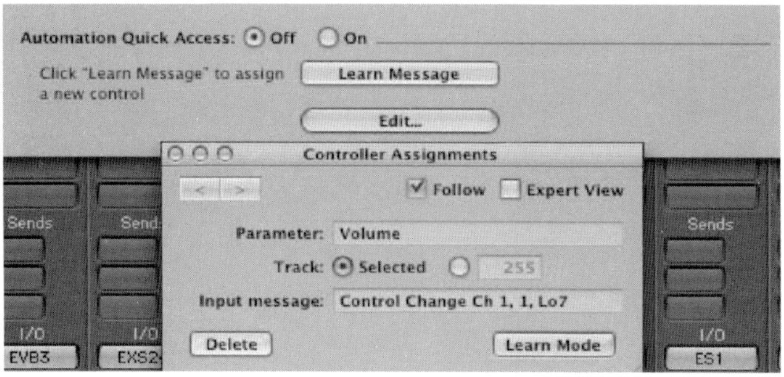

Figure 16.20

- You can see that Controller 1 is set to Volume automation.

For more on controller assignment see Chapter 17.

Other automation modes

The usual automation mode you'd use is Latch. This is the mode that replaces automation data when you move a control with the data generated by that control. When you let go of the control, the Track continues with previously recorded data. You'll notice that other modes are available when you click and hold on the pop up menu.

The other modes are:

Figure 16.21

- Off – this disables the automation data on a track. It doesn't delete it – just stops Logic Pro from responding to it.
- Read – in this mode, Logic Pro reads the previously written automation data. You can't overwrite data accidentally in this mode.
- Touch – latch is pretty much like Latch mode except that when you release a control, the last automation data continues until you stop the sequencer.
- Write – in write mode the data is written according to the settings in the Track automation Settings as described earlier.
- MIDI – in this mode, the automation data is written into regions as 8 bit MIDI data as in previous versions of Logic Pro.

Once the mix has been set up to your satisfaction you can then record your stereo master. There are two ways to do this, depending on whether you are using an external mixer or not.

- Use Read mode when you've perfected you mix to make sure you don't accidentally edit automation data.
- Holding the ALT key while selecting the automation mode will change all the channels that were previously set to the same as the channel you choose will change to the new setting. For example, If a channel is set to Touch and you change to Read while holding the modifier key, all channels set to Touch will change to Read.

There are several Key Commands regarding easy selection of automation modes. Search for 'automation' in the Options>Settings>Key Commands window.

Info

Loop around a section when automating parameters to get it just right.

Mixing to an external recorder

If you are using a set up similar to that in Figure 16. with an external mixer, this is how you'd mix your song down. Don't worry about fade ins and outs or noise at the start or end of the track – this can be addressed during mastering.

First of all you need to set the input levels on the recorder. If it's a digital one, you should aim to get the levels peaking just below 0dB. Analogue machines should peak on or just above 0dB. Play back the track and record.

If you are using a DAT machine to mix down to, don't change the sample rate between songs. It'll make life a lot easier if you just use 44.1kH sample rate – the rate used on CD.

Mixing using the Logic Pro Bounce feature

If you are just mixing down audio tracks and virtual instruments within Logic Pro, or using an audio interface that allows you to bring the audio outputs from your external MIDI devices and effects units into Logic Pro, you can bounce the mix directly to hard disk.

• Select the range you want to bounce down using the left and right locators

Figure 16.22

• Open the File>Bounce window.

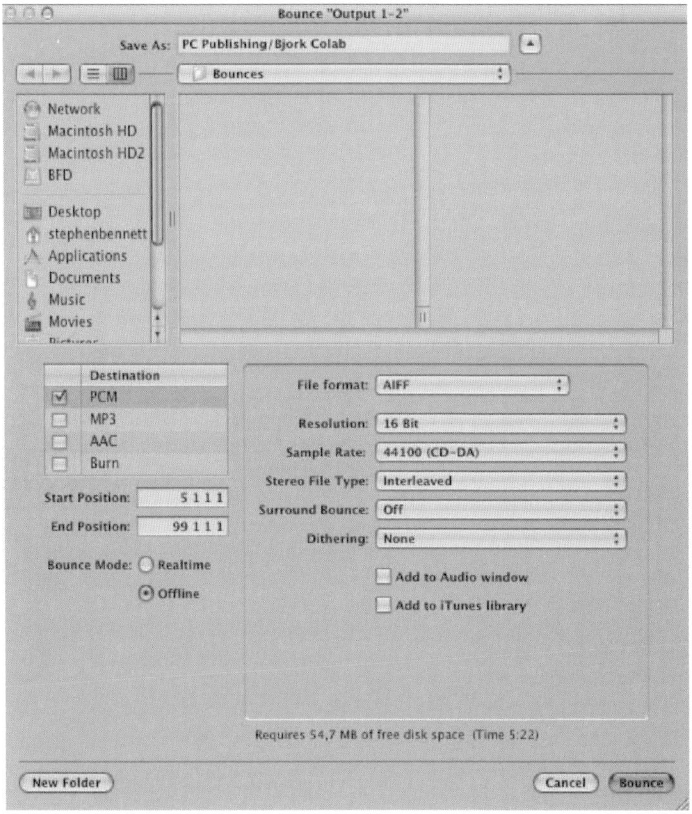

Figure 16.23

Here you can choose the file type and file format you want to bounce to and you can choose the location of the bounced mix file. Make sure dithering is set to None.

• Choose the same Sample Rate and Resolution as your original recordings. These will need to be 'dithered' down to 16bit/44.1Hz during Mastering. More on this later in the chapter.

- Choose the destination PCM for the highest quality file.
- Choose the following File Formats

  * AIFF for general Mac use.
  * Sound Designer II if you want to master on a DigiDesign Pro Tools rig.
  * WAV if you are transferring the mix to a Windows PC

- Click on Bounce and the mix will be recorded to the disk with the automation you have set up.

This file can then be easily imported into Logic Pro for mastering using the Audio window

POW-r dithering algorithm

Figure 16.24

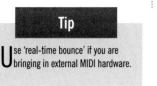

Logic's internal resolution is 32 bit floating point. However, you will often bounce down to 24 bit for mastering or 16 bit files for CD creation. Dithering reduces unwanted graininess and quantisation noise produced during this bit reduction. The POW-r algorithm has three types of dithering. Which one you use depends on what you are recording. As usual, let your ears be the judge. However, some use examples are given below.

- None – no dithering occurs. Use this if you want to re-import audio for mastering or adding to an already recorded track.
- POW-r #1 – uses a dithering curve to reduce noise. Use on acoustic music that has been recorded at a decent level or natural sounding music.
- POW-r #2 – uses noise shaping to add an extra 10dB to the dynamic range. Use on low level recorded acoustic or anywhere you need the added dynamic range.
- POW-r #3 – uses noise shaping to extend the dynamic range by 20dB in the 2 to 4 kHz range. This is the range most sensitive to the human ear. Use on pop, rock or dance music or music destined for the radio. Or voice recordings.

In general you should only dither audio once. If you plan to reintroduce files into Logic turn dithering to 'None' before the bounce.

Some mastering tips

Once you have your song mixed into stereo, that's not the end of the story. Before you let the world hear your masterpiece, there are several things you can do your recording using Logic Pro.

Making Music guide to mastering

First we need to get the stereo recording into Logic. If you 'bounced down' the track during mixing you can skip this step.

Record the mix back into Logic Pro. If you can, use the digital inputs of your audio interface to maintain quality. Use a stereo Audio object as this will produce a stereo file. Rename the audio file to the song name.

If you 'bounced down' the mix, just import the file into Logic Pro using the Audio>Import audio file.... window. Drag the audio into the Arrange window.

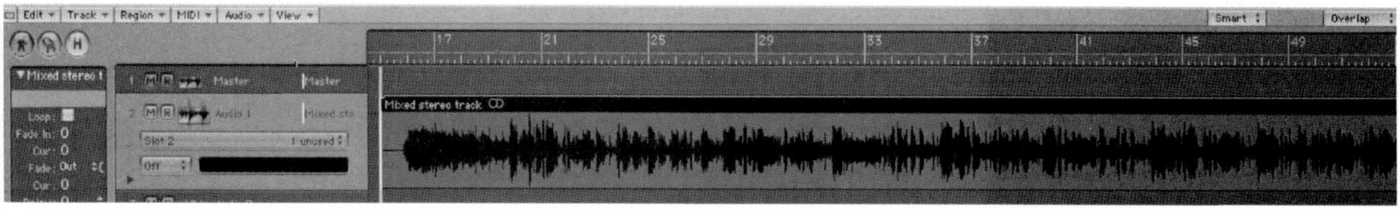

Figure 16.25

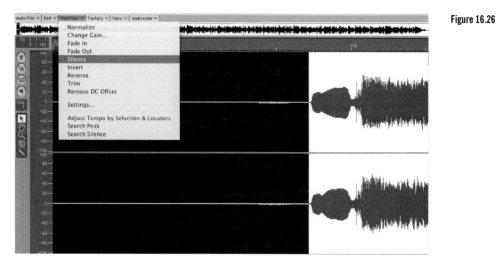

The first thing to do is remove residual noise at the start and end of the song. Double click on the audio region to open the Sample editor.

Remove the noise as described in Chapter 4.

Figure 16.26

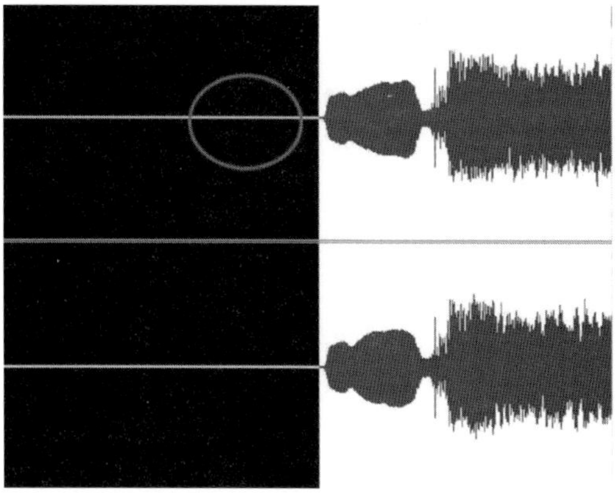

Figure 16.27

Fade out the song if needed as described in Chapter 4.

Figure 16.28

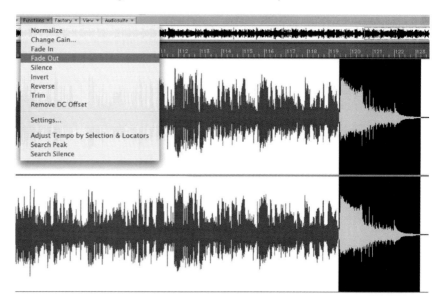

Figure 16.29

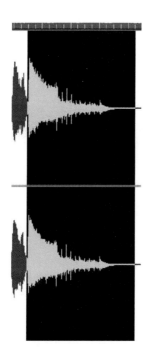

Now we will use plug-ins to process the song. There are two ways to do this in Logic Pro. You can either:

- Use the destructive plug-ins within the Sample editor, if you are using Pro Tools Audiosuite. If you process in this way, the actual audio file will be changed and no further action will be necessary.
- Use the real-time plug-ins and record the output or bounce it down as if it were a mix.

Or use a combination of the two. Process destructively then re-import the file for further treatment. It all depends which particular plug-ins you have available. The following section describes the use of some common uses of the plug-ins and provided by Logic Pro when mastering.

EQ

EQ is covered in more detail in Chapter 6.

Compression

Compression is used to 'level out' an audio signal. For example, if a vocalist sings too quietly in some sections of a song, you could use a compressor to make sure the level of the vocal is consistent throughout. Compressors usually have the following parameters – but there may be others:

Figure 16.30

Threshold

This sets the level at which the compression starts to work. Over this threshold, the compressor reduces the level according to the ratio.

Ratio

Sets the amount of gain reduction. A ratio of 4:1 will reduce the level by 1dB for every 4dB rise above the threshold level. 1:1 would be no compression.

Attack

This sets the rate at which the compressor attenuates the output.

Release

Sets the rate at which the signal returns to normal output when the signal is under the threshold level.

Gain makeup

By its very nature, compression will reduce the overall level of a signal. You can use the gain makeup to bring the level up.

Compressors often have a 'knee' control. If this is set to hard knee, compression starts exactly at the threshold. Soft knee begins gradually a few dB below the threshold.

Limiter

If the threshold is set to 'Infinity' or a high ratio, the signal will never get louder than the threshold. This will 'Limit' the upper level of the audio, hence the name.

Some compression tips

While the effect of the compressor depends upon the input signal, there are some basic rules you can follow. As with many things in music, it pays to experiment. If it sounds good to you – it is good!

• Set a ratio between 2:1 and 10:1 for most signals
• Set a slow attack time if you want more of the original signal to come through.
• Set a fast release time if you want to avoid 'pumping' effects.

Reverb

Info

Use a reverb plug-in on a Buss Audio object and use the sends on individual Audio objects to add reverb. Many sounds can use the same reverb type, such as vocals or drums. This will reduce processor overhead.

Reverb, or reverberation to give it its full name, is probably the most useful effect in modern music production. Reverb plug-ins attempt to simulate the natural reflections that exist in most real rooms. Any of you who sing in the bathroom, will be aware of the effect! Recreating these effects make reverb plug-ins the most processor-hungry of all effects, with the quality of the reverb effect being directly proportional to the amount of computer power the effect uses.

Reverb plug-ins can have many parameters, but the most important are

Reverb time or room size

This determines the amount of reverb. Low values are toilets while high values are caverns.

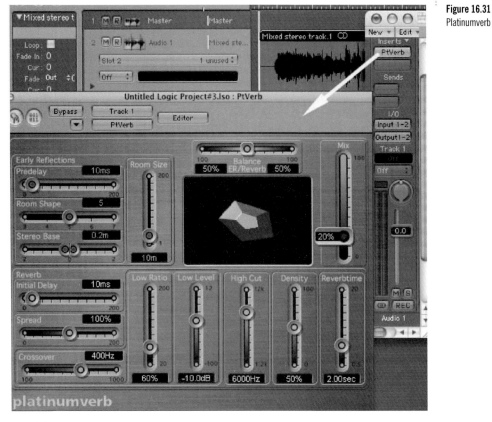

Figure 16.31
Platinumverb

Pre-delay

This determines when the reverb effect starts. A small pre-delay will help the sound 'sit' better with the reverb, almost as if the reverb was part of the sound rather than added to it. If the pre-delay is set too long an audible echo will be heard.

Density

This adjusts the quality of the reverb. Higher density gives a smoother, more complex reverb, but at the expense of processor power.

Mix

Sets the balance of wet (reverb) and dry signal passing through the plug-in.

High Frequency damping or EQ

Natural reverb loses high frequency information compared with the original. Use this control to simulate this effect.

Quality

As stated before, reverb uses a lot of processing power. Occasionally you can use lower quality, and therefore less processor intensive, reverb.

Surround sound

Each Audio object output can be set to output to a Surround sound format. This output mode is used for creating various mixes for multimedia and films in formats such as 5:1, 7:1 and Pro Logic. Stereo has two outputs and requires two amplifier channels and speakers to reproduce. To hear surround sound properly, you'll need the appropriate number of amplifiers and speakers i.e. for 5:1 you need six amplifiers/speakers; three front, two rear and a low frequency woofer.

You'll also need a multiple output sound card to send each channel to a separate surround output. These outputs are set in the Audio> Surround main menu.

Figure 16.32

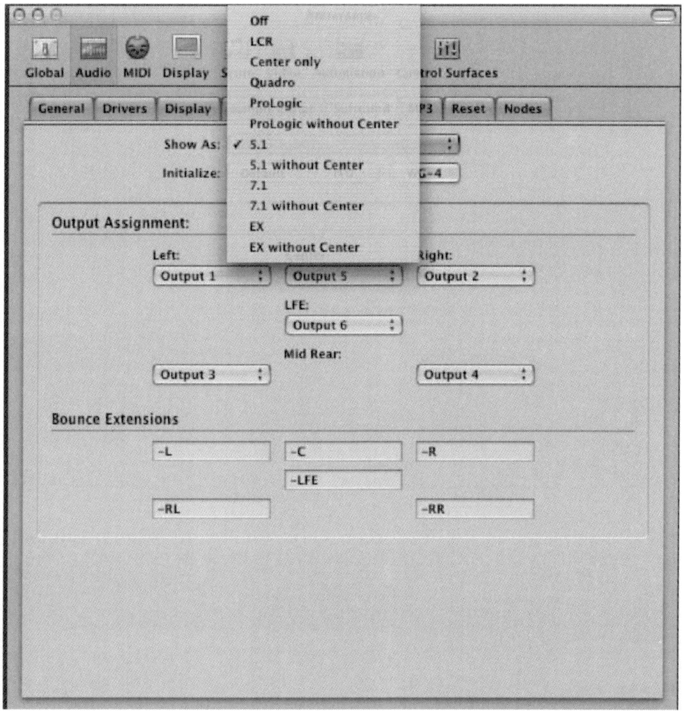

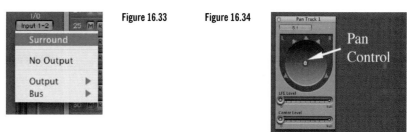

• Select the type of surround from the pop up menu (Figure 16.33) and the outputs you want to send the different channels to.
• Select 'Surround' on the Audio objects that you wish to send to the surround outputs from the pop up menu.
• Now double clicking on the output button opens the surround pan window (Figure 16.34).

Figure 16.33   **Figure 16.34**

- Select the type of surround sound required using the pull down menu (Figure 16.35).
- Drag the blue ball around to pan the audio into the surround space (Figure 16.36).

Figures 16.35 and 16.36

The LFE control sends the 'low frequency effects (or enhancement)' audio to the subwoofer channel. You should insert a low pass filter on this channel and set a cut-off frequency of 120Hz. This will ensure only low frequency information is sent to the sub woofer channel. The Center level control adjusts the center speaker of a 5:1 system.

When you're bouncing Surround sound to disc internally within Logic, you need to set the output to the correct Surround type in the bounce dialog.

Figure 16.37

Other useful information

Step time input

You can input note data in step time in all of Logic Pro's editors. Here's how you do it.

- Create a blank sequence in the Arrange window using the pencil tool. Drag the sequence to the desired length.
- Open the sequence in an Editor window, lets use the Matrix Editor as an example.
- Switch on the IN button (right) in the editor.
- Move the song position line to the beginning of the sequence.
- Press the a key on your MIDI keyboard. Notes will be entered. As you enter

Figure 17.1

each note or chord, the sequencer will move on to the next step by the division (Figure 17.2 (a)) setting. You can change this setting at any time as you add notes.

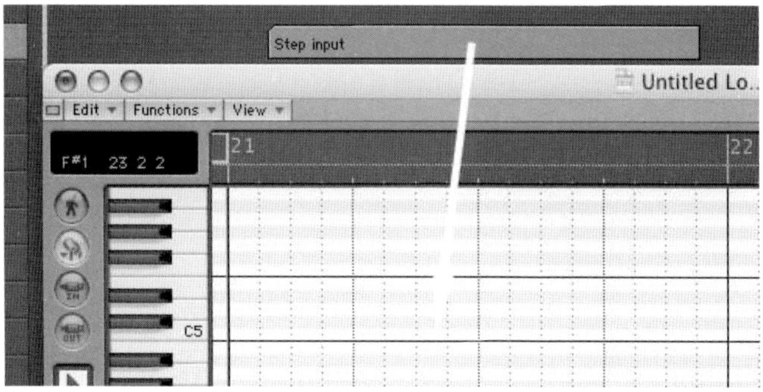

Chords are entered one note after another. When you release the last note, Logic Pro moves on to the next step. Rests are entered with the sustain pedal of your MIDI controller.

There are several computer keyboard keys that have special functions when step editing, which, if they haven't been re-defined, can be used during step input.

Figure 17.2
Various notes have been added using different division settings

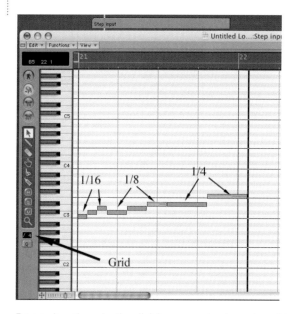

When step editing in the score editor do not use the Default quantize value as the note display would change with every note input.

Remember though, the divisions can also be entered in the transport bar or directly in the editor you are using for step input.

These keys are:

n   jumps to the next bar division. So in 4/4 time, to the next quarter note
m   jumps to the next bar
b   moves back a step and erases the event there
a   sets the division to 1/4
s   sets the division to 1/8
d   sets the division to 1/16
q   sets the division to 1/32
w   sets the division to 1/64
e   the current division value is set to the next highest triplet value. For example from 1/16 to 1/24
e   the current division value is set to the next lowest triplet value. For example from 1/16 to 1/12

These commands will continue adding up these values if the MIDI keyboard key is held down.

The Caps lock keyboard

Pressing the Caps lock key will bring up a small on-screen keyboard (Figure 17.3).

- When this is visible, you can play the computer keyboard as if it was a MIDI keyboard – very useful for Laptop composing.
- Pressing Esc will send an 'All Notes Off message'
- The numeric keys change the octave of the keyboard

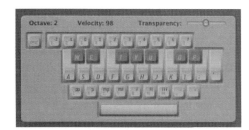

Figure 17.3

- The lower keys change the Volume level and thus MIDI volume value. The lowest volume is to the left, the highest to the right.
- Spacebar is sustain
- You can also make the keyboard more or less transparent.
- You can switch on the Caps lock keyboard and various other parameters from the Logic Pro>Preferences>Global>Caps Lock Keyboard menu item.

Using SysEx to store the patches on your MIDI devices in a Logic Pro song

Another way of using Logic Pro to make sure your MIDI devices have the correct banks of sounds and other parameters for a song is to store a Systems Exclusive (SysEx) dump of their memory and store it in your Logic Pro song. Of course, your devices will have to be capable of sending MIDI Systems Exclusive dumps. It's 'consult your manual' time again! Here's how you do it:

To store the dump

Connect the MIDI out of your MIDI device to the MIDI in on your computer. Tip: Use a Multi IN MIDI interface or MIDI patchbay to make these connections easier.

Move the song position line well before the song is to begin. SysEx data demands a lot of bandwidth and if you try and send it when the song is playing, timing will suffer.

On your MIDI device, select the mode allowing you to 'bulk dump' the contents of its memory. Some devices allow you send the whole memory, patches only, effects only and so on. Choose the mode you want. Don't press send yet!

Select an Instrument on the Arrange page. SysEx has no regard for MIDI channel, so it doesn't matter which instrument you select, only that it is connected to the same MIDI OUT as the device you are saving the SysEx from. However, it may be best to use the same instrument name just for clarity.

Put Logic Pro into Record and let the sequencer start. Press Send on your MIDI device. When the dump is complete, press Stop. A region is created. Rename the region to something useful.

To send the dump back to your MIDI device

Move the song position line to the beginning of the region containing the SysEx data. Set your MIDI device to receive SysEx dumps if it needs that. On some devices you will have to switch off memory protect. Press Play on Logic Pro. The sequencer may 'hiccup' as it sends out the data – this is normal! Again, the MIDI channel the region sends out on is irrelevant. The Sysex code itself contains the information regarding the dump and the MIDI device it came from. Your MIDI device will now contain the original data.

In this fashion, you could store the patches and other information in all your MIDI devices and pump the data back into each device at the beginning of each song.

Import/export

Logic Pro can import and export many different file formats.

MIDI files

OMF import/export

OMF (Open Media Framework) is a file import and export option to enable you to transfer data between other programs. The most notable example is Digidesign's Pro Tools. OMF files can be imported using the File>Import OMF/Open TL File to song ...

You can export to an OMF file using the File>Export>OMF export menu item. This opens a window containing several OMF export commands. The various options are there to enable the OMF files to be compatible with both Logic and the OMF capable program.

Open TL Import/export

Open TL is a file format usually used to transfer data between various Tascam hard disk recorders. It's a simple import and export protocol and is accessed through the File main menu item.

AAF

This is Apple's low-loss compression format used in iTunes and the iPod.

XML

This format allows you to exchange Logic songs with Apple's Final Cut Pro video editing software.

SysEx

Logic can Import standard SysEx files.

Logic help

There is help system available from your computer's help menu. Amongst other things, this has detailed information on Logic's built in plug-ins and synthesisers. These are standard PDF files.

Recycle file import

Logic can import files generated from Propellerhead's 'ReCycle' software. They can also be imported into Emagic's EXS24 sampler. You import these files in the same way as normal audio files. You can import various different ReCycle formats. If Logic's tempo isn't compatible with the imported ReCycle files, a window will open where you can either leave the ReCycle file tempo as it is, crossfade the files to fit, or place the ReCycle regions on individual Logic Pro tracks.

You can also copy and paste ReCycle audio files via the clipboard between ReCycle and Logic if you have both open at the same time.

Nodes (distributed processing)

As stated many times in the book, Logic Pro requires a lot of CPU power when using Virtual Instruments and effects plug-ins. Even a modern powerful computer, such as the Power Mac G5 may not be enough for some applications. You can offload some of the processing power, with some limitations, to another Macintosh running OSX.

Limitations of Logic nodes

- You can only distribute Logic Instruments and plug-ins except the EXS24 and Ultrabeat. You cannot offload processing if the track has a third-party plug-in instanced.
- You can only distribute the processing of tracks and not Auxes or Busses.

The computer that will do the extra processing is called the 'node. The computer you are actually working on is called the 'host'. Here's how you set up distributed processing.

- Connect the two computers via an Ethernet cable.
- Copy the Logic node program from the installation DVD to the Applications folder of the node computer
- Run the node program. The node computer doesn't need to be running Logic.
- In Logic Pro on the host computer, make sure the Track node buttons are visible from the View menu.
- Open the Logic Pro>Preferences>Audio>Node pane.
- You should see the node computer displayed here. Check the Enable Logic Nodes box. Make sure the node you wish to use is checked (Figure 17.4).

Info

Though Apple recommends you use a powerful computer with Gigabit Ethernet as the node, you can use less powerful computers. However, you may not get much in the way of performance.

Figure 17.4

- Click on the Track's node button (Figure 17.5).

Figure 17.5

- This will offload that tracks processing to the node. Click again to disable node processing. If you hold down the Apple key while clicking, all tracks will be offloaded to the node, if this is possible (Figure 17.6).

Figure 17.6

- When the node button glows (Figure 17.7), the processing on that track is offloaded onto the node.

Figure 17.7

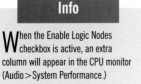

> **Info**
>
> When the Enable Logic Nodes checkbox is active, an extra column will appear in the CPU monitor (Audio > System Performance.)

> **Info**
>
> If you drag the Logic node program into the startup items section of your account in the Accounts pane of the System Preferences, you can get the node to automatically run when you boot the Mac. As you don't need a screen or mouse, this is ideal if the node is only used for distributed processing.

Latencies incurred by the offline processing are automatically compensated for in Logic. See Appendix 2 for more on Latency.

AU (Audio Unit) validation

When you first run Logic, it checks that any third party AU plug-ins pass the stringent AU validation criteria set out by Apple. If they all pass, Logic will boot normally. However, if they fail, Logic will disable the AU plug-ins. If this happens, you should check with the plug-in company whether there is a 'Logic 7 or later' version and install that.

You can, however, allow failed plug-ins to be used in Logic. Be aware though that you do this at your own risk; unstable plug-ins can cause Logic to crash.

Enabling plug-ins that has failed the AU validation.

Start the Logic AU Manager from the Logic Pro>Start Logic AU Manager menu item.

- Logic will quit and the AU manager loads.
- Enable failed AU plug-ins by clicking on the Use check box (Figure 17.8).
- When you have enabled all the plug-ins you want, click on OK. Logic will reload and the new AU plug-ins will be available in the usual way.

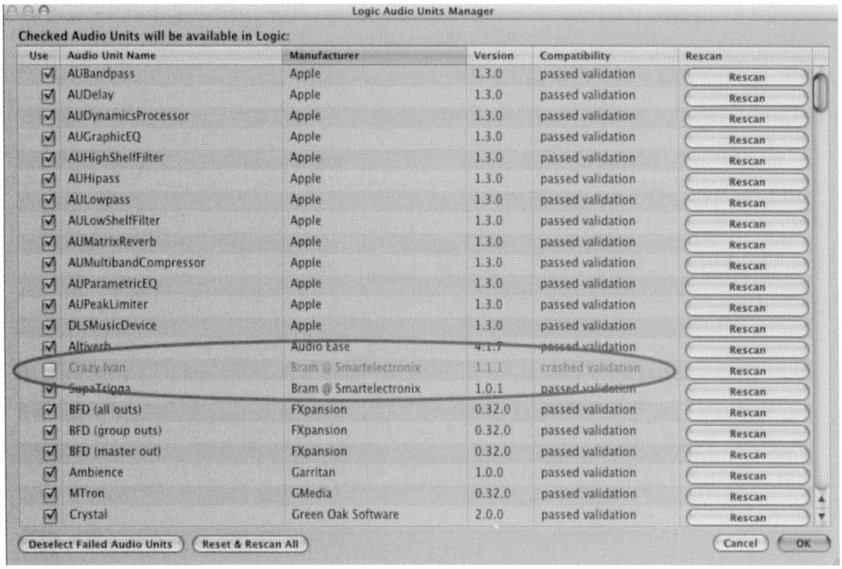

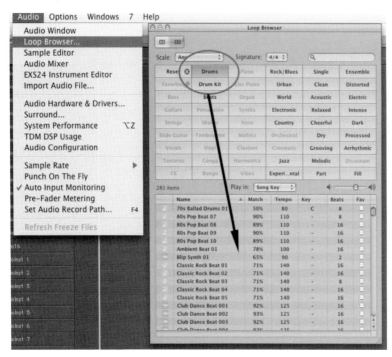

Figure 17.8

Apple loops

These are specialized audio files that can easily be tempo matched to a song. Apple loops can also contain information about their content, making them searchable. Logic ships with many Apple loops and you can make your own using the supplied Apple loop utility. It's easier to see how Apple loops fit into the scheme of things within Logic by an example.

Open the Loops browser from the Audio>Apple loops menu item.

Figure 17.9

Info

You can store Apple loops anywhere you like and load them into Logic by dragging to the Arrange page or using the Audio>Import audio file menu item. But if you want them to appear in the browser you'll need to place them in /Library/Application Support/GarageBand

If you have any Apple loops installed in the default location,, /Library/Application Support/GarageBand , you'll see them displayed here.

- To audition an Apple loop click on it.
- To add an Apple loop to a song, drag it to the Arrange page.

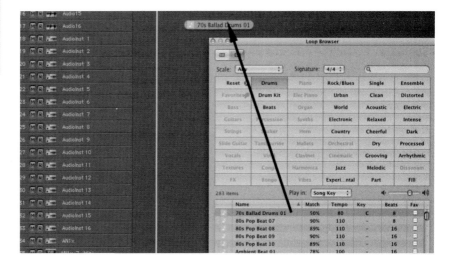

Figure 17.10

- Now change the tempo in Logic. You'll hear that the audio in the Apple loops changes tempo too.

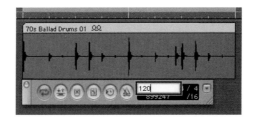

Figure 17.11

- Apple loops have Tags associated with them. These tags provide information about the audio in the Apple loop, so you can use the search window in the browser and the scale and signature information to find the loops you need.

Figure 17.12

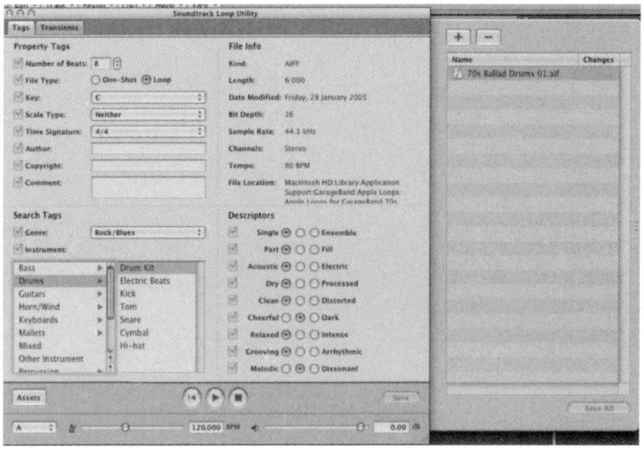

The Apple loops Utility

This is a separate program stored in the Applications folder. Figure 17.12 has the drum Apple Loop shown above, loaded. Let's create an apple loop from a 4 bar recording of a drum kit. The original tempo is 130 bpm.

First load in the audio file. Click on the + in the file management (Assets) window. If it's not visible, click on the Assets button at the bottom left of the Apple Loops utility.

Figure 17.13

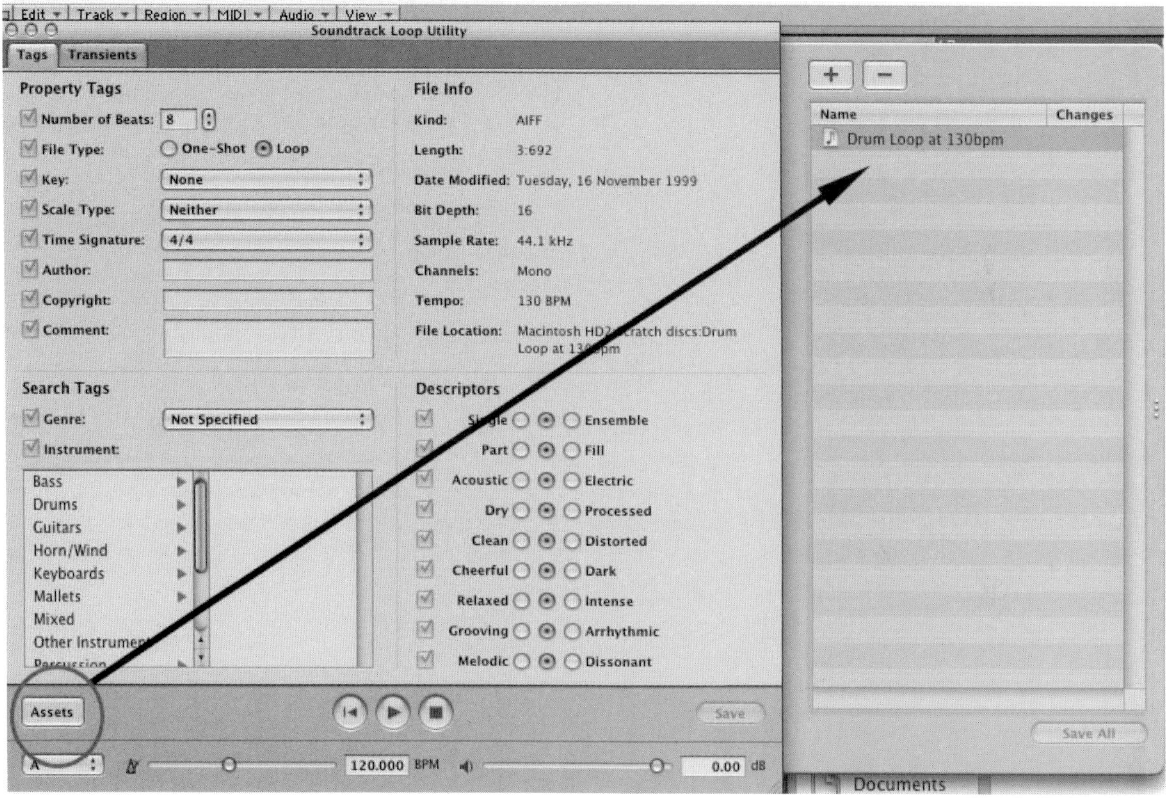

Once the file is loaded, you can fill in the Tag fields. In this example we might have:

Number of beats =16
File type = loop
Key = none (as it's a percussion loop)
Scale=none (as it's a percussion loop)
Time signature =4/4
And so on.

The Transients pane

In a percussion-based audio file, you may not know the tempo of the file. The transients pane can be used to determine tempo from the 'beats' in the file.

Figure 17.14

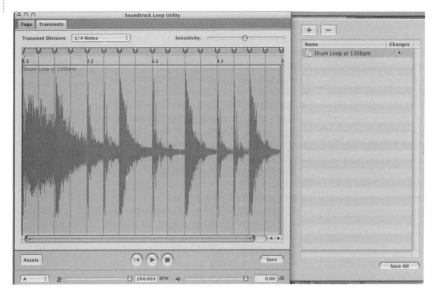

You can fine tune the Apple loops utility's beat detection using the following parameters.

Transient division – a high beat value (1/8th notes or less) will mean fewer transients being detected. This is useful for slow tempo recordings. A low beat value (1/6th notes or higher) will mean more transients being detected. This is useful for faster tempo recordings.

Sensitivity slider – this sets the amplitude or volume that the software will detect as being a transient. Low sensitivity means less transients being detected – i.e. only loud beats pass though.

Transients detected – can be edited directly in the Transients pane. You can also add new transient information if the automatic system isn't suitable (for non- percussive audio files)

Adding a transient – click in the area below the Transient division pull down menu.

Figure 17.15
Fade in dialogue

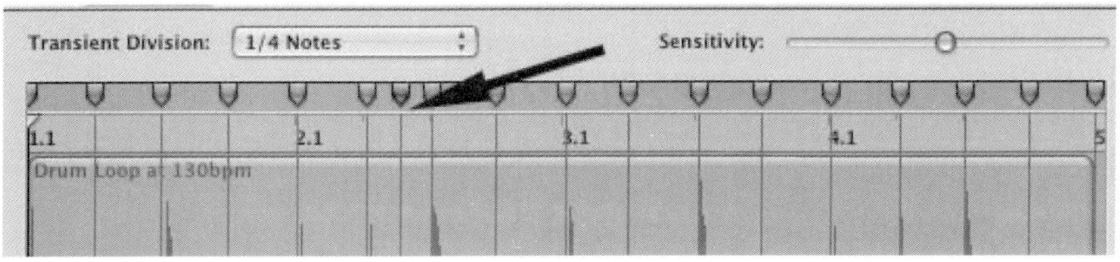

Moving a transient – drag the marker in the below the Transient division pull down menu.

Deleting a transient – drag the marker out of the area below the Transient division pull down menu, or select it and press Delete.

You can play back, and check out the effects of tempo changes of a created Apple loop.

Saving an Apple loop

Once you have created your loop, save it using the program's 'Save' button. Remember to save in the ,/library/Application Support/GarageBand directory if you want to audition the loop in the Apple loop browser.

Controller assignments

If you have a hardware controller that can send out data such as MIDI controllers from the controls, you can use these to control various parameters in Logic. These could be anything from the Modulation, Pitch bend wheels and Expression pedals on your synthesizer to a dedicated hardware box with lots of knobs, faders and switches. Some hardware controllers have 'pre-set' assignments within Logic.

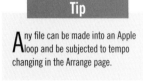

Tip

You can also create Apple loops from audio regions in a song by selecting the region and opening the Apple loop utility with the Audio > Open in Apple loops utility menu item.

Tip

Any file can be made into an Apple loop and be subjected to tempo changing in the Arrange page.

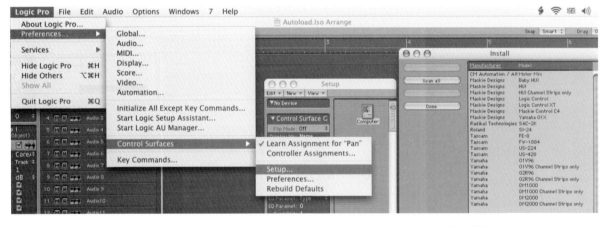

Figure 17.16

However, you can easily allow your hardware controller control of any Logic on-screen parameter manually. You could, for example, use knobs on a synthesizer that send MIDI controllers to adjust parameters on the ES-1 Virtual instrument.

Here's how to do it.

Figure 17.17

- Choose menu item 'Logic Pro > Preferences > Control Surfaces > Controller Assignments'.
- Click Learn Mode.
- Move the on-screen knob you want to control – pan knob on a Channel strip, for example.
- Move the physical knob or slider you want to use on your hardware controller.
- Repeat steps 3 and 4 as necessary.

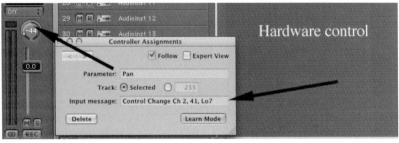

Exporting tracks and regions as Audio files

You may want to convert whole tracks of audio or Virtual instruments, or regions on a track to audio files for re-importing into Logic. Us the File>Export menu to do this. You can then drag the exported files back into Logic.

Appendix 1
Modifying the Setup Assistant song using the Environment

Open the Environment from the Windows>Environment menu item. When you first open the Environment it will look something the following Figure A1.1.

Those little icons are called 'objects' and represent your MIDI devices; MIDI output ports and various MIDI data modifiers. Logic Pro also will set up an Environment layer containing Audio tracks. You may wish to modify various aspects of the Environment. As stated before, Logic Pro is a flexible program. This means that there are often many ways to achieve the same ends. Here, we'll concentrate on getting the program to do what you want, rather than to show you dozens of ways of doing it. The information detailed below isn't the whole truth, just enough of it to get you up and running.

MIDI data flow through Logic Pro

Figure A1.2 shows how MIDI data flows through Logic Pro.

Figure A1.2

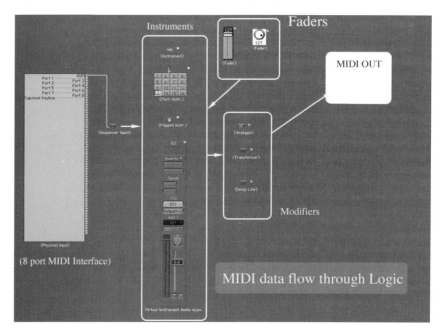

We'll use this model, as far as is possible, when we modify the Environment in Logic Pro. As you can see it's a fairly 'Logical' path! The data from your MIDI controller (keyboard, wind controller, percussion etc.) passes into Logic Pro through the MIDI interface and then through the Environment objects. The MIDI data is recorded and edited in the Arrange page or the editor windows.

MIDI data is passed in via the physical input object to the sequencer input object, where it is recorded into Logic Pro. These two objects are cabled together but you don't need to cable them to anything else – the connection to the rest of Logic Pro is a 'hidden' one. The data is then passed through an Instrument object, where selection of the patches on your MIDI devices is done, or to a Virtual instrument Audio object, where you instance Virtual instruments. Data from the Instrument is passed through modifier objects, if desired, and then out of the MIDI ports, where your synthesisers and other MIDI devices will play the sounds or respond to the MIDI controller data and so on. You can see from this data path that all the modification of MIDI data is done after the sequencer records it. All processing is non-destructive and performed in real time.

Figure A1.3 shows a typical set-up like the one you may have in your studio. We have a MIDI keyboard connected to the MIDI interface for entering note data. This is also a multi-timbral synthesiser, able to play 16 different sounds at the same time on different MIDI channels. Make sure this instrument is in 'multi mode'.

Connected to the MIDI OUT of your MIDI interface is a drum module (say an Alesis D4) and a mono timbral synthesiser (say a Roland D50), which can only play one sound at a time on one MIDI channel. We're assuming the MIDI interface just has a single MIDI in and OUT.

Tip

Remember to switch the keyboard you are using to enter MIDI data to 'Local Off' if you are also going to use it as a sound module. Otherwise you'll get double notes playing.

Figure A1.3

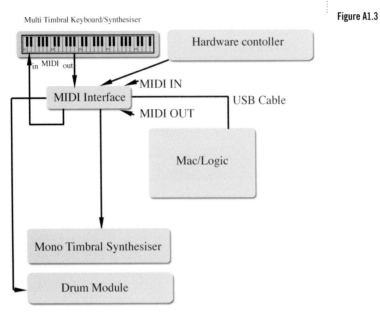

Multi Timbral Keyboard/Synthesiser

Figure A1.4

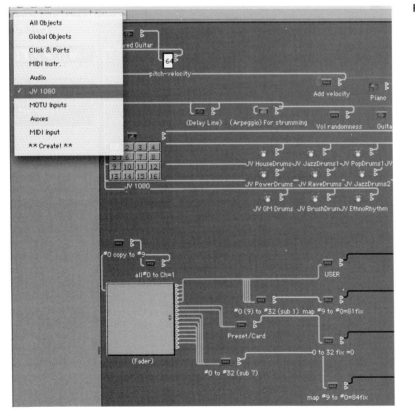

- The Kurzweill 2000 receives on MIDI channels 1, 2, 3, 4, 5, 6, 8, 9, 11, 12, 13, 14, 15 and 16
- The Roland D50 receives on channel 7
- The Alesis D4 receives on channel 10

Remember a single MIDI interface can only transmit on 16 channels. So how do we go about creating a basic Environment for this set-up? Open a Logic Pro Environment window, if one isn't already open. Click the 'link' icon (see left) so it is grey.

Figure A1.5

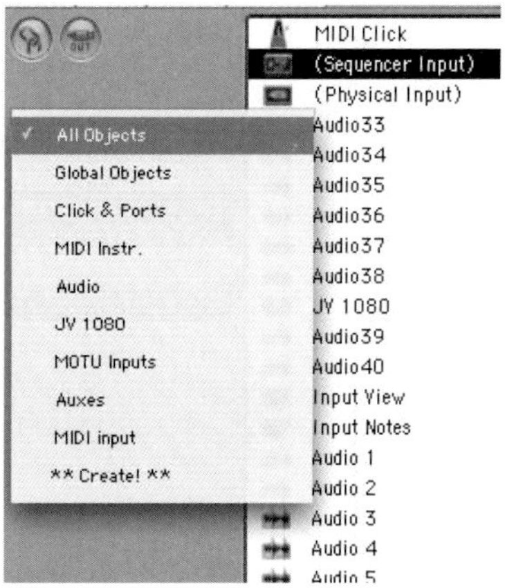

The Environment window consists of several 'layers' like pages in a book. You can flick through these layers by holding and clicking on the 'MIDI instr' text in the figure below left. This will produce the pop up menu shown below right.

Now go to the 'All Objects' layer. If it isn't there, switch it on from the Logic Pro> Preferences> Display> Other menu item. When an object is selected, the Parameter box to the left of the window will show parameters relating to that object. If there isn't one, switch it on from the View>Parameters menu item (Figure A1.5).

Click on each object in turn. If the box next to the Icon in the Parameter box has a cross in it, remove it. If you can't see the Icon box, click on the little arrow next to the name of the object to drop-down the box and make it visible. If you can't see the Parameter box at all, turn it on from View>Preferences menu item (Figure A1.6).

Next create a layer by selecting ** Create ** from the pop up menu. Rename the Layer by double clicking on the '(unnamed)' text. Call it 'Synths'. You can now create objects that represent your synthesisers on this empty layer (Figure A1.7).

Figure A1.6 (left)

Figure A1.7 (right

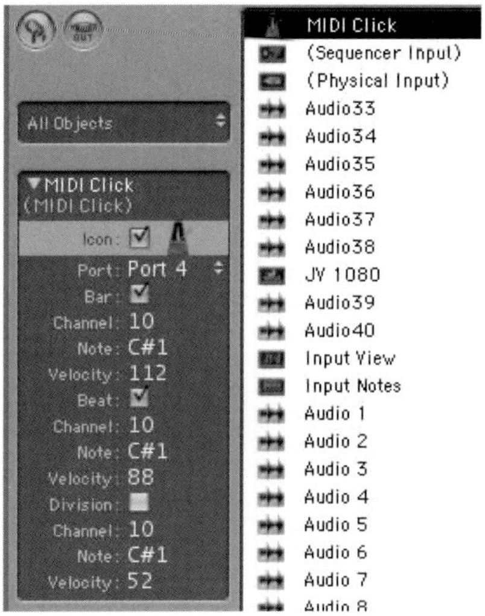

Click on 'unnamed'

Rename it 'synths'

Multi-timbral synthesiser set-up

From the New menu, create a multi-instrument and drag it to the top left of the Environment window. Make sure there is not a tick in the box next to Icon in the Parameter box for this object.

Rename the object to the real name of your MIDI device by highlighting it and double clicking on the name in the Parameter box – 'Multi Instr.'.

Tip

A multi-timbral synthesizer is one that can play back many different sounds on 16 or more different MIDI channels.

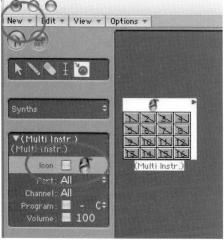

Figure A1.8

Now select the port the MIDI device is connected to using the pull down menu on the Parameter list.

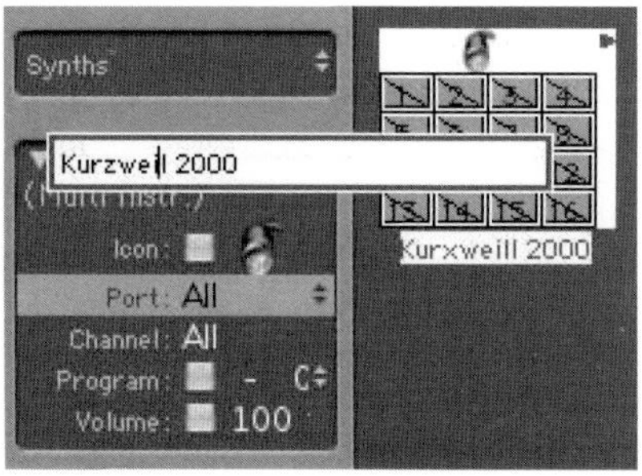

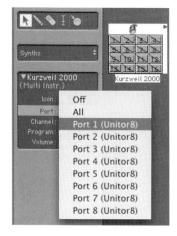

Figure A1.9 (left)

Figure A1.10 (right)

Click on the '1' on the Multi instrument so it is uncrossed and highlighted. This selects the sub-instrument that will use MIDI channel 1 on your synthesiser. Click on the box next to Program, so the instrument will receive program changes. Make sure the box next to Icon is crossed too. Notice that the Parameter box changes too. It now displays the Parameters for the sub-channel rather than the whole multi-instrument object.

Figure A1.11

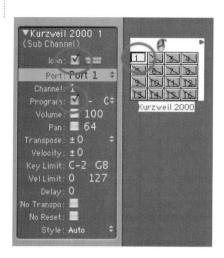

Now open an Arrange page. You can select the Kurzweil 2000 MIDI channel '1' from the pull down menu in the Instrument Column. Notice that the Environment layers are shown here. Select 'Kurzweil 2000 1 Grand Piano' from the 'Synths' layer. Play a note on your MIDI keyboard. You should hear sound out of your synthesiser. It probably won't be Grand Piano though!

Figure A1.12

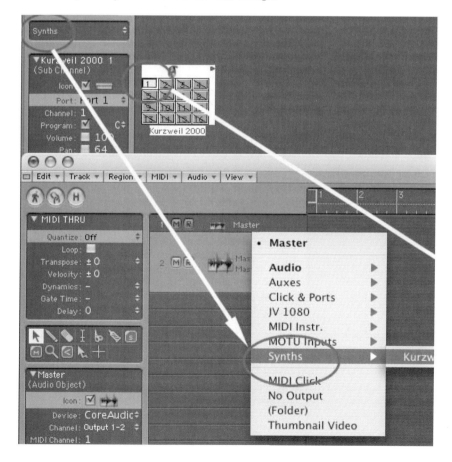

If you don't hear a sound, check the following:

- Make sure all your MIDI cables are connected correctly and your synthesizer is connected to an amplifier or headphones.
- When you press your MIDI keyboard, do you see values appearing in the IN and OUT boxes on the transport bar (Figure A1.13)?
- If there are no IN values, check the connections between the MIDI OUT and MIDI IN on your computer. If there are no OUT values make sure you have set the correct port in the Multi-instrument and the MIDI cables.

  If all has gone well, you have now made the first basic connection. Well done!

Figure A1.13

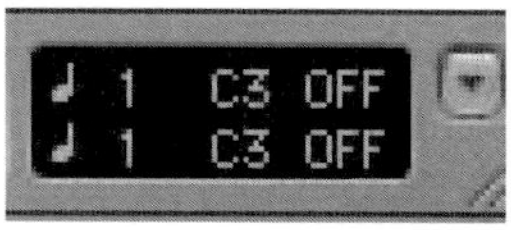

Now, click on the '2' on the Multi instrument so it is uncrossed and highlighted.

Click on the box next to Program, so the instrument will receive program changes. Make sure the box next to Icon is crossed too.

Figure A1.14

Repeat this for all 16 MIDI channels, leaving out channels 7 and 10. These two channels will be used for the other two MIDI instruments we have in our basic set-up. The Pull down menu on the Arrange page should now look something like this:

Figure A1.15

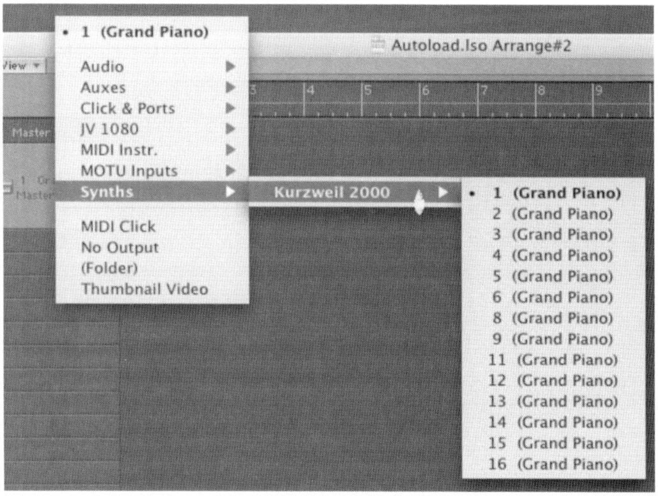

Of course all the sounds on the Kurzweil 2000 aren't Grand Pianos! Fortunately, Logic Pro provides a way to name all the patches residing in your synthesiser. You can then select these by name, rather than just a choosing a patch number. Who can remember that patch 100 on bank 4 is a 'Snort Horn' anyhow? Double click on the top of the Multi Instrument. This will open a patch name box (Figure A1.16).

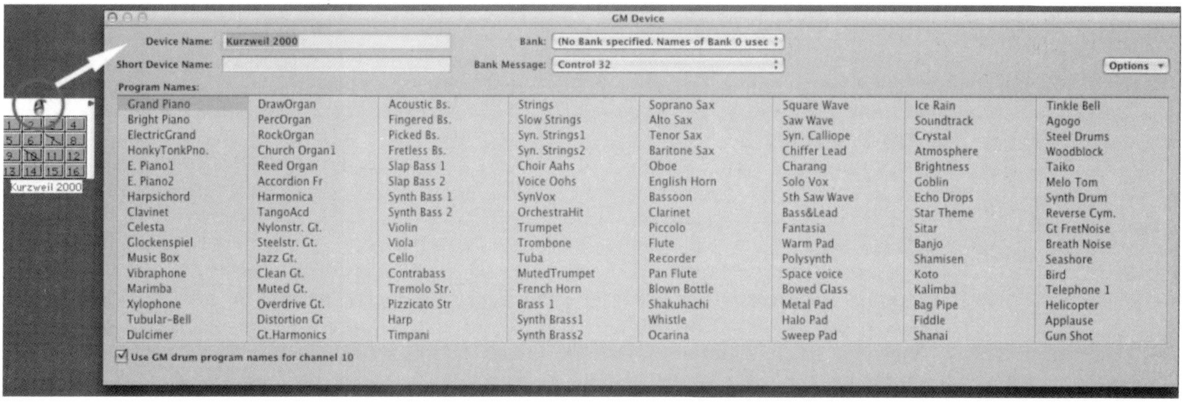

Figure A1.16

Of course these default names are unlikely to be the ones on your synthesiser, so you'll have to rename them appropriately.

Figure A1.17

Select bank 0 from the pull down menu.

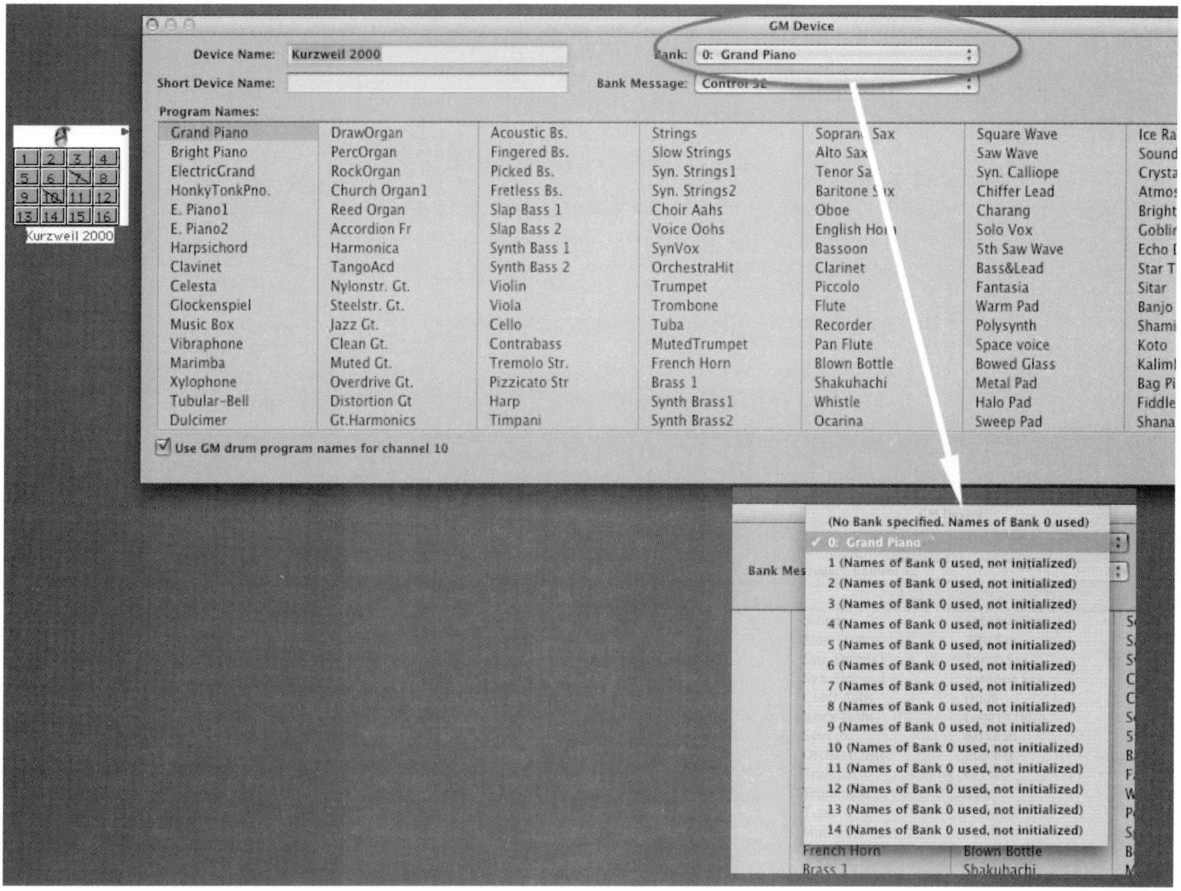

Your synth may need special bank change parameters. You'll need to look in the manual of your MIDI device, and select the appropriate Bank Message from the menu.. Now delete all the names in the window by choosing 'Cut all names' from the pull down menu.

Now you can type in the names of the patches on your synthesiser. Double click on each of the boxes in turn and type in the correct name of the patch. When you have finished typing in all the names in a bank, change to the next bank. Logic Pro will initialize it for you, and then you can continue to enter patch names.

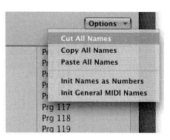

Figure A1.18 (above)

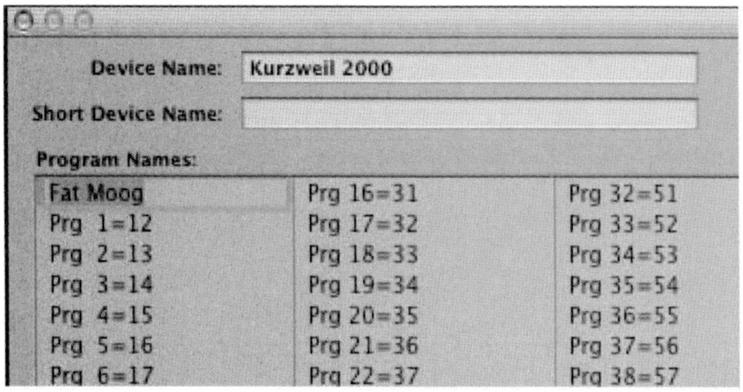

Figure A1.19 (left)

As you can imagine, it can take quite a while to type in patch names on a synthesiser that has 16 banks of 128 sounds! Luckily you can copy the patch names from either a patch editor or another Logic Pro song that has the names of the patches for your synth already entered – by someone else who obviously has too much time on their hands! You can find a lot of Logic Pro songs containing this sort of thing on the Internet. See Appendix 7 for more details.

Loading standard Logic Pro set-ups

Once you have downloaded the your required Environment with the MIDI devices you need , you can load in these and paste the names into your Autoload Environment. Here's how you do it. These 'Environments' are actually Logic Pro songs that can be loaded directly into the program.

From Logic Pro, open the required Environment from the File>Open menu item. When Logic Pro asks you if you want to 'Close current songs', select 'Don't Close'. Load the required 'Environment'. (Note: Logic Pro can load many songs at the same time and copy data between them).

You need to find the Multi-instrument that corresponds to your hardware.

Figure A1.20

Double click on the top of the required Multi Instrument to bring up the patch name box

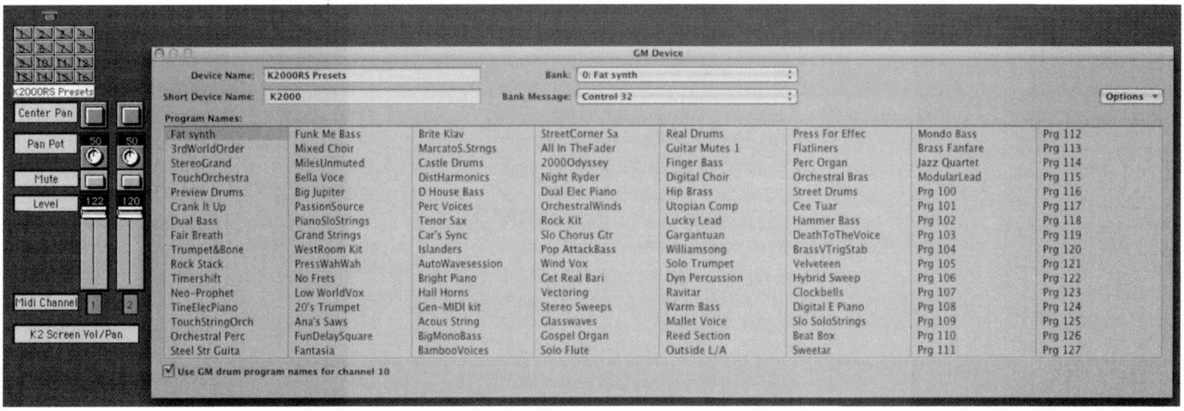

Figure A1.21

Copy all the patch names by selecting 'Copy all names'.

Figure A1.22

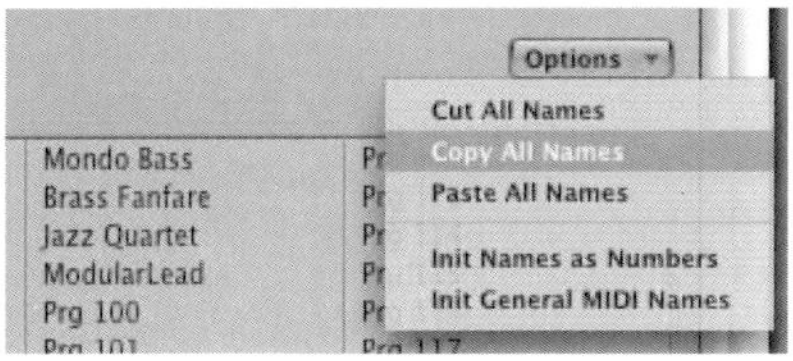

From the Windows menu bring the Autoload song to the front.

Figure A1.23

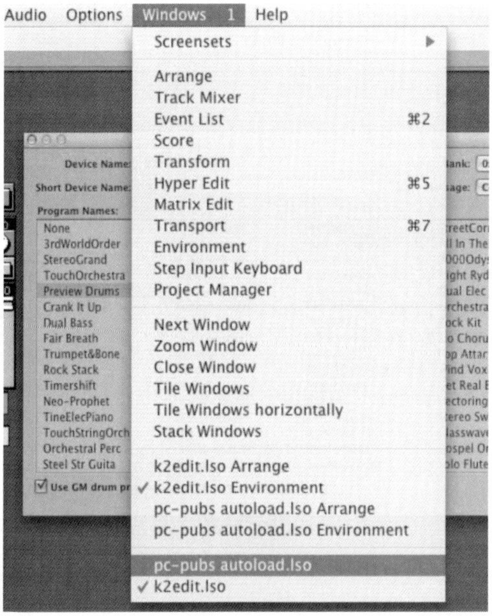

Select the correct bank from the Bank: Pull down menu. Double click at the top of the Kurzweil 2000 Multi Instrument to bring up the patch name box. Paste all the names into the box using 'Paste all names'.

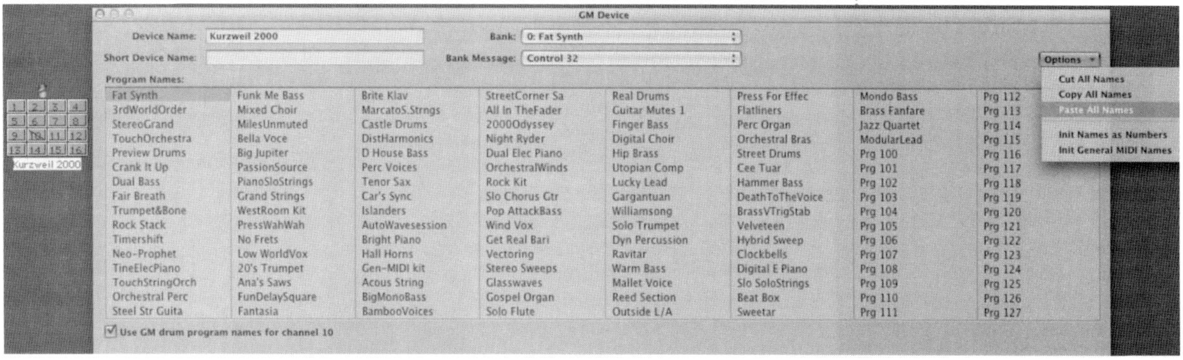
GM Device
Device Name: Kurzweil 2000
Short Device Name:
Bank: 0: Fat Synth
Bank Message: Control 32
Options
Cut All Names
Copy All Names
Paste All Names
Init Names as Numbers
Init General MIDI Names
Program Names:
Kurzweil 2000
Fat Synth
3rdWorldOrder
StereoGrand
TouchOrchestra
Preview Drums
Crank It Up
Dual Bass
Fair Breath
Trumpet&Bone
Rock Stack
Timershift
Neo-Prophet
TineElecPiano
TouchStringOrch
Orchestral Perc
Steel Str Guita
Funk Me Bass
Mixed Choir
MilesUnmuted
Bella Voce
Big Jupiter
PassionSource
PianoSloStrings
Grand Strings
WestRoom Kit
PressWahWah
No Frets
Low WorldVox
20's Trumpet
Ana's Saws
FunDelaySquare
Fantasia
Brite Klav
MarcatoS.Strngs
Castle Drums
DistHarmonics
D House Bass
Perc Voices
Tenor Sax
Car's Sync
Islanders
AutoWavesession
Bright Piano
Hall Horns
Gen-MIDI kit
Acous String
BigMonoBass
BambooVoices
StreetCorner Sa
All In TheFader
2000Odyssey
Night Ryder
Dual Elec Piano
OrchestralWinds
Rock Kit
Slo Chorus Gtr
Pop AttackBass
Wind Vox
Get Real Bari
Vectoring
Stereo Sweeps
Glasswaves
Gospel Organ
Solo Flute
Real Drums
Guitar Mutes 1
Finger Bass
Digital Choir
Hip Brass
Utopian Comp
Lucky Lead
Gargantuan
Williamsong
Solo Trumpet
Dyn Percussion
Ravitar
Warm Bass
Mallet Voice
Reed Section
Outside L/A
Press For Effec
Flatliners
Perc Organ
Orchestral Bras
Street Drums
Cee Tuar
Hammer Bass
DeathToTheVoice
BrassVTrigStab
Velveteen
Hybrid Sweep
Clockbells
Digital E Piano
Slo SoloStrings
Beat Box
Sweetar
Mondo Bass
Brass Fanfare
Jazz Quartet
ModularLead
Prg 100
Prg 101
Prg 102
Prg 103
Prg 104
Prg 105
Prg 106
Prg 107
Prg 108
Prg 109
Prg 110
Prg 111
Prg 112
Prg 113
Prg 114
Prg 115
Prg 116
Prg 117
Prg 118
Prg 119
Prg 120
Prg 121
Prg 122
Prg 123
Prg 124
Prg 125
Prg 126
Prg 127
Use GM drum program names for channel 10

Figure A1.24

There you have it! Better than typing in banks of 128 names, I'm sure you'll agree. Repeat this with the other banks on your syntheiser.

Save the song if you haven't recently using the File>Save menu item. You can now play the sounds on this synthesiser. On the Arrange page, select the instrument and channel you want to use.

Tip

You don't have to copy and paste from another Logic Pro song. You could paste the names from a patch editing program, such as Apple's SoundDiver or indeed from a text editor.

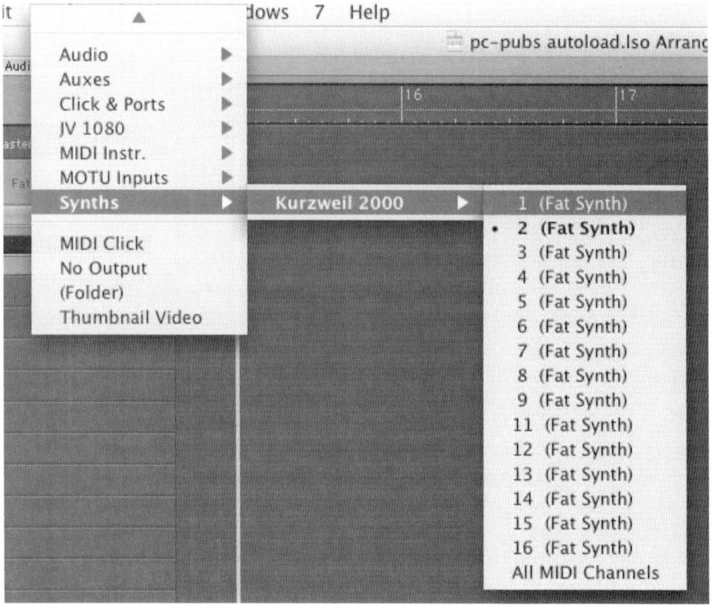
dows 7 Help
pc-pubs autoload.lso Arranç
Audio
Auxes
Click & Ports
JV 1080
MIDI Instr.
MOTU Inputs
Synths
Kurzweil 2000
MIDI Click
No Output
(Folder)
Thumbnail Video
1 (Fat Synth)
2 (Fat Synth)
3 (Fat Synth)
4 (Fat Synth)
5 (Fat Synth)
6 (Fat Synth)
7 (Fat Synth)
8 (Fat Synth)
9 (Fat Synth)
11 (Fat Synth)
12 (Fat Synth)
13 (Fat Synth)
14 (Fat Synth)
15 (Fat Synth)
16 (Fat Synth)
All MIDI Channels

Figure A1.25

On the Arrange page, click at the top right of the Parameter box (in this case, on the '2000' to the right of the downward arrow) (Figure A1.26).

From the patch change box choose the sound you want. Use the bank change pull down menu to change banks. Close the patch change box and you will see the patch name in the Instrument column of the Arrange page (Figure A1.27).

Playing the MIDI keyboard should now play the correct sound. No more trying to remember which patch number and bank number relates to which sound on your synthesizer!

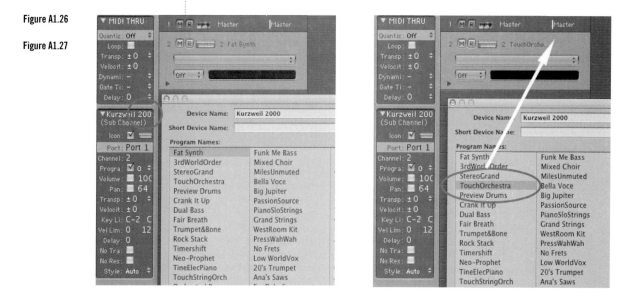

You can select all the instruments on the remaining MIDI channels in the same fashion. Remember to leave out 7 and 10 for the other two synthesizers though!

Mono timbral instrument set up

Now let's set up the mono timbral instrument (Roland D50). This synthesiser can only play one sound at a time and it may seem, at first glance, sensible to use an Instrument object rather than a Multi instrument. However, you cannot assign patch names to an Instrument object, so it's more sensible to use a Multi instrument object and only switch on one of its MIDI channels. Here is how you do it. It's similar to the previous Multi Instrument object.

Click on the Environment windows' title bar to highlight it. Select the 'Synths' layer if it isn't already selected.

Figure A1.28

- From the New menu select Multi Instrument.
- Move it to a convenient position.
- Rename it by clicking on its name in the Parameter box.
- Make sure the box next to the icon in the Parameter box is not checked.
- Select the Port the D50 is connected to from the Port: pull down menu in the Parameter box.
- Click on '7' on the Multi instrument.
- Make sure there is a tick in the icon and Program boxes (Figure A1.28).
- Click and hold on the Instrument column in the Arrange page. You should now see the new Instrument in the list (Figure A1.29).

You can select this instrument and play it just like the Kurzweil. Now you can type in, or cut and paste patch names and select them from the Arrange page, as described for the Multi timbral instrument.

Figure A1.29

Drum module – the Mapped Instrument

This section applies also to a drum machine or drum sound patch on Multi timbral instrument.

Drum and percussion voices are often played on an instrument that only responds to one MIDI channel but every key plays a separate drum sound. Of course, you could use a normal Multi instrument to play these, but there are advantages in using a Mapped instrument. This object allows you to name each key separately, so you don't have to remember that the 'Quacking bongo' is on the G key in the second octave on your keyboard.

The Mapped instruments' other advantages are:

- When editing, the names of each key will appear in the List and matrix editors, rather than just the notes.
- You can set up a kind of Drum edit page in the Hyper Edit window (See Chapter 10).
- It ignores any transpose parameters, so you won't get your bass drum played by a tamborine!

How to set up a Mapped instrument

In the Environment window select the New>Mapped Instrument menu item. A window will open. Close it. Move the Mapped instrument to a convenient place.

In our example, the Mapped instrument would control the Alesis D4 drum module which is set to respond to MIDI channel 10, but it could just as easily be a drum machine or sound on a Multi timbral synth.

Highlight the mapped instrument and change the MIDI channel to 10 in the Cha field in the Parameter box. While it's Highlighted, rename it, make sure there is a cross in the box next to the Icon in the Parameter box and make sure you can see the cables from the View>Cables menu item. Set the Port: to OFF – this mapped instrument will only be used to control the Alesis D4 instrument, which already has its port set.

Cable the Mapped instrument to the Alesis d4 Multi instrument by dragging the cable from the little arrow at the top right.

Figure A1.30

Figure A1.31

Figure A1.32

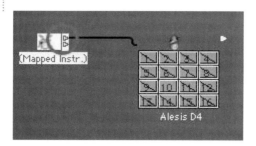

Rename the Mapped instrument to something useful – 'Alesis D4 Mapped Instrument'

Figure A1.33

If you look in the instrument menu on the track column in the Arrange page you will see the Mapped instrument. Select it and check it plays your drum sounds.

Figure A1.34

If you want the Mapped instrument to play a Virtual plug-in (such as Ultrabeat or the EXS24 sampler, cable the Mapped instrument to the Audio object the Virtual instrument is on. Remove the channel port setting when asked by Logic (Figure A1.35).

Double click on the Mapped instrument to open the window again (Figure A1.36).

Figure A1.35

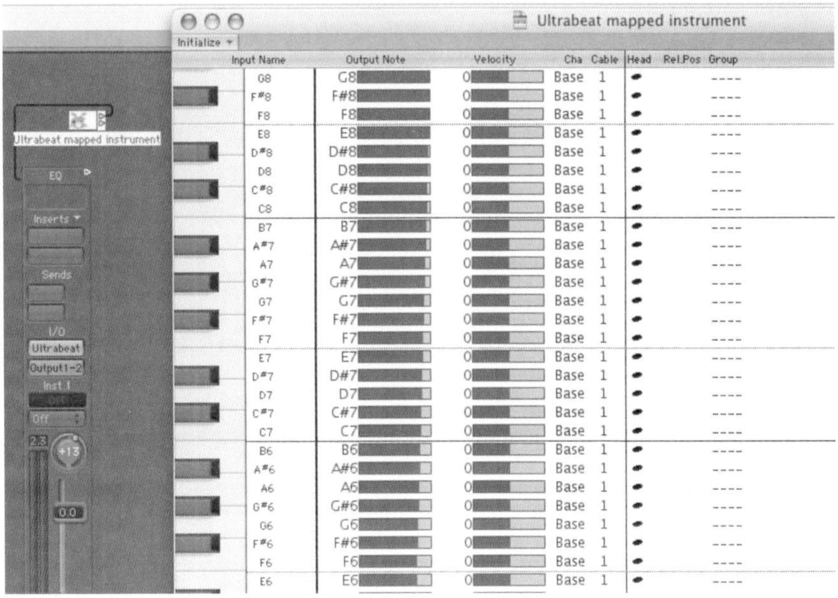

Figure A1.36

The window has the following properties:

- Click on the keyboard to the left of the window; it will play the sounds assigned to that key.
- Double click on the name of a drum sound to change it.

Figure A1.37

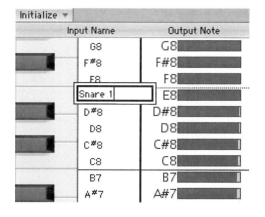

- You can then give each drum (or key) its own name.

Figure A1.38

Input Name	Output Note	Velocity	Cha	Cable	Head	Rel.Pos	Group
L CONGA	E3	0	Base	1	●		Congas
OH CONGA	D#3	0	Base	1	●	↓1	Congas
MH CONGA	D3	0	Base	1	●	↓2	Congas
L BONGO	C#3	0	Base	1	●		Bongos
H BONGO	C3	0	Base	1	●	↓1	Bongos
RIDE 2	B2	0	Base	1	×		Cymbals
VIBRA	A#2	0	Base	1	●		----
CRASH 2	A2	0	Base	1	⊠		Cymbals
COWBELL	G#2	0	Base	1	△		Cowbells
SPLASH	G2	0	Base	1	⊠		Cymbals
TAMB.	F#2	0	Base	1	●		----
RIDE BELL	F2	0	Base	1	×		Cymbals
CHINA	E2	0	Base	1	×		Cymbals
RIDE 1	D#2	0	Base	1	×		Cymbals
High TOM 1	D2	0	Base	1	●		Toms
CRASH 1	C#2	0	Base	1	⊠		Cymbals
High TOM 2	C2	0	Base	1	●	↓1	Toms
Mid TOM 1	B1	0	Base	1	●	↓2	Toms
Open HH	A#1	0	Base	1	⊠		HiHat
Mid TOM 2	A1	0	Base	1	●	↓3	Toms
PED HH	G#1	0	Base	1	×		HiHat
Low TOM 1	G1	0	Base	1	●	↓4	Toms
Closed HH	F#1	0	Base	1	×		HiHat
Low TOM 2	F1	0	Base	1	●	↓5	Toms
SD 2	E1	0	Base	1	●		Snare
HANDCLAP	D#1	0	Base	1	×		Snare
SD 1	D1	0	Base	1	●		Snare
SIDESTICK	C#1	0	Base	1	◆		Snare
KICK 1	C1	0	Base	1	●		Kick
KICK 2	B0	0	Base	1	●		Kick
METROBELL	A#0	0	Base	1	●		----

The Initialize menu has several helpful parameters to assist you in setting up GM presets and output velocities and so on.

Using existing Mapped instrument set-ups

As with Multi instruments, there are sources of several Mapped instrument set-ups with the names of the drum sounds already entered. However the method of getting these into your Autoload song is slightly different. Here's how to do it.

Open the song or Environment containing the Mapped Instrument you want to import. Remember not to close the Autoload song when you open the new one. Select the Mapped instrument you desire from the new songs Environment page. You can double click on this object to see how it is set up if you like. Close the window. Copy the object to the clipboard by highlighting it and selecting Edit>Copy from the Environment window menu. Move to the Autoload song by selecting it in the Windows menu.

In the Autoload song's Environment window and click on the background of the window to de-select any objects. If you want to paste over an existing Mapped instrument, select it first. Logic Pro will warn you if you are going to paste over an existing object. Paste the Mapped instrument into your Environment using the Edit>Paste menu item.

You assign a MIDI port to this instrument as described earlier. Make sure the box next to the Icon on the Parameter box has a cross in it, so it's visible in the Arrange page.

Creating Mapped instruments for each drum sound on a MIDI module.

As you can see below, you can have many Mapped instruments with different sounds assigned. Say, for example, your Multi timbral MIDI device has several sets of drum sounds, you could make a Mapped instrument for each.

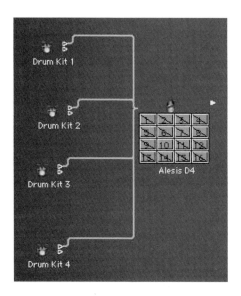

Figure A1.39

You can change which set you assign to which Mapped instrument by sending a program change to your synth using the program change parameter (Program:)

in the Mapped objects Parameter box. Hold down the mouse key over the program change number and you will get a pull down menu.

Figure A1.40

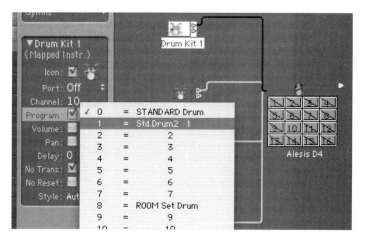

You can easily make copies of objects by clicking and dragging an object while holding the Option/Alt key while you do it. Rename the instruments separately. Each one will appear in the Arrange page as long as you have the Icon box clicked in the Parameter box for each object on the Environment page.

Figure A1.41

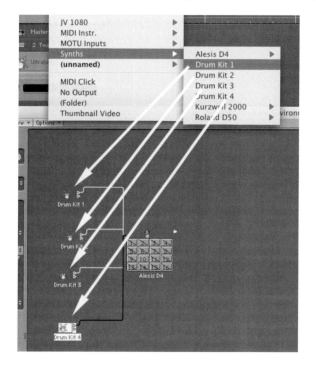

Other Mapped instrument features

There are some other things you can change in the Mapped instrument window. Double click on the Mapped instrument to open it.

Figure A1.42

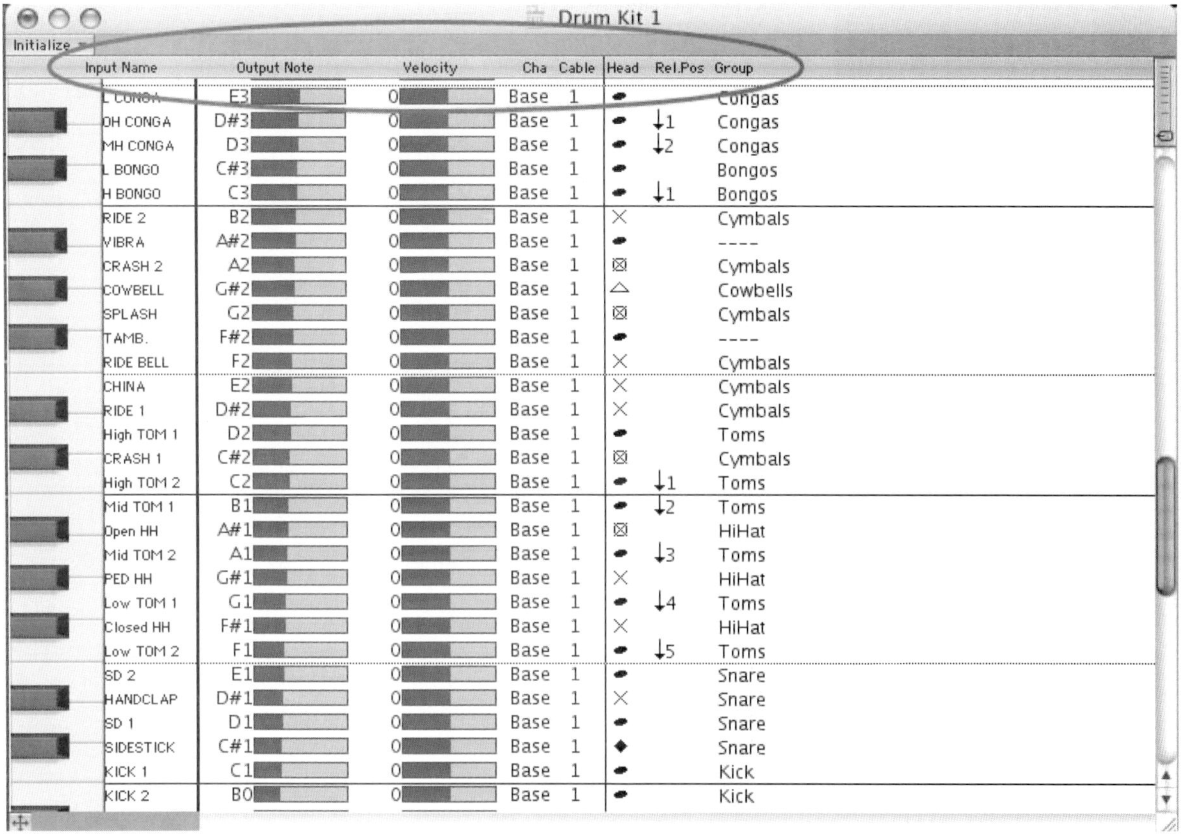

Input Name	Output Note	Velocity	Cha	Cable	Head	Rel.Pos	Group
L CONGA	E3	0	Base	1	●		Congas
OH CONGA	D#3	0	Base	1	●	↓1	Congas
MH CONGA	D3	0	Base	1	●	↓2	Congas
L BONGO	C#3	0	Base	1	●		Bongos
H BONGO	C3	0	Base	1	●	↓1	Bongos
RIDE 2	B2	0	Base	1	×		Cymbals
VIBRA	A#2	0	Base	1	●		----
CRASH 2	A2	0	Base	1	⊠		Cymbals
COWBELL	G#2	0	Base	1	△		Cowbells
SPLASH	G2	0	Base	1	⊠		Cymbals
TAMB.	F#2	0	Base	1	●		----
RIDE BELL	F2	0	Base	1	×		Cymbals
CHINA	E2	0	Base	1	×		Cymbals
RIDE 1	D#2	0	Base	1	×		Cymbals
High TOM 1	D2	0	Base	1	●		Toms
CRASH 1	C#2	0	Base	1	⊠		Cymbals
High TOM 2	C2	0	Base	1	●	↓1	Toms
Mid TOM 1	B1	0	Base	1	●	↓2	Toms
Open HH	A#1	0	Base	1	⊠		HiHat
Mid TOM 2	A1	0	Base	1	●	↓3	Toms
PED HH	G#1	0	Base	1	×		HiHat
Low TOM 1	G1	0	Base	1	●	↓4	Toms
Closed HH	F#1	0	Base	1	×		HiHat
Low TOM 2	F1	0	Base	1	●	↓5	Toms
SD 2	E1	0	Base	1	●		Snare
HANDCLAP	D#1	0	Base	1	×		Snare
SD 1	D1	0	Base	1	●		Snare
SIDESTICK	C#1	0	Base	1	◆		Snare
KICK 1	C1	0	Base	1	●		Kick
KICK 2	B0	0	Base	1	●		Kick

The parameters are:

Output note – when you play a note on your MIDI controller keyboard, you can change which actual note is output here. Slide the black line to the left or right to change it . You can reset this in the Initialize>Output notes menu.

Velocity – this sets a velocity offset to be added or subtracted to a note.

Cha – this defines which MIDI channel the note is output on. Normally this is set to Base (the same channel as the incoming note), but you may want to change this if you want an individual note to be sent out on a different MIDI channel, perhaps to a separate module.

Cable   – each Mapped instrument can be connected to up to 16 ports or other instruments. Choose which one you want the note to be sent to here. It's normally set to 1.

The last three parameters, Head, RelPos and Group refer to the notation parameters of the drum parts in the Score Edit window.

Getting a click to play along with

The KlopfGeist Virtual instrument is a built-in metronome. You insert it as you would any Virtual instrument.

Figure A1.43

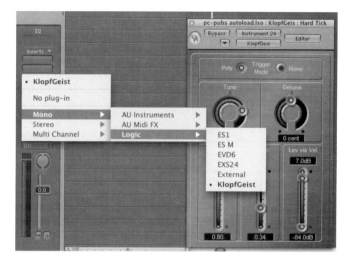

Setting up Logic Pro as a MIDI mixer to control your MIDI devices

The fader objects available in the Environment can be used to send out MIDI controller data to modify parameters such as volume, pan, reverb amount etc. on your MIDI devices. Of course, your synthesiser or whatever must be capable of receiving and acting on these incoming MIDI controllers.

Figure A1.44

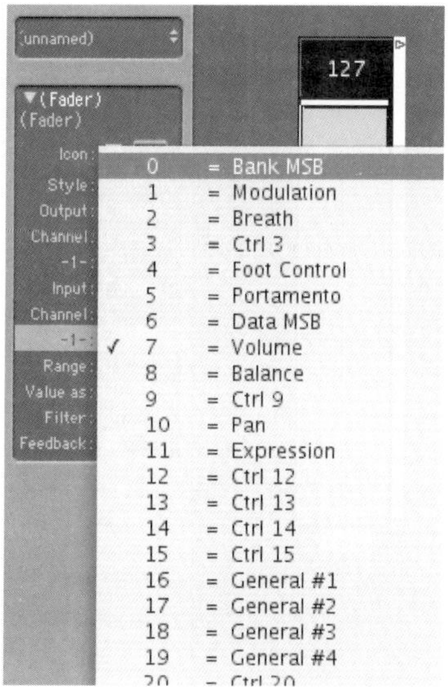

Setting up a ' channel strip' to control a Multi timbral synthesiser

Say we have a 16 MIDI channel Multi timbral synthesiser (the Kurzweil 2000 described earlier perhaps) and we want to set up a mixer surface to control the following parameters on the synth:

- Volume
- Mute
- Pan
- Reverb
- Chorus

This is how we would set it up in our Autoload song:

- Open the Environment window and move to the 'Synths' layer
- Select the Kurzweil 2000 Multi instrument object
- Click on the box next to Icon in the parameter box. This will make it appear in the list of instruments
- Create a new layer and rename it 'Synth Mixer'
- From the New menu select the following faders from the Fader sub menu

  * Vertical
  * Knob (You'll need three of these, so create one, and drag while holding down the ALT key to make two more)
  * Button

Figure A1.45

Select which style you prefer! Arrange them as in Figure A1.45.

You may want to have the View>Snap-positions on to make it looks neat! From top to bottom it's

- Knob
- Knob
- Knob
- Button
- Vertical

You may want to rename the faders. Highlight a fader and double click on the name next to the down arrow in the parameter box (Figure A1.46).

You can now cable up the mixer by dragging cables from the little arrows at the top of the objects, making sure the View>Cables menu item is set (Figure A1.47)

Figure A1.46

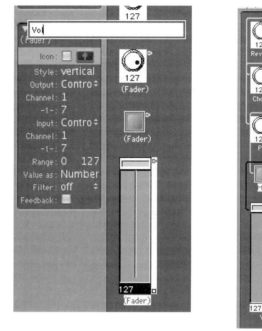

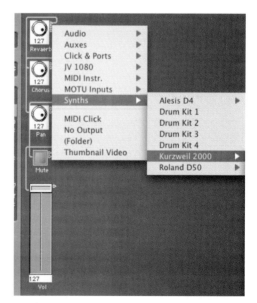

Figure A1.47

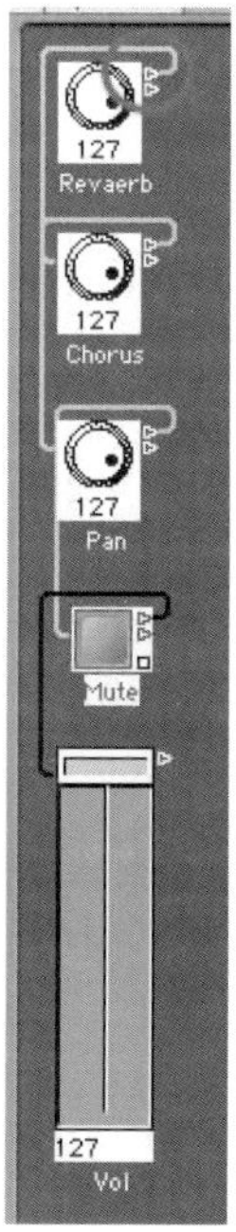

Now we need to connect the 'Mixer Strip' to the correct Multi instrument. To do this we have to make a connection between this layer and the 'Synth' layer. This means we can keep each layer neat and with a specified function, while not creating multiple objects and eating up memory.

Click on the arrow coming out of the 'Reverb knob' while holding down the Alt key. You will see a list of available objects. This is why we made sure that the Kurzweil 2000 Multi Instrument was available in this list at the beginning of this section by putting a cross in its Icon box. Select the Kurzweil 2000 instrument from this list.

Figure A1.48

You will see a little stubby cable coming from the top of the 'Reverb' object. This shows you have a link 'through' the layers (Figure A1.49).

Now select the correct controller parameters. This strip will control MIDI channel 1 on the synthesiser.

- Highlight the Vol slider
- Make sure there is not a tick in the box next to the icon: parameter to stop the object appearing in the Arrange page.
- Set the (MIDI) Channel to 1
- Select the correct controller number from the pull down list next to the –1- parameter. Volume is controller number 7.
- Set the range the controller will act over.
- Set the Val as number
- Set the filter to match (Figure A1.50).
- Select each control in turn and repeat steps 1–7 for each fader. Of course, you need to change the controller numbers to the correct ones (i.e. Pan, Chorus etc.)
- Now select MIDI channel 1 on the Kurzweil 2000 from the Arrange page.
- Play the keyboard and adjust the faders and knobs. You'll hear the effect that each controller has on the instrument.

To make the next Channel strip, select all the objects (Rubber band or use Edit>Select All) and click on the selected objects while holding down the Alt key. Then drag the whole strip sideways to make a copy.

While the new strip is still selected, change the Channel parameters in the Parameter box to 2. As all the objects are still selected, they will be changed to MIDI channel 2.

In this fashion, you can create a channel strip for all 16 MIDI channels.

Figure A1.49

Figure A1.50

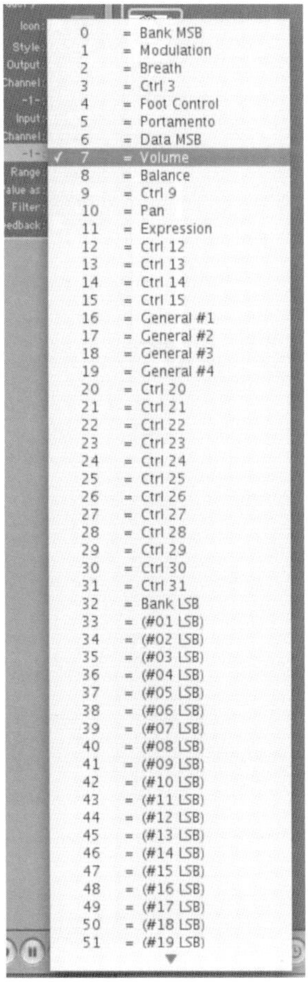

Figure A1.51

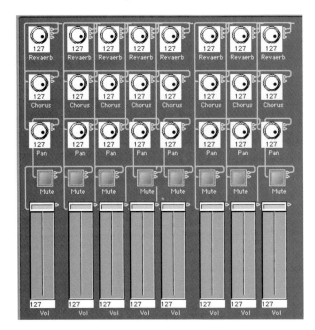

To make the mixer look nicer and to prevent accidentally moving objects, you might want to do the following:

- Click off the View>Parameters menu item.
- Click off the View>Cables menu item
- Click off the View>Protect cabling/positions menu item.

Now you have a nice MIDI mixer for the Kurzweil 2000. As you can imagine, you can create faders to adjust any MIDI controller that a synthesiser can respond to. It doesn't need to be a synthesiser either. A Digital mixer or Effects unit that responds to MIDI controllers can be adjusted in this fashion.

Setting up Logic Pro to adjust parameters on your MIDI devices via SysEx

MIDI devices don't only respond to controller information. They can receive and generate Systems Exclusive (SysEx) data. This has a much more complex format than controller data and is generally used to adjust things like filter cut off, selecting waveforms and the like, and allows you to build up an on-screen representation of your MIDI devices within Logic Pro, with the advantage that any changes can be recorded into Logic Pro.

Here is an example of what you can do with a SysEx fader. Create a fader object from the New>Fader>Vertical menu item. In the Parameter box, change the Out value to SysEx.

Figure A1.52

This opens a window like Figure A1.53. You can add SysEx data in two ways. If your MIDI device can send out SysEx information, connect its MIDI out to the MIDI in of your computer. Make sure the IN button in the SysEx window is ON. Change the required parameter on the MIDI device. The SysEx information should appear in the window. Close the window and cable the fader to the required Instrument object in exactly the same fashion as that for a MIDI controller fader. When you move this fader, the SysEx information stored is sent to your synthesiser.

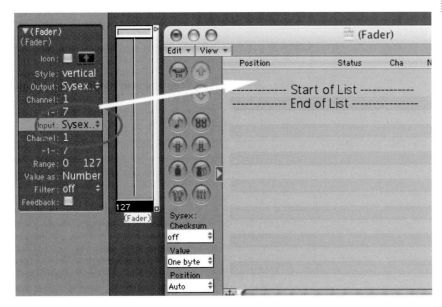

If your MIDI device doesn't send out SysEx then you'll have to delve into the manual to see what SysEx information controls which parameters, and enter this data directly into the SysEx window. To do this, Click on the SysEx button with the Apple key down. A Sysex event will be created which can be edited.

Creating complex SysEx set ups is beyond the scope of this book, but remember, someone has already probably created 'front panels' for your synthesisers, effects units and mixers. Yours may be available on the Logic Pro support disks or the Internet. Don't re-invent the wheel!

Logic Pro and GM devices

GM or General MIDI is an attempt to standardise the way that MIDI files are played on different synthesisers. A GM MIDI file played via one GM MIDI module should, in theory, play back exactly the same on another GM synthesiser .It should have the correct sounds, pan, reverb and chorus settings. In fact, as with many standards, GM is a flexible beast and this is not always the case. There have also been several 'extended' GM's such as GS and XG.

GM MIDI Mixer
Logic Pro provides an 'off the shelf' GM MIDI Mixer. Use it like this:

- Make sure your GM sound module is in its GM mode
- First, create a Multi Instrument from the File menu. The Multi Instruments default to a GM mode
- Select the Multi Instrument Port that the hardware GM device is set to
- Create A GM Mixer from the New menu
- Cable the GM mixer to the GM Multi Instrument. Remove the Port connection when asked.
- This will now control the external GM hardware directly.

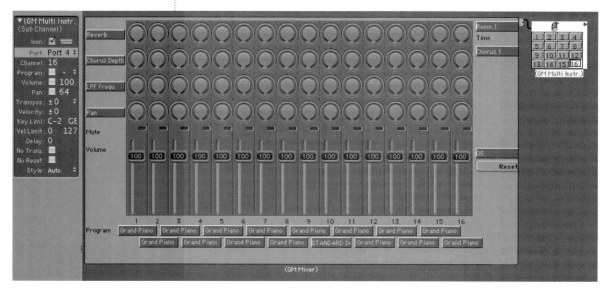

Figure A1.54

You can double click at the top of the GM instrument to see the GM patch names. These will be correct for a GM synth, so no editing or copying is required! Now look at the instrument list in the Arrange page. You will see the GM devices listed there. Choose one and play the GM sound. This GM Multi instrument is just the same as the other Multi instruments described earlier in the chapter.

Figure A1.55

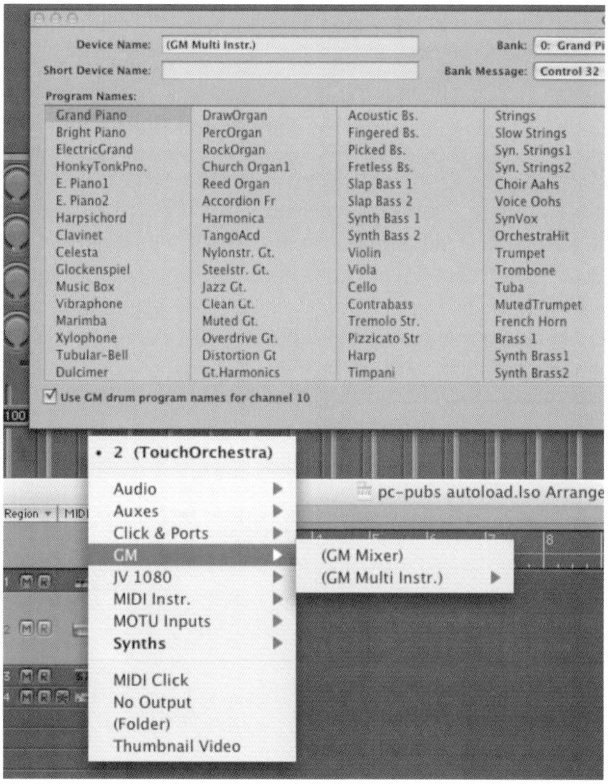

If you look in the instrument list on the Arrange page, Channel 10 is set to 'Standard Drums'. You may want to create (or copy from the 'untitled' song) a Mapped instrument with its Cha parameter set to MIDI channel 10 to play the drum sounds.

The GM mixer can now be used to control the respective channels on your GM MIDI instrument. You can change which MIDI controllers the knobs send out by choosing them from the pull down menu displayed by clicking and holding on the boxes to the left of the knobs.

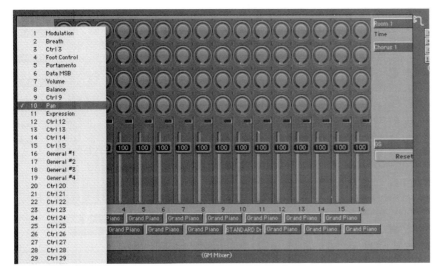

Figure A1.56

You can also choose GM, GS and XG modes from the pull down menu (Figure A1.57). Different modes have other variable parameters.

The GM mixer is just a variation on the 'homemade' mixer detailed earlier. As such, it can be used in songs in exactly the same way. See earlier in the Chapter for more on this.

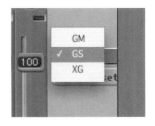

Figure A1.57

Using modifiers in Logic Pro

By modifiers we mean the following Environment objects, selected from the New menu in the Environment. Most of these work only while Logic Pro is running.

- Arpeggiator – creates arpeggios.
- Transformer – changes the MIDI data passing through it
- Delay line – acts like an echo or delay unit, but with MIDI data
- Voice limiter – limits the number of voices a synthesiser plays
- Chord memorizer – plays a chord from a single note played on an external MIDI controller

As usual in Logic Pro, there are several ways to use these objects, but perhaps the most 'Logical' way is to create a special instrument to take advantage of their features. Here's how to set them up. It's the same for all these objects, but let's take the example of the Arpeggiator

Figure A1.58

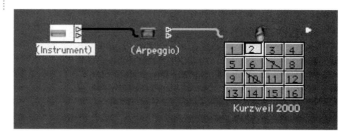

Select the 'Synths' layer in the Environment window and create an Instrument and Arpeggiator object. Move them to a convenient place. Rename them and cable them to each other as follows, and then to the Multi Instrument you want to use to play the actual sound. Make sure the box next to the icon in the instrument Parameter box is crossed, and that the one in the Arpeggiator is not.

Figure A1.59

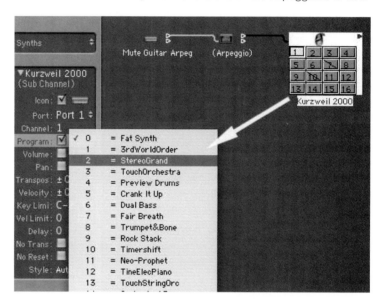

Change the patch on the instrument by holding down the mouse key over the number on the Program box on the Parameter box. To change banks, use the + value to the left of the program change number. Rename the Arpeggiator object something useful; let's call it 'StereoGrand Arpeg'.

Figure A1.60

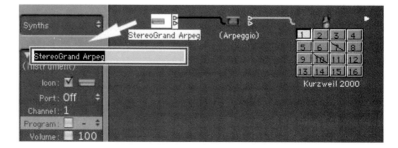

Select the instrument in the Arrange page instrument list (Figure A1.61). To adjust the parameters on the Arpeggiator, select it in the Environment window, and adjust its parameters in the Parameter box. Start Logic Pro, play the keyboard and adjust the parameters to hear the results (Figure A1.62).

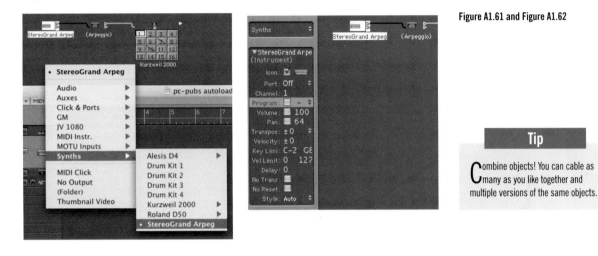

Figure A1.61 and Figure A1.62

> **Tip**
>
> Combine objects! You can cable as many as you like together and multiple versions of the same objects.

Of course, you can patch these objects anywhere in the MIDI flow within Logic Pro.

Touch tracks (MIDI data only)

Touch tracks allow you to play whole regions at the touch of a single key on your MIDI keyboard, drum pads or wind controller. Here's how you set Touch tracks up.

Create a Touch tracks objects from the New menu in the Environment window. A window will open up. Play the desired key on your MIDI keyboard. The key will be highlighted, in this case F2.

Figure A1.63

Input Name	Group	Region/Folder	Trp	Velocity	Trigger	Start	Delay
G#3							
G3							
F#3							
F3							
E3							
D#3							
D3							
C#3							
C3							
B2							
A#2							
A2							
G#2							
G2							
F#2							
F2							
E2							
D#2							
D2							
C#2							
C2							

Drag the desired region from the Arrange page to the Touch tracks window (Figure A1.64).

> **Tip**
>
> You can highlight several notes and drag the region to the group highlighted. When each note is played, the region will be transposed.

Figure A1.64 and Figure A1.65

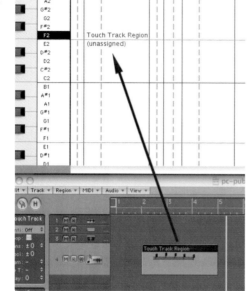

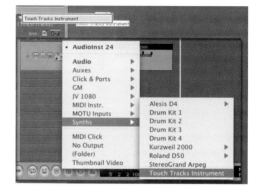

Close the window. Rename the Touch tracks objects as desired. Make sure there is an tick in the box next to the Icon in the Parameter box. Select the Touch tracks object in the Instrument list in the Arrange page (Figure A1.65).

Start Logic Pro. Playing the F2 key on the keyboard will play the region. You can change various Touch tracks parameters by double clicking on the object in the Environment and opening the Touch Tracks window (Figure A1.66).

Figure A1.66

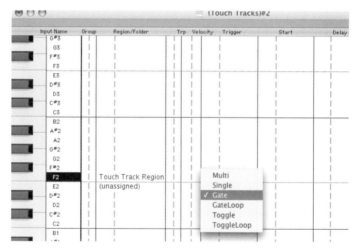

> **Tip**
>
> You can highlight several notes and drag the sequence to the group highlighted. When each note is played, the sequence will be transposed.

- Group – when grouped, sequences can only be played back one at a time, so there are no overlaps.
- Trp – transposes the sequence.
- Velocity – changes how much the velocity values of the regions are affected by the velocity of the note which controls the sequence.
- Trigger – there are several trigger modes accessed by the pull down menu.
- Multi – the sequence is always played right to the end even if you release the key.
- Single – as Multi but the sequence stops when the same trigger note is played again.

- Gate – the sequence is played for as long as the trigger note is held down
- Gate Loop – like gate, but the sequence is played repeatedly until another note stops it.
- Toggle – a trigger note starts the sequence until another trigger note stops it
- Toggle Loop – like toggle, except that the sequence is repeated until another trigger note stops it.
- Start – quantize how sequences start and stop, select from the pull down menu
- Delay – delays the sequence. Another pull down box.

Importing Screensets, score styles and stuff from other songs

You can import the following items from one song to another. Here's how you do it. Close all songs except the one you want to import things into. Select the Options>Import Settings menu item from The Arrange page. The following box opens:

Click on the options you want to import and select the Logic song you wish to Import settings from. Click on Open. Note you can't undo this! Use the File>Revert to Saved menu item to get the old settings back.

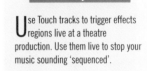

Tip

Use Touch tracks to trigger effects regions live at a theatre production. Use them live to stop your music sounding 'sequenced'.

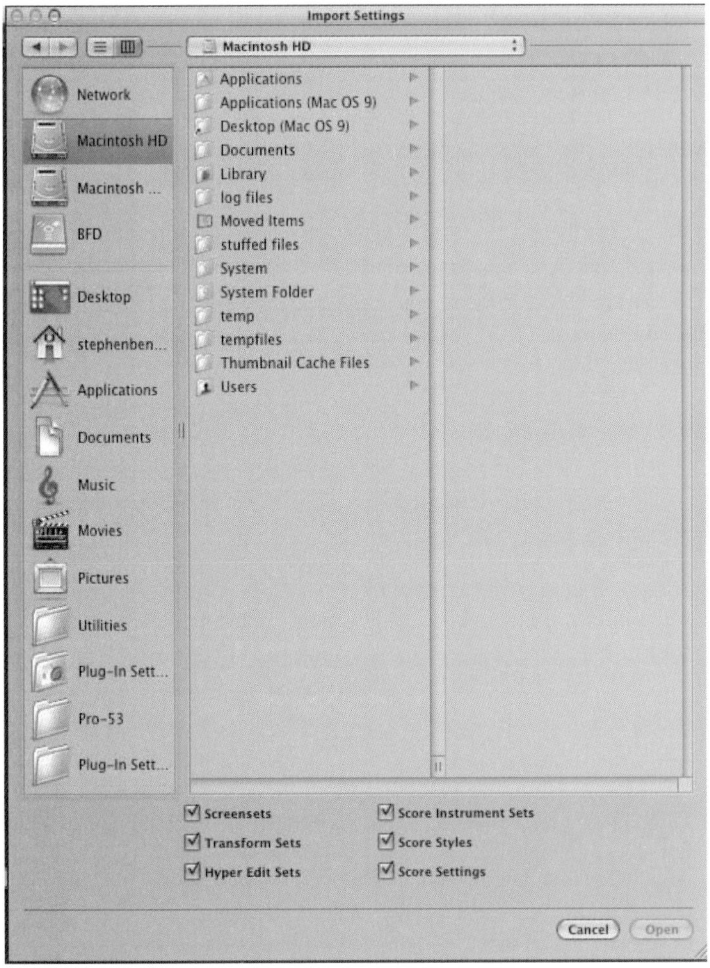

Figure A1.67

Appendix 2
Latency and plug-in delay compensation

Overview

Latency is the bane of all 'native' Digital Audio Workstations. It's defined as the length of time the audio signal takes to move through various parts of the recording system. Latency can exhibit itself in various ways.

Latency when playing a Virtual instrument

When you play a key on a MIDI master keyboard, the signal is sent down the MIDI cable into the MIDI interface, into Logic Pro and into the Virtual instrument plug-in. Then the Virtual instrument needs to do the calculations needed to produce the sound. Finally, the Virtual instrument needs to output the sound to the speakers via Logic. All this takes time and is exhibited as a delay between playing and hearing a sound, which we call Latency.

Latency when using effects plug-ins

In a similar fashion, when audio is passed through one or several plug-ins, Latency is introduced.

Latency when recording audio

This is extremely important when trying to overdub alongside previous recordings. If a vocalist or guitarist, for example, is hearing the audio in their headphones delayed by passing through Logic Pro and any plug-ins, it can really spoil a performance!

Dealing with latency when recording

If you set the i/o buffer size to a low value, you can reduce the latency in your system. However, too low a value may cause CPU overloads or clicks and pops. Buffer size is set from the Audio>Audio hardware & drivers window (Figure A2.1).

Info

The playback latencies exhibited when playing back Virtual instruments or audio through plug-ins can be compensated for using the Logic Pro>Audio>Plug-in delay compensation feature. You should always leave this feature ON.

Info

When Audio>Audio Hardware & Drivers>Software monitoring is ON, you can use Logic Pro's plug-ins to add reverb to a vocalist when recording.

Preferences

Global Audio MIDI Display Score Video Automation Control Surfaces

| General | Drivers | Display | Sample Editor | Surround | MP3 | Reset | Nodes |

| Core Audio | DAE | Direct TDM |

☑ Enabled

System Memory Requirement: 70.0 MB

Driver:

I/O Buffer Size:

      32
      64
 ✓ 128
   256
   512
   1024

Recording Delay: 0

Max. Number of Audio Tracks: 124

☐ 64 Busses

☑ Universal Track Mode

☐ Larger Disk Buffer

☐ 24 Bit Recording

☑ Software Monitoring

Process Buffer Range: [Medium]

Rewire behavior: [Playback Mode (Less CPU Load)]

Maximum Scrub Speed: [Normal]

Scrub Response: [Normal]

Use the Audio>CPU Performance window to see how changing i/o buffer values affect performance (Figure A2.2).

- Use as low a buffer size as possible when recording. If you get too many CPU overload messages or clicks and pops, increase the buffer size until you have a value you can work with. You may have to use Logic's Freeze feature (see below) to free up CPU power to obtain the lowest latencies.
- Use a buffer size of 32 to 128 when doing recordings that require critical timing such as vocals or percussion.
- Use a buffer size of 128 to 512 when recording MIDI or virtual instruments.

Freezing

You can automatically bounce down an Audio or Virtual instrument track along with all plug-in processing using Logics Freeze function. This bounced file, then replaces the original recording in the Arrange page. Freezing a track reduces the CPU power needed to play back that track drastically.

Freezing does have some limitations:

CPU

Audio Disk I/O

Tip

When mixing downs a song, increase the buffer size to 512 or larger to allow more plug-in effects to be used.

- When a track is frozen, only Volume, Pan, Sends and output assignment can be changed. If you try and edit any of the other parameters of the plug-ins a box will open asking if you want to unfreeze the track.
- Regions on frozen tracks cannot be edited in any way until unfrozen.

You can unfreeze a track at any time for further editing by clicking on the Freeze button. Here's how you freeze a track

- Make sure you have made the Freeze button visible from the Arrange page View menu

Figure A2.3

- Click on the Freeze button and press play.

Figure A2.4

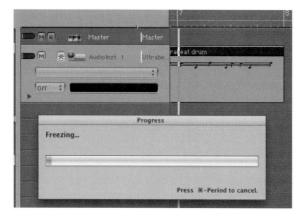

- The SPL will drop back to bar 1 and move across the song, freezing (or rendering to audio) the track.
- When the SPL is past the last region on the track you want to freeze press the Apple key and '.' To stop freezing.

You can freeze multiple tracks at the same time.

Appendix 3
Hardware requirements

Computer

Logic is Macintosh only so you'll need a USB equipped G3, G4 or G5 computer. Realistically, a powerful G4 or G5 will allow you to exploit more of Logic's features; but if all you want to do is audio or MIDI recording using external instruments, a slower computer may suffice. Whatever computer you use, it needs to have the following hardware and software specification;

- It needs to be running the latest version of Mac OSX
- It needs to have at least 512MB to 1GB of RAM. Software like Logic continues to use more and more RAM, so get as much as you can afford.
- You need a hard disk drive, preferably one running at a minimum speed of 7200 r.p.m. You'll want to play back many audio tracks and disk speed is important for this.
- The larger the storage space the better. You may want to have two disk drives: one for programs and samples and one for your audio recordings. This set-up will make your work easier to back up too.

CD and/or DVD burner

You'll want to produce audio CDs from your recordings, so you'll need a CD burner. If you want to back-up to a larger capacity format a DVD burner is a useful addition.

Audio interface

The internal analogue outputs and inputs of a typical Macintosh computer are not really suitable for recording or playback at a semi-professional or professional level. Ideally you'll want to use an external audio interface. The choice of interface is dependent on several things;

- What maximum sample rate and frequency you want to use. Some simple interfaces are limited to 16 bit/44.1KHz recording while others can record up to 24 bit/96KHz or above.
- How many tracks you wish to record at the same time. If you are just recording by yourself you'll probably only need to record two tracks at a time (stereo). If you want to record a band you'll need more.
- How many outputs and inputs you need. You may want to use extra inputs to bring in external hardware synthesisers, mixing desk or hardware effects units.

- What type of connection to the computer do you need? For portable computer users, USB or Firewire might be the best choice. For desktop users, an internal PCI card might be more suitable.

MIDI interface

If you want to use a keyboard or other electronic instrument to enter musical information, or play back recordings using external MIDI hardware, such as synthesisers or samplers, you'll need a MIDI interface. These usually connect via USB and can have several MIDI inputs and outputs. If you are using just Virtual instruments you'll probably need a single in and out. For more complex set-ups a multiple in and out system will be needed. Some keyboards combine MIDI in and outs with an audio interface into a single unit.

Appendix 4
About audio files

Audio files can come in many formats. The main files used in Logic Audio are as follows:

- WAVE or .WAV file (PC and Mac)
- AIFF (Mac) – often generated by CD 'rippers'
- SDII or Sound Designer II files (MAC)

So if you want to use Logic Pro on Macs and transfer to Windows PCs, you would save all the audio files within Logic Pro as Wave files.

Files supported by Logic Pro can have the following sampling rates 44.1KHz, 48kHz, 88.2kHz, 96kHz, 176.4kHz or 192kHz. Bit depths can be 8, 16 or 24. The sampling rate is the number of 'slices' taken by the recording software per second. The bit depth is the number of discrete volume level steps recorded. Basically, the higher the sampling rate and the higher the bit depth the more 'accurate' the recording.

If you imagine a very low recording level, only a few bits will be used to describe the sample thus increasing the noise level. In the following diagram waveform A is described by 5 bits whereas waveform B is described by 15 bits. The more bits used the smoother the waveform and the more like the analogue waveform being recorded.

However, CDs are fixed at 16 bit, 44.1kHz so, whatever sample rate you record within Logic Pro, you will have to mix down to this format if you want to make CDs. The higher the bit depth/sample rate you use, the more hard disk space you will need for storage.

The sample rates and bit depths Logic Pro can handle are limited by the type of audio hardware installed and the power of the CPU on your computer.

Audio files created by Logic Pro can also contain regions. These are created when you cut up audio in the Arrange page, or create them explicitly in the Audio window or Sample editor. Regions can be independently copied, moved and cut. But any destructive processing of a region will also affect all copies of the region as it works on the original audio file. To avoid this, you need to make regions into new audio files using Audio>Convert regions to individual audio files in the Arrange window, or Audio file>Save regions as in the Audio window.

Figure A4.1

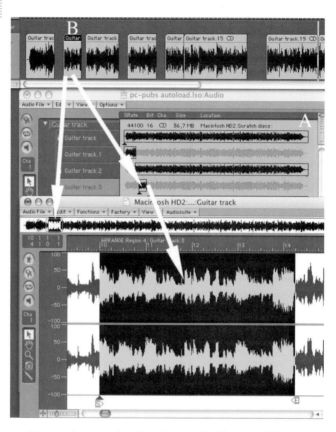

A is a region covering the whole audio file called 'Guitar track'. B is a region created by cutting in the Arrange page. B is a region In the Arrange page that is selected in the Sample editor and Audio window.

Stereo audio files can be in two formats:

- Split stereo – these have two separate left and right portions, often with the extensions .L and .R.
- Interleaved stereo – the left and right portions of a stereo file are combined into one file.

Logic Pro can freely use both types of stereo file, and can convert between them.

Appendix 5
Glossary

Analogue to digital converter (ADC)

Converts analogue signals (guitars, drums, vocals) into digital signal (bits) that a computer can read.

AES/EBU

A digital input/output, usually on XLR sockets.

Amplitude

The 'loudness' of an audio signal.

Analog(ue)

With respect to audio signals, analogue refers to a continuous waveform, as opposed to a digital one that is described a series of steps. Americans use the term analog.

ADC

Analogue to digital converter. The opposite of a DAC.

ASIO

Audio stream input output. A generic system for handling audio input and output on audio interfaces.

Audio interface

This is the hardware that allows audio to be input and output from your computer. It could be as simple as the stereo in/out card or built in soundcard or as complex as a multi in and out system with extra DSP processing.

Bank select

A combination of MIDI controller numbers 0 and 32. This command allows you to change the banks in a MIDI device and was introduced to overcome the limitation of 128 patch change numbers accessible via MIDI.

Bit

The smallest unit of digital information described as a '1' or a 0'.

Byte

An 8 bit binary number. A kilobyte is 1024 bytes, a megabyte is 1024 kilobytes and so on.

Buffer

A portion of computer memory that stores information before it is read to and from a hard disk. A buffer basically speeds up hard disk recording.

CD ripper

A program which allows the direct transfer of data from an audio CD to a hard disk audio file.

Clipping

Clipping occurs when audio levels exceed 0dB or 90 withing Logic Pro. This is a bad thing. You should not exceed these levels unless you deliberately want to make your audience's ears bleed.

Control change

MIDI control changes are used to control a wide variety of functions on a MIDI device. Some are universal such as:

Different manufacturers use other controller values for different applications. For example a MIDI controlled mixer may use MIDI controllers to adjust its values, or a MIDI effects unit may use MIDI controllers to adjust the various parameters. The upshot of this is that using a MIDI sequencer like Logic Pro you can set up 'virtual interfaces' for MIDI devices and record the changes into the sequencer.

Core Audio

All audio software under OSX uses the Core Audio drivers built into the operating system. This means that a single audio interface only needs one driver (the core audio one) to be available for all installed software such as Logic Pro and iTunes.

Core MIDI

All MIDI software under OSX uses the Core MIDI drivers built into the operating system. This means that a single MIDI interface only needs one driver (the core midi one) for it to be available for all installed software such as Logic Pro and iTunes.

CPU

The 'brain' or Central Processing Unit of a computer.

Cut, copy and paste

You may be familiar with these terms for cutting out or copying a portion of a sequence and pasting it into a new position. Logic Pro, confusingly, uses the terms 'Snip, splice and insert' to perform the same functions.

Cycle

The process of cycling or looping around a pre-defined section of a song.

DAC

Digital to audio converter. Converts digital data to analogue data.

DAT

Digital audio tape. A 16 bit digital tape recorder that records at sample rates of 44.1Khz and 48kHz.

Decibel (dB)

dBs are used to describe the loudness of audio signals on a logarithmic scale.

Defragment

When a hard disk fills up with files, the data that the files contain become spread across the whole disk, filling up the spaces between data. This non-contiguous file storage slows down hard disk access. Defragmenting often will speed up hard disk access – very important when recording Audio.

Digital

With respect to audio, digital signals are made up of discrete steps representing analogue waveforms. For example if you sample an analogue waveform at 44.1kHz you will have 44100 steps every second. The amplitude of the waveform is described by the number of bits. CD is 16bit, 44.1kHz digital recording. In general the more bits and the higher the sample rate, the more accurately the digital representation of the analogue waveform.

Driver

Software providing communication between a piece of hardware (audio interface, display) and the computer operating system. OSX uses a Core Audio driver.

Dongle

A hardware key allowing Logic Pro to run. Alternatively, a source of immense annoyance when it breaks down, doesn't work, or you leave it behind when you take Logic Pro out of your studio!

Drop in

Like Punch in. An automatic way of putting Logic Pro into record at a predefined point in the song.

DSP

Digital signal processing. Term used for any audio feature that uses the computer to emulate hardware units such as synthesisers, effects units and so on. DSP can be done either using the computer's main processor or additional external DSP chips, depending on which audio interface you have.

Editor

A window within a sequencer where you can edit MIDI data.

Environment

In Logic Pro, the Environment is the window where you will define your MIDI devices, patch in MIDI modifiers and set up virtual mixing desks and editors.

EQ

Equalisation. Tone manipulation. EQ can vary from simple bass and treble controls to sophisticated multi-band parametric EQ.

Event

In Logic Pro, an event is MIDI data. It can be note data, controller data, SysEx data or meta events and so on.

Fixing

Making edits in MIDI events, such as volume changes and quantization permanent. Also known in Logic Pro-speak as Normalization.

Folder

A folder in Logic Pro is analogous to a folder or directory on a computer. A folder can contain other sequences.

Formants

Harmonics contained in a sound that often define the quality of that sound.

GM or General MIDI

An attempt to standardise MIDI file play back so that a song created on one sequencer will play back exactly on another, using the same sounds and effects. GM is often available as a 'mode' on a synthesiser, and like most standards, there are various variations and additions, such as GS and XG.

Hard disk recording

The term used to describe recording using a computer through an audio interface to a computer hard disk drive.

Headroom

The difference between an input signal and the maximum signal an audio system can take without distorting.

Hertz

Unit for measuring frequency. It describes the oscillations per second.

Hyperdraw and Hyper editor

Hyper in Logic Pro parlance means visual editing of controller and other MIDI events.

Instrument

In Logic Pro, an instrument is a representation of a patch or sound on a MIDI device. You use an instrument to record or play back MIDI data. They are defined within the Environment window. It's also used to refer to Virtual instrument plug-ins.

Key commands

Most of Logic Pro's parameters can have a Key command assigned to them, if you prefer not to use menus and on screen buttons. Some of Logic Pro's parameters only have Key commands.

Layer

In the Environment, a layer is a 'page' containing Environment objects. Its main function is to keep the Environment tidy and easy to use by grouping together related objects.

Mac

Apple's Macintosh computer.

Main volume

The volume of a MIDI device is adjusted by MIDI controller 7.

Meta event

These are events internal to Logic Pro, and are used to control various things, such as the automatic changing of Screensets.

Metronome

The 'click' you play along with in Logic Pro.

MIDI

MIDI stands for Musical Instrument Digital Interface. This was first established to allow the connection of two or more electronic musical instruments. This serial communication protocol has gone on to become the method of interfacing keyboards, computers and a wealth of MIDI devices and has become one of the most enduring 'standards' of modern times. MIDI data is also used when recording and playing back Virtual instrument plug-isn.

MIDI channel

MIDI devices send and receive data on up to 16 MIDI channels. these are not to be confused with the number of tracks a MIDI sequencer can record on which can, on modern computers, be almost infinite. Well a pretty large number anyway.

MIDI clock

A timing message embedded in the MIDI data enabling instruments such as drum machines to keep in time with another MIDI device, such as a sequencer.

MIDI controller

This is MIDI information used to control other MIDI parameters than notes themselves. Controllers can be used to adjust volume, pan, balance etc.

MIDI event

Any MIDI data recorded into Logic Pro is an Event.

MIDI file

A 'standard' song file designed to be universally playable on MIDI sequencers. There are three types of MIDI file. For maximum portability, use Type 0, in Logic Pro. It's a good idea to normalize all sequence parameters prior to saving the song as a MIDI file.

MIDI interface

The hardware interface, containing the 5 pin DIN sockets that MIDI needs to communicate. These can come in many forms from the inbuilt MIDI IN and OUT on the Atari ST, through simple single port interfaces connected to a computer's USB ports, to complex multi channel interfaces allowing a sequencer to access more than 16 MIDI channels.

MIDI IN, MIDI OUT and MIDI THRU

These sockets are found on MIDI devices. MIDI IN and OUT are pretty self explanatory while MIDI THRU allows the MIDI data to pass through the device unaltered.

MIDI machine control (MMC)

MMC allows a sequence to control various parameters on some tape machines and other MIDI devices. You could, for example, use MMC to put a Fostex R8 8 track tape machine into record, and select the track to be recorded on.

MIDI message

The data passed between MIDI devices. MIDI messages can be note data, controller data, SysEx data and the like.

MIDI modes

MIDI modes determine how a MIDI device will respond to, or send out, MIDI data.

MIDI module

A sound generating, MIDI controlled device with no keyboard or other controller.

MIDI remote

You can assign many of Logic Pro's functions to an external MIDI device, so you could for example control Environment faders with a slider on your synthesiser, or put Logic Pro into play with an unused key on a keyboard.

MIDI time code

Unconfusingly, time code sent via MIDI. Most usefully used for converting SMPTE time code to a format that sequencers understand to keep them in sync with external devices such as tape and video machines.

Modifier keys

Keys on a computer keyboard, such as Control, Shift and Alt that modify the action of other keys.

Multi timbral

The ability of a synthesiser or module to produce several different sounds on different MIDI channels at the same time.

Normalize

See Fixing.

Object

Logic Pro is an 'object orientated' sequencer. What this means in practice is that everything is defined as an object – notes, sequences, MIDI modifiers, output ports etc. All the objects in Logic Pro have similar parameters, making it easy to move from one part of the program to another.

Parameter

In Logic Pro, objects can have parameters that can be changed. Often, these parameters are changed in a Parameter box.

Patch

On a MIDI device, a patch is a sound, or easily recallable set-up, for example, on a effects unit.

PC

An IBM type computer, usually running the Windows Operating System.

Plug-ins

These are software representations of Instruments or effects units that run under Logic Pro.

Program change

Program changes are MIDI events used to change patches on MIDI devices.

Quantize

Quantizing is 'bringing into time' unruly MIDI note data. It's used, for example, to bring drum parts into time. Quantizing can be used as a creative or restorative tool. It's non destructive within Logic Pro.

RAM

The memory in a computer where programs are run when they are loaded from hard disk RAM stores data temporarily and all data is lost when the computer is switched off.

Real time

This is the term for recording into a sequencer as if it was a tape machine, or for replaying controller data to control an external MIDI device. See Step time.

Region

Within Logic Pro, a sequence is a part recorded on a track in the Arrange window, or a section of an audio recording.

ROM

The permanent memory in a computer that runs essential operating software.

Sample rate

The number of times an analogue signal is measured per second in digital conversion.

Screensets

Within Logic Pro, a Screenset is a screen arrangement which can be stored and recalled.

SCSI

Small computer system interface. A fast communication system used for hard drives, CD ROMs etc.

Signal to noise ratio (S/N)

The ratio of signal level to noise level in an audio system expressed in dB.

SMPTE

A code, sounding not dissimilar to a modem or left field techno group, usually recorded on a video machine or tape recorder, and used to synchronise a sequencer with those devices.

Song

Logic Pro stores its sequences as Songs. When you are working in Logic Pro you are always in a Logic Pro song.

Soundcard

See Audio interface.

S/PDIF

Sony/Phillips Digital Interface. A low cost option digital interface. Similar to AS/EBU but using phono connectors.

Step time

Entering MIDI note data with the sequencer stopped, a note (or chord) at a time. See Real Time.

SysEx or System exclusive

A series of MIDI messages which enables different manufacturers to produce their own 'custom' MIDI data. SysEx is usually used to edit a synthesiser from a sequencer, or to store a whole memory dump from a MIDI device.

Toolbox

A toolbox, within Logic Pro, is a series of icons which, when selected, allows the mouse cursor to perform a different function. For example, select the pencil tool to draw MIDI data, the eraser tool to delete it.

Track

In Logic Pro, a track is where sequences are recorded in the Arrange page. A track always has an object assigned to it, most usually an instrument.

Transformer

An object that changes, or transforms, one type of MIDI data to another.

Transport

Logic's on screen representation of tape recorder style functions such as play, record etc.

Virtual instruments

These are DSP based representations of real instruments, such as samplers and synthesisers. Within Logic Pro, Virtual instruments are inserted as plug-ins on Audio objects and their parameters adjusted in the same way as more traditional plug-ins. Virtual Instruments use a lot of computer processing power.

Appendix 6
Optimisation

While modern computers are powerful and perfect tools for recording, there are still certain optimisation procedures you can follow to get the last drop of performance from your machine.

Close all unnecessary programs

Logic Pro uses a lot of memory and CPU power. If you have other, unnecessary programs running at the same time, performance can suffer. Use the highest buffer size you can get away with.

While low buffer sizes lead to lower latencies (see Appendix 2), they eat into CPU power. You'll be able to use more plug-ins with higher buffer sizes. Buffer sizes are set in the Audio>Audio Hardware & Drivers menu.

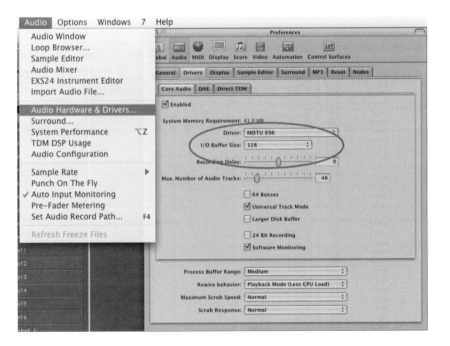

Figure A6.1

Turn off Journaling on the Audio hard drive

Journaling is a method by which OSX stores a 'map' of all the files and folders on your hard drive. If you have a crash, a journaled drive is easier to recover from. However, journaling also continuously writes data to the hard disk. This will reduce the number of audio tracks you'll be able to use. If you have a separate hard drive just for Audio, turn off journaling on that drive only and leave it on for the system and program hard drive. Use the Disk Utility in the Applications/Utilities folder.

Figure A6.2

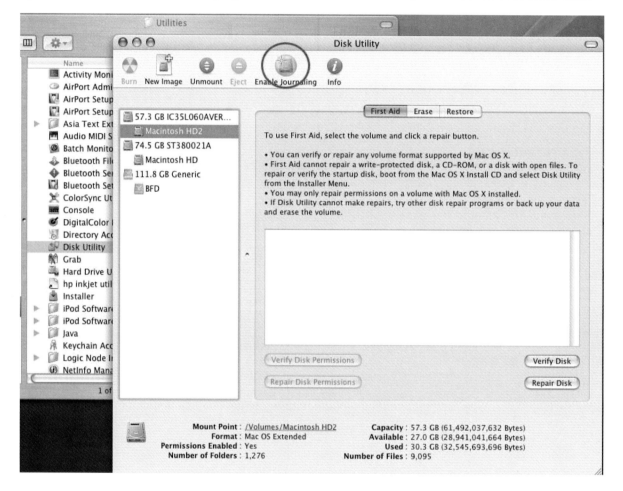

Repair permissions regularly

OSX is very sensitive to the permissions each file has been set too. Occasionally, these settings get confused and files can fail to be written to disk properly. Do this on a regular basis. Use the Disk Utility in the Applications/Utilities folder.

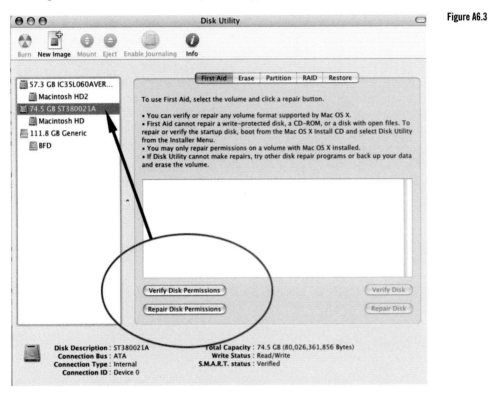

Figure A6.3

Turn off any virus checkers

Virus and spyware checkers are constantly checking the memory and files on your computer. This is bound to have an adverse effect on performance, so disable them. You may want to disconnect from the net when you do this.

Turn off screensavers

These may also adversely affect performance so turn them off.

Appendix 7
Logic and the internet

Logic Pro is well represented on the internet. There are mailing lists, web sites containing Environment set-ups and other useful files, along with other resources useful to the Logic Pro user. As the Internet is a volatile area, with sites coming and going willy-nilly, all we are providing here is a pointer to the PC Publishing web site:

http://www.pc-publishing.com/logiclinks.html

At this address you will find links to other useful Logic Pro sites and resources that will be updated as and when new information becomes available.

Index